Christ In You

The Hope of Glory

Ron Johnson

1st Edition

Contents

Foreword

Ron Johnson is an amazing man with an amazing story. If you do not know his story, I encourage you to start by reading his first book, *Love Never Fails*. In that book, you will learn about his dear wife Jenny and the process that God took him through to become like Him.

In each book he has written since then He has taken another step toward God. In *Joy of the Lord*, you can find surprising answers from the heart of Jesus to many questions that bother many people. In *One Heart at a Time*, Ron shares a vision Jesus gave him of how can walk as love to those around and truly bring Him Joy.

In his last book, *A Precious Walk With Jesus*, he begins to share not just the answers Jesus gives Him, but how to know Jesus in such a way that you too can experience the life that Ron does. And now in this book, *Chris in You the Hope of Glory*, Ron takes you on the next step – inviting you to the life of oneness that He is so earnestly pursuing. I encourage you to read them both together.

Having known and followed many Christians over the course of my life, what stands out most about Ron is His sincere and pure passionate love for Jesus. So many of us are caught doing our religious duties because we know we must, but we easily lose the love that makes it all worthwhile. Ron is a living testament that it does not have to be this way. You can have a passionate and fulfilling romance with Jesus.

Ron has given his life to be a blessing to others and he wants to bless you. If you have questions or a testimony that comes from reading this book, please call him at 513-377-1727. He wants to hear from you. But then, so does Jesus.

-- Will Riddle

Introduction

Have you ever thought of yourself as being the hope of glory for our Abba Father and Jesus? Paul declared we are the hope of glory in Colossians 1:27:

> **Colossians 12:7** To whom God would make known what is the riches of the glory of this mystery among the Gentiles; which is Christ in you, the hope of glory

Let us take a moment to think about the responsibility of being the hope of glory for God. What is our responsibility in this scripture? We are the chosen ones. We believers are the ones who God has made known the riches of His glory for we are His believers. We born again believers have the responsibility to be ambassadors for Jesus Christ. An ambassador represents the person that he is an ambassador for – *Jesus*. The ambassador does this by living and making decisions, having been granted power and authority by the one who commissions him.

That is an awesome responsibility isn't it? This might seem hard or even unrealistic at first but read on and you will find Jesus gave us everything we need to do the job of being His ambassador. Yes, we will live as Jesus lived by living a life so intimate with Him that we can have the compassion of Jesus, the thoughts of Jesus, the heart of Jesus and we will see as Jesus sees.

The blueprint for becoming an ambassador is written in our Holy Bible. We will come to know God through our Holy Bible but Jesus showed us an intimate life style of loving others that is only possible through His Holy Spirit becoming one with us. We simply have to lay down our life of earthly needs and earthly wants to become hearers of the word and give the Holy Spirit permission to start the transformation process that will bring us into intimacy with Abba Father and Jesus.

I pray that this book will bring you into a desire to know our Lord and Savior so intimately your heart will delight in spending time hearing and being prompted to do the things that seem impossible to a non-believer. To me, a non-believer includes people who study their Bible and quote their Bible but the Word has never come alive in their heart. These would be likened to scribes and Pharisees who Jesus called hypocrites. True believers have a relationship with God in their heart, mind and soul. True believers never struggle with the '*Is God real?*' question because they have settled the fact that God is real in their mind, heart and by faith. True believers never struggle with man's knowledge versus God's wisdom and faith.

Have you heard or thought of Christians as *Bible thumpers and hypocrites?* I know for a fact Jesus was none of these things and I know for a fact that Jesus didn't come to raise an army of hypocrites or what some preachers call '*pick and choose believers.*' True believers have a desire to become one with God by allowing the Holy Spirit of Jesus and Father God to live in us, talk to us and have their way in us. True believers have laid down their life to follow Jesus. Jesus called this process *dying to self.*

To truly die to ourselves we need more than a relationship with our Holy Bible. If we read the words on the pages of our Holy Bible and they are just knowledge to us, then we will never know how to follow Jesus. We actually follow Jesus by allowing the Holy Spirit of Jesus and Abba Father into our heart. This process is described in His Holy Bible but we must allow the word of God to become flesh to us as it was in Jesus and allow the word to become alive in our heart as it was in the heart of Jesus.

John 1:14   And the Word was made flesh, and dwelt among us, and we beheld his glory, the glory as of the only begotten of the Father, full of grace and truth.

Jesus is actually revealing His heart to us through His words in His Holy Bible but if we just read the words and they remain knowledge to us then dying to ourselves becomes very hard. People who simply study His Word to know it and quote it will not understand following and becoming the heart of Jesus. Trying to live a Christian life by knowing Jesus in word only is really a hard place to be. Most of these Christians are living to become pleasing to God but believe they live in a state of unworthiness. The devil and this world will usually suck Word only believers back into worldliness and they will become known as hypocrites or pick and choose believers.

We will overcome by the word of our testimony. Jesus didn't tell us to seek the knowledge of God and Jesus didn't tell us to pick and choose what words of His to believe. Jesus is asking us to seek first the kingdom of God and His righteousness. Seeking the kingdom of God is making God your priority. I pray that as you read this book you will realize we do not try to achieve a testimony to overcome. We simply make living for God our priority and God will give you a testimony.

If you have ever fallen in love with someone then you will recognize the depth of your love for this person by how much you make this person your priority. You will know your heart longs to be with that person. Jesus is the same way. Jesus does not want you to just study His Word. Jesus wants you to let His Word into your heart and come alive in your heart so the Holy Spirit can transform your heart in to the loving forgiveness of God. You will find yourself making God and His needs your priority.

Please right now, ask God for His heart. Yes, if we seek God and not just the knowledge of God then we are seeking His heart. This is actually simple. We ask God to reveal His heart to us in His Word and the Word we read will become alive in our heart. You see if we allow His Words in the Holy Bible to become alive in our hearts we will start hearing form God as we read. The apostles did this as they walked with Jesus. They were always asking Jesus to explain Himself to them. I want you to know that Jesus is still explaining Himself to us if we are not too busy to listen.

Here is an example. Please read again John 1:14:

John 1:14 And the Word was made flesh, and dwelt among us, (and we beheld his glory, the glory as of the only begotten of the Father,) full of grace and truth.

When I read John 1:14 and ask my Jesus "How do I become your flesh? I want people to see your glory manifested in us believers like I read in your Holy Bible." I asks Jesus to help me become *the only begotten of the Father* and I want to live a life full of grace and truth. This is possible for Jesus tells us all things are possible.

John tells us that Jesus is the word made flesh. You just read it, so it is in your heart. You can memorize it and study it but will it be in your heart? To receive the Word into your heart you must ask Jesus what He is teaching you personally in this scripture. When you ask Jesus, understanding will come into your heart in the form of the Holy Spirit. Jesus is telling us to become the Word and we are to be His Word made flesh today.

I ask you, "Who wants to follow the Word?" No one! Who will follow glory, joy and truth? *Everyone.* Yes, everyone will follow glory, joy and truth by the grace of God. In the same scripture we are told Jesus is the glory and the joy and the truth of His Father and we are to be the glory and joy and truth of our Father also. The glory of God is for us to manifest His grace and truth and joy toward others the way Jesus did.

The life of Jesus brought glory to Father God, and we are given the same opportunity Jesus had. We have to choose. Will our life bring glory to God or to ourselves? We are all capable of being made in the image and likeness of God and bring glory to God by believing in His truth. Please read Genesis 1:26.

Genesis 1:26 And God said, Let us make man in our image, after our likeness: and let them have dominion over the fish of the sea, and over the fowl of the air, and over the cattle, and over all the earth, and over every creeping thing that creeps upon the earth.

We have been given dominion over the entire earth but we are never to dominate over other people. Think about the life of Jesus and you will come to realize Jesus asks us to follow Him but Jesus never demanded us to follow Him. Jesus never put non-believers into a concentration camp for not believing. Instead Jesus gave us a choice to believe or not to believe.

As we read on we will realize Jesus never started different denominations. Man started all these denominations by picking and choosing the scriptures to believe in. Please I beg you to set aside these differences long enough to let Jesus show you the joy of being on the narrow path and how to stay on His narrow path.

When we choose Jesus and His path we will become aware of the Father's love for us. Jesus knew His Father loved Him and His Father's love gave Him a goodness that He knew would change the hearts of men. Jesus walked in His Father's joy and strength. We can have the Father's love and the same joy and strength Jesus has by believing His word and allowing the word to become flesh in us.

I believe we become one with our Holy Spirit when we receive baptism into our hearts. Think about what His Father said the moment Jesus was baptized. Abba Father said:

Matthew 3:17   And lo a voice from heaven, saying, this is my beloved Son, in whom I am well pleased.

Jesus was human flesh and blood when our Father called Him His Son. Why did Father God wait until Jesus received baptism before He called Him his Son? Naturally, I cannot speak for God but I believe Father God got so excited about the baptism because Jesus was our living example of how to become sons and daughters of God.

I was born into the Charles Johnson family as an infant. I had no choice back then, but I thank God my parents were believers and gave me a desire to be born into the family of God. I didn't hear the words of Matthew 3:17 when I was baptized but I hope to hear these same words of love from my Father someday and I pray to hear them while I am here on earth. I choose to accept by faith that I am loved as Jesus was loved. I choose to walk the narrow path because I have never before experienced such joy.

I believe the second step to seeking the Lord is to become aware that Jesus wants to be our teacher just like he taught the apostles. We simply must ask Jesus to be our teacher. If you ask Jesus to be your teacher Jesus will jump for joy at the chance to teach you.

7

In John 14:26, Jesus was talking to the apostles about His upcoming human death and that He would be leaving them. But Jesus reassured them that He was still going to walk with them and teach them all things.

> **John 14:26** But the Comforter, which is the Holy Ghost, whom the Father will send in my name, **he shall teach you all things**, and bring all things to your remembrance, whatsoever I have said unto you.

Sadly, today we can read John 14:26 and study it and know it is true. But until we ask Jesus to be our personal teacher, our comforter, and the reminder of all His words then we won't have the life of the scripture in our heart. Our life will change with the awareness that Jesus is our teacher; our only teacher but Jesus wants us to choose to believe Him so we can receive Him.

In Matthew 23:8 Jesus was talking to the Pharisees who loved to be called Rabbi meaning master or teacher. The Pharisees loved this title so much they were willing to kill Jesus for not following them and for not teaching as what they taught. This is serious business and Jesus made it very clear to the apostles and to us believers who our teacher is.

> **Matthew 23:8** But you, do not be called 'Rabbi'; for **One is your Teacher, the Christ**, and you are all brethren.

Jesus is talking to the apostles telling them they are not to be called Rabbi meaning teacher or master by others or each other. I pray you ask Jesus into your heart and I pray you ask Jesus to be your personal teacher because with the revelation of who Jesus is *'for One is your Teacher.'* We will be made part of the flock of Jesus and when we become teachable we will have the honor of being called His brethren. Jesus will come into us through His Holy Spirit and teach us believers who will lay down their life by turning off the distractions of this world and listen to follow Jesus into His righteousness.

This is how we become the Word of God made flesh by simply allowing the Holy Spirit of God to dwell in us. You must die to yourself by following Jesus on His journey to glorify our Father as described in His Holy Bible. The knowledge gleaned from reading our Holy Bible will lead us to understanding how the love of God will transform us into the caregivers of His love.

Today there are so many distractions to snare us away from God and it might seem impossible to stay focused on being the love of Jesus to all. I tell you to seek first the kingdom of God and His righteousness for if you do His Spirit of wisdom and His understanding will come and Jesus will transform your heart so your desire for the distractions of this world will gently dissolve. Jesus tells us He will sprinkle us clean of an evil conscience.

SPEAKING IN JAPANESE

Here is a short story that will hopefully bring a desire into your heart to ask the Holy Spirit of God into your heart. As you might have guessed by now, I love to talk about having an intimate heart to heart relationship with God.

A couple weeks ago my friend Will and I got together and had some really good talk about Jesus. Will told me I talk in English and write in English but people hear me in Japanese. Please understand that Will is very, very smart and he will use his smartness to see if I understand him or not. Will desires me to understand him. I believe the smartness of Will is not just in his intelligence but his smartness is in how he asks God to help me understand him and he relies on God to give me revelation.

Will continued, "You see Ron, when you talk about your heart to heart relationship with God and how personal your relationship is with God, most people don't understand. Most people have a relationship with their Bible but not with God."

Will knew I didn't understand too well what he was trying to tell me. He said, "Don't worry, Ron. God will bring understanding to you." I rested for I knew Will was right and Jesus will give me understanding.

The next morning, we went to a little church service in the campground. I was given a chance to share with a man there how much Jesus wants to talk to us personally. I told him a story about my wife Jenny. Oh, if you haven't read *Love Never Fails* or my other books I need to back up a little. If you have read the other books, please bear with me for the sake of new readers.

My wife was diagnosed with a disease called Pick's disease which started when Jenny was 43 years old. Pick's is disease where your brain starts to die. Jenny wasn't able to brush her teeth on her own so I brushed her teeth for her. A problem arose when Jenny didn't understand that she needed to spit out the toothpaste. I mean, how do you make someone spit it? After brushing Jenny's teeth in the evening, I put her to bed without being able to rinse her mouth. In the morning, her breath gotten so bad it would stop a freight train. The problem is the toothpaste will turn rancid in her mouth during the night.

Jenny was also incontinent at this time and so I needed to bathe her every morning. I would carry her to our tub and prop her up in the corner of the tub so I can shower her. I had to put my foot in front of her feet to keep her feet from sliding. One particular morning, her breath was totally horrible. I cried out to Jesus and ask Him for help. I said "Jesus, Jenny's breathe smells worse than her feces. Please Lord, help me. I don't know what to do." I asked Jesus if her breath smells this bad to me, what does her breath smells like. I ask how this will affect her gums and her eating. I asked Lord to please help me.

Immediately, Jesus told me to brush her teeth now. Somehow, I managed to reach for the toothbrush and hold Jenny from falling over in the tub. I turned the toothbrush on and brushed her teeth like I was told. When I was finished brushing Jenny's teeth I put down the toothbrush and Jesus lead my hand to the showerhead. I turned it on and pointed it at Jenny's mouth and Jenny responded by spitting out the water.

I tell everyone how Jesus answered all my questions in seconds and I continued to brush Jenny's teeth that way for ten years. I thank Jesus for Jenny never had bad breath again and her teeth were always clean and pretty.

After sharing Jenny's story at the campground church service, a man came up to me and told me I was either superstitious or borderline to witchcraft. He said no one hears from God that way because God doesn't talk to people like that. I felt prompted by my

Jesus and so I told that man another story about hearing from God. My friend Will also talk to the man.

Will and I went back to the camper and Will told me that man's reaction was the Japanese he was telling me about last night. He said that man has a relationship with the Bible and not God. Will said, "The Bible will never tell someone how to brush their wife's teeth. Ron, you have a relationship with Jesus and Father God which allows them to talk to you directly." I then replied, "I pray for everyone to come to know God personally for I know Jesus told me how to brush my Jenny's teeth and Jesus and I live in the same house."

Will smiled at me and said, "You know Ron, that man came up to you and basically accused you of being into witchcraft and you simply started telling him another story about hearing from God." I replied, "I believe God prompted me to tell him the second story in the hopes the man might understand." Will just smiled and said, "I know, Ron."

After Will left that day, I asked my Jesus how to explain this relationship Jesus and I have. Jesus said, "Ron you have a walking, talking relationship with me because you read your Bible not just to know God or to quote God, but you read with a desire to receive all I have for you and you have opened your heart to make me your priority in life."

Jesus said, "I love how you read a story in my Holy Bible, like Job and you tell me you want the steadfast faith of Job. Ron, I love when you tell me you want my compassion and I love how you want and desire so earnestly to manifest my love and my Father's love to everyone you meet. Ron, I love your desire to have the same close relationship I have with our Father God. I love how you want my truth, my faith, my wisdom like you read about in your Holy Bible flowing out of me to flow out of you."

Yes, my dearest Jesus I want your wisdom and discernment to know your voice from a stranger's voice! I asked God to give me His forgiveness so I too can forgive as God forgives. I believe God is the ultimate forgiver and so I desire to forgive like God forgives. I ask Jesus for these gifts because I know by faith all things are possible because I know for sure I have the Holy Spirit of God in me.

Here are a few more of my wants. Lord helps me comfort whoever He brings into my path. Lord let me bring your joy and light into this world because I know from your Word it is your joy and your light that attracts others and leads men to true repentance. Lord, let me bring your peace to those around me and most of all let your strength be my strength. Lord, let your dreams be my dreams for I know I dream to small. I thank you for giving me the Holy Spirit who brings your loving truth and peace and so I know I have it all. Lord, I thank you for your Holy Bible that tells me all these things are possible to those that believe. Lord I thank you for loving me.

Jesus and I talk every day and I have questions every day. Read on and you will hear his answers and how my Jesus makes understanding His ways very simple to me.

Again, I want to say this book is being written to give the readers a desire to have an intimate relationship with our loving Jesus and Father God. I know the desire of God is to have an intimate relationship with us for Jesus reveals His desires to us through His Word.

Is It Reasonable for God to Ask Us to be His Hope of Glory?

We may have thought or been taught that there are requirements that we have to learn or maybe we must attain some deep meaning from the scriptures for us to be His hope of glory. Yet, Jesus tells us in His Word that we have all the requirements to be His hope of glory and we will lack nothing if we in faith simply seek first the kingdom of God.

> **Matthew 6:31-33** Therefore take no thought, saying, what shall we eat? Or, what shall we drink? Or, how shall we be clothed? For after all these things do the Gentiles seek: for your heavenly Father knoweth that ye have need of all these things. **But seek ye first the kingdom of God, and his righteousness**; and all these things shall be added unto you.

You see we will lack nothing if we seek FIRST the kingdom of God and His righteousness. Our priority, thoughts and our life has to be focused on bringing heaven to earth like Jesus did. When we believe the Words of Jesus and prove our belief by living like Jesus lived – fearlessly.

You know the kingdom of God is at hand, we are sent like Jesus was sent from the Father and so we are sent to the lost sheep. I don't need to go to some foreign country to find lost sheep because Jesus shows me lost sheep everywhere and Jesus will show you lost sheep also.

> **Matthew 10:6-10** But go rather to the lost sheep of the house of Israel. And as ye go, preach, saying, the kingdom of heaven is at hand. Heal the sick, cleanse the lepers, raise the dead, cast out devils: freely ye have received, freely give. Provide neither gold, nor silver, nor brass in your purses, Nor scrip for your journey, neither two coats, neither shoes, nor yet staves: **for the workman is worthy of his meat**.

We read in Matthew 10:6-8 that we have the power in His name. Yes, that is correct. We have been given the authority to call on the name of Jesus and we have the kingdom of heaven at hand or at our command so we lack nothing. As the Father sent Jesus so has Jesus sent us. Jesus lacked nothing and we lack nothing when we believe by faith. We are loved by the Father as Jesus was loved by our Father.

We read in Matthew 10:9-10 that we have everything provided if we believe. Jesus is telling us that we have everything we need physically – shoes, clothes and food. For true believers in the Word of Jesus Christ will know our Father God will provide. The devil has some of us believing in him and some of us have listened to the wisdom of man and we have decided we lack worthiness. Sadly a lot of believers think they are not worthy to go preach the kingdom of God is at hand. But I know the devil is the only source of unworthiness. Read on and you will see God has made us worthy.

Let us talk about being worthy for a moment. I was in a church a couple weeks back where they sang the words over and over 'You are worthy Lord' and I started thinking and wondering how many of these people singing this song, think of themselves as being worthy. I thought, "God knows He is worthy. He is God."

God has commissioned us to go to the lost sheep so we must be worthy. Jesus didn't make the apostles pass a worthy test so why do we give ourselves a worthy test? I haven't read where Jesus told the apostles to go search your past for years and years to make yourself worthy before you go to the lost sheep. I haven't read where Jesus told the apostles, "Now that you are worthy to go." On the contrary Jesus tells us to follow Him, to seek ye first the kingdom of heaven and God will transform you into worthiness.

God has commissioned us. God knows all things, even our past so God must know we are worthy if we simply believe and put our faith in Him. By faith and trust in God we have been given everything we need to preach His Word, we have His power and the authority in the name of Jesus if we believe. We lack nothing when we believe we are His chosen ones and we prove our belief with our steadfast faith and trust that God is with us as we go.

Think about the Samaritan women at the well. Jesus tells her, she had, "five husbands and the man you are living with now is not your husband." The apostles came back with food and she ran to town to tell everyone in her town, "Come see the man that told me everything I have ever done." And the people went to see Jesus and they ask Jesus to teach them and Jesus taught them and they believed.

The Samaritan woman didn't go to Bible school for years or dig up her past for years. She simply heard from Jesus and became so full of His love she ran to town and His love over flowed to give everyone there a desire to know God. Jesus told me the woman hadn't even repented yet. Jesus knew she would repent for her sins and change her ways because His Word says that repentance comes when we become aware of the goodness of God.

I believe the love of God is a gift to us and the power of God is a gift to us and the authority of God is a gift to us from God. We have all these gifts of the Holy Spirit if we simply trust God will manifest His gifts to us if we by faith believe we are worthy. Ask the Holy Spirit into your heart and he will transform you into worthy. Read on and you will see how the transformation happens.

When we trust in God we will believe we have it all. Does all include protection too? Paul trusted in God and some would say God didn't protect Him at all. Paul suffered many things while on this earth but not more than he could handle. Look at the protection God gave Paul when Paul needed it. Paul says Acts 22:17-18:

> **Acts 22:17** "When I had returned to Jerusalem and was praying in the temple, I fell into a trance and saw Jesus saying to me, 'Make haste and get out of Jerusalem quickly, because they will not accept your testimony about me.'

I know Jesus lives inside of me. I know I have His undivided attention as we walk together. I know sometimes I get distracted and I thank God for His perseverance in dealing with me. I am worthy of God's love not because of anything I can do or achieve but because I simply believe I am a child of God and therefore God does love me. My simple belief that *I am a child of God* allows God to love me and God puts a quiet rest in me that I know if I am in a danger I cannot handle, Jesus will tell me to get out of there.

I know if the devil makes the fire seven times hotter, or the giant bigger or the lion roar louder, that with faith in Jesus I will still have peace because I believe in the protection of my Jesus. I hope you realize in all the persecutions that we read about in our Holy Bible that they had a choice to deny Jesus and live for the moment or live by faith in God and live forever.

I remember when Jenny said the words *'I do love you'* on our wedding day. Jenny made a commitment to love me and it was the happiest day of my life. All my happiness came from the simple belief that Jenny really loved me. I never thought at the time anyone could bring this kind of happiness to me. Deep down inside of me I never felt worthy of her love. I never thought I could prove my love for her enough to be worthy of her precious love. Now I know I was deceived by my own thoughts. Jenny didn't love me because I was worthy of her love. Jenny loved me because she knew Jesus intimately and had taken our love – our marriage to Jesus and Jenny knew Jesus approved our marriage.

Please, if you feel unworthy of God's love then please seek God for discernment. God is not waiting for us to be worthy. Jesus tells us we are His children. Can a new born baby be worthy of all the love, the time and the patience the parents will willingly give? Yes, the baby is worthy because God created the baby for us to love. We are created by God and God created us to love us! I ask you to consider, will loving parents protect their children? Will our loving God protect us, His children? Yes! Simply believe you are His child because you are His child and the word of God says so.

We have a God given commission to preach the Word of God to all the nations. We will fall short of our commission if we don't understand the love God has for us first. When Saul was killing Christians, was he worthy of God's love and grace and mercy? I believe God saw the child He created Saul to be and by the mercy of God, He gave Saul a chance to repent. Saul was smart enough to accept the mercy of God and the love of God allowed God to transform Him into Paul. Paul believed he became a child of God when he accepted God into his heart. I believe Paul allowed the Holy Spirit of God to come into his heart and Paul was transformed into the hope of God's glory by doing so.

I am a child of God if I believe I am His child. I will bring glory to God by believing I am His child. I do believe I am His child, I know the Holy Spirit of God dwells in me and I love having the Holy Spirit of God living in me. Like the happiness I had when Jenny said '*I love you*' on our wedding day. The acceptance of the love of God comes with an eternal joy that is complete. Jenny has gone to live eternally with my Jesus and her memories bring great joy to me. Unlike the momentary happiness of the things of this world I have great joy when I think about Jenny's love for me; the love of God is joy that is eternal. I have eternal joy in knowing Jenny is with my Jesus eternally.

Nothing of Jesus is in a momentary time frame, like the momentary love of a wife or a child. Jesus is in my heart and my heart will live somewhere forever. I hope you realize right now today we are all choosing where our forever will be spent. I choose to let God possess me. Yes, I believe Jesus Christ lives in me so I can be His hope of glory here on earth. Please read again Colossians 1:27:

> **Colossians 1:27** To whom God would make known what is the riches of the glory of this mystery among the Gentiles; which is **Christ in you, the hope of glory**

Please put your name in this scripture. **Christ in Ron Johnson, the hope of glory.** Actually, to do so is our reasonable service to God. As we read in Romans 12:1:

> **Romans 12:1** I beseech you therefore, brethren, by the mercies of God, that ye present your bodies a living sacrifice, holy, acceptable unto God, which is **your reasonable service.**

This scripture gives me a picture of a good marriage. I wanted to keep myself pure for my wife Jenny. I wanted to present myself holy and acceptable to her for I saw her purity every day of our life. Now I have found the love of Jesus and I believe it is my reasonable service to present myself a living sacrifice to Him. What am I sacrificing for God? I am sacrificing what I now know is the natural man's foolishness of this world.

My goal is to stand naked and unashamed in front of Jesus like I did Jenny and this time to look into His eyes and see His loving eyes looking at me. Thank you my loving Lord for transforming me with thy mercies and for allowing me to follow you into the joy of the Lord for eternity.

Please understand, I have been talking about being worthy to do the work of the kingdom of God. There is a place called heaven and we will be given a test of worthiness before entering into heaven. Our life here on earth is the test of worthiness for going to heaven but not for service to God. We are being sprinkled clean if we desire to be partakers of God's glory; but if we decide not to repent and not to serve, I don't think we will be worthy of entering into the kingdom of God. I hope you understand, God will give us grace and love to do the kingdom work here on earth but to enter in the Kingdom of God for eternity we have to become worthy.

You see we become a hope of glory by the mercies of God. I believe it is reasonable for God to expect me to present my body a living sacrifice, holy and acceptable to God. I mean, God does give me everything I need to become who He created me to be. I don't lack any good thing if I believe in His mercy that I'm being forgiven and focus all my attention on seeking first the kingdom of God. I believe seeking the kingdom of God is simply laying down my life for another.

KNOWLEDGE PUFFS UP

Tomorrow I am going to meet with Bill. He is a man I have met a couple times last year and twice this year. This man studies the Word of God diligently and probably more than anyone else I know. He reads more and quotes more men's writings about God that I knew existed. He says he has read one of my books but he said I misquote the meanings in the scriptures so he will not read any more of my books.

For example, I tell everyone to fear not when talking about Jesus because Jesus himself said, *"The Holy Spirit of Jesus will give you the words to speak in that very hour."* Read these words from my Jesus:

> **Luke 12:11-12** And when they bring you unto the synagogues, and *unto* magistrates, and powers, take ye no thought how or what thing ye shall answer, or what ye shall say: For the Holy Ghost shall teach you in the same hour what ye ought to say.

I ask my Jesus who is my magistrate? I have never been called before a magistrate or powerful ruler or judge. Jesus answered me, saying, "Your magistrate is anyone I put before you Ron." I tell everyone how Jesus takes the pressure off us believers and kingdom builders because I now know Jesus will give me the words to speak to anyone that He puts in front of me.

I told Bill that my desire is to give you a desire to know the Lord and now with this revelation of Jesus living in me; I know the Holy Spirit of Jesus will give me His words and I am free to go and do as Jesus commanded us 'feed my sheep.'

I found this freedom in the book of Mark also.

> **Mark 13:11** But when they shall lead *you*, and deliver you up, take no thought beforehand what ye shall speak, neither do ye premeditate: but whatsoever shall be given you in that hour, that speak ye: **for it is not ye that speak, but the Holy Ghost.**

When Bill read these paragraphs, he said to me, "There you go again, misquoting the scriptures." He said, "If you had any depth in your knowledge of Jesus you would know these scriptures are for the end times when Jesus comes back, then Jesus will give us the words to speak. This scripture is not for our everyday walk with the Lord. This scripture is clearly for the end times, meaning that Jesus will give us the words to speak only in the end times."

According to Bill, I am very shallow in my knowledge of God's Word and that I need to study more of the Word before I go out into the world, for as he says the Bible is very deep in meaning. He told me my faith is not faith but presumption. He said there are allegories in the Holy Bible and he asked me if I knew what an allegory was. I answered I don't know what an allegory is. You are probably wondering why I went back to meet this man again.

This year I was going through Bill's town. I ask Jesus whether or not to stop and see Bill. I felt prompted by Jesus although I really didn't want to stop to see him. But I still stopped and visited with him.

I just gave you a picture of Bill and what I see with my fleshly eyes. In my heart I see a man hungry for the Lord. I see a man trying to the best of his ability to find some hidden meaning in the scriptures. I see a man who wanted to be used by God but think he must know more or have more knowledge of God before he actually goes out and talks about God. I see a man in love with the Bible. I see a man who knows there is a kingdom of God but has not entered into it.

When we meet this year I mentioned to Bill that as I travel in the motor home I realize I go not to teach or bring some deep meaning or some great discovery I found in the Holy Bible but I go to simply be who God created me to be – that is the love of Jesus Christ and Jesus makes being His love so simple. Yes, I knew I will probably get beaten up by Bill's words again but I will learn also and I will be enlightened and in the process I pray to be able to demonstrate the love of Jesus and be an example of the kingdom of God.

After talking to Bill, I looked up the scriptures and I quoted what Mark was talking and it is about the end times. But in that passage we are told what to do now. We are told to watch for the signs and how to pray and I believe that we are told what to say today.

I mentioned to Bill that there are a number of scriptures where the apostles referred to their days as the last days and they referred to the days they walked the earth as the end times. So I think I can assume we are in the last days now. I mean, the apostles thought they were in the last days so why shouldn't we think so. Most people today believe we are in the last days but no one knows for sure when Jesus will return, not even the angles.

Taught by the Spirit

Here are some more scriptures that talk about how things are revealed by the Spirit. We read how the Spirit spoke to Samuel and the words of the Holy Spirit were on the tongue of Samuel in 1 Corinthians 2:13. These things we also speak, not in words of man's wisdom or in the words of man's teachings but we speak by faith the words the Holy Spirit teaches us, comparing spiritual things with spiritual.

1 Corinthians 2:13 These things we also speak, **not in words which man's wisdom teaches but which the Holy Spirit teaches**, comparing spiritual things with spiritual.

In the past, before Jesus came to dwell with me, I literally and almost always spoke the word of man's wisdom. I spread man's wisdom as if it were true and is worth repeating. I thank God for His loving forgiveness and I thank God for showing me a more excellent way.

Ephesians 3:4-5 Whereby, when ye read, ye may understand my knowledge in the mystery of Christ which in other ages was not made known to the sons of men, **as it has now been revealed by the Spirit** to His holy apostles and prophets

We believers are the apostles of today and I pray we the Holy apostles of today will have discernment to discern between man's knowledge and the spiritual wisdom of God. We will have spiritual discernment when we put down the distractions of this world and turn our hearing to the Lord's voice. The choice is ours.

We read here in 2 Samuel 23:2 the Spirit of the Lord spoke through Samuel.

2 Samuel 23:2 "The Spirit of the LORD spoke by me, And His word was on my tongue.

Please read 1 Corinthians 2:13 again. Hearing the voice of God is very important and we must understand the Lord desires to have intimacy with us and to speak not only to us but also through us the words of His Holy Spirit.

1 Corinthians 2:13 These things we also speak, **not in words which man's wisdom teaches but which the Holy Spirit teaches**, comparing spiritual things with spiritual

Jesus tells in a number of scriptures that He is our teacher and by faith I believe Jesus is my teacher. Yes, Jesus gave us His Holy Spirit and the Holy Spirit of Father God and I am smart enough to believe them and by faith I hear their voice. By faith in Jesus and Father God being my Holy Spirit and my teacher, I live in a wonderful world of hearing and allowing the Holy Spirit to speak through me.

1 Corinthians 2:14 But the natural man receives not the things of the Spirit of God: for they are foolishness unto him: neither can he know *them*, because they are spiritually discerned.

Remember in your prayers to ask Jesus for His heart, His mind, His discernment and His eyes and expect He will give you them. How did Jesus bring Glory to Father God? Jesus said He only did what He sees His Father do and Jesus gave us Himself as our example to follow. I believe in 1 Corinthians 2:14 where Jesus was talking about having spiritual discernment. I hope that does not sound like foolishness to you because in 1 Corinthians, Paul says the natural man receives not the things of the spirit and being a natural man would be a tragedy, for a natural man seeks after the things of this world.

Please open your heart to the love of Jesus and simply stop trying to figure Him out and simply believe by faith that Jesus is real and His words are for you today. You will see your heart transformed and your life will reflect the light in your heart and you will hear your friends say, *"What happened to you and how did you change like this?"* The answer is I simply believe the Word of God to be true and allowed His Spirit into my heart.

Personally I remember when my son came to the realization his dad had changed and Jason said to me, "Dad, you are not the same dad that raised me." I looked at Jason and said, "God will transform your heart too if you let Him."

I remember when my son Ron gave me a keychain for Christmas that said *Man of God* on it.

I never got knocked off a horse. I never had a day where I woke up and felt some big change but I did ask Jesus into my heart and I did hear the Holy Spirit tell me that He wanted to have coffee with me. I cried as I made coffee and asked Jesus out loud, "Do you really want to have coffee with me?" Jesus answered, "Yes, Ron. We need to talk every day." I still have my quiet coffee time with my Jesus everyday and I love the fact Jesus is so intimate with me. I have written a story called *Coffee Time With Jesus* and I believe the day Jesus asked me to have coffee with him was a turning point in my life.

Preparation

Are most Christians prepared to go out and preach the gospel today? If not, then what is needed? Some would say it took Jesus three years to prepare the apostles. What do you say about this?

Almost every Christian will tell you Jesus taught in parables and this is true. I believe Jesus taught more by the way He lived than the words He spoke. When reading your Holy Bible you will notice how much is written about the way Jesus lived. When I hear non-Christians talk about Christians today and I hear the non-Christians saying, "I cannot tell Christians apart from the rest of the world because Christians sometimes live the opposite of what they profess Christianity to be. I believe our walk declares our Christianity more than our words and therefore many Christians are called hypocrites."

The sad news is some Christians are actually taught more by man's wisdom than by the Word of God and so they live by man's wisdom. The Pharisees lived in man's wisdom and let us read what Jesus called the Pharisees in Matthew 23. I believe Jesus would talk about most Christians the same way today. There are thirty-nine verses in Mathew 23 and here are a few.

> **Matthew 23:5-8** But they do all their works in order to be seen of men. They make their phylacteries broad and enlarge the borders of their garments. And they love the first couch at feasts, and the chief seats in the synagogues, and greetings in the market-places, and to be called, Rabbi! Rabbi! by men. But you must not be called Rabbi, for One is your teacher, Christ, and you are all brothers.

I believe Jesus could make these comments about the Christian's of today. We Christians talk about living a Christian life and some of us can quote the Bible but the non-Christians don't see us living our morals. They don't see our belief of forgiveness in action and for these reasons they don't see our Christ-like love flowing out of us. This is the tragedy of living in man's wisdom of knowing of God by reading your Bible for knowledge but not spending quiet intimate time with God and not walking and talking with Him.

Jesus lived the perfect Christian life and so we have an example to model our life after. Jesus told us He fulfilled all the law and He did. I believe Jesus fulfilled the law by simply dying to Himself. If we live to be the love of our Father God to everyone we meet as Jesus did, we will fulfill the law also. Jesus asks us to die to our self but most of the times I find some reason to put my needs above the needs of others.

Consider the example of speeding. If no one went over the speed limit, then there would be no need for the police to monitor our driving speed. You see, if we Christian never let our need to get to somewhere supersede the safety of the people around us then we will never over speed. Over-speeding is actually putting our need to be somewhere above the safety of others. If we die to ourselves then we will put the safety of others above our needs to be somewhere. What if a non-believer was with us in the car and asks us, "Why are you driving so slowly?" and you answered, "I am simply thinking about the safety of others."

Wow, how simple is that? How much preparation does going the speed limit takes? I am sure the person in the car will be thinking about your answer for a long time. I believe that is a mustard seed of faith planted and God can move a mountain with a mustard seed. Think about this: Did you have to preach, did you need some big revelation from God, or did you simply let your actions speak louder than your words?

Remember not everyone needs to be knocked off their horse but everyone needs to see the difference between a Christian and a non-Christian. Jesus wants Christians to fulfill the law by living within the law. The preparation needed to fulfill the law is to die to oneself.

Just one more comment about speeding. What if the person in the car with you knew that you were really in a hurry and saw that you still keep the law despite of your timeline? You are showing your passenger you are dying to yourself by not letting your need to be somewhere superseding the safety of others. This will have a bigger effect on their mind. I believe God can use our simple obedience to start the process of transforming our world around us.

Some people tell me that I am too simple-minded. I like being thought of as simple-minded because for me it's saying that I have my faith in God and Jesus tells us with faith the size of a mustard seed He will move a mountain. Thank you Jesus I am prepared because I believe you. Thank you Jesus for your example of how to live and I pray to be a child of God with child-like faith in the Holy Spirit of God living in me and speaking through me as I am driving the speed limit. Think about what Jesus told the apostles in Matthew 10:24:

> **Matthew 10:24** "A disciple is not above his teacher, nor a servant above his master.

To avoid being a Christian hypocrite, do as Jesus did and live within the laws of our land. Jesus even paid taxes! We have our example in Jesus so I don't think we will have any excuse for not living with in the laws of our land when we stand before Jesus for judgment.

I think it is important to see how Jesus thought of the apostles. Jesus had prepared and taught the apostles for years and yet when Father God gave them revelation Jesus referred to them as babes.

> **Matthew 11:25** At that time Jesus answered and said, I thank thee, O Father, Lord of heaven and earth, because thou hast hid these things from the wise and prudent, and hast revealed them unto babes.

Remember when Jesus sent out the 12 and the 70 apostles. Remember when they came back from their missionary trip. Remember how excited they were, telling Jesus, "Even the devils are subject to us in your name."

> **Luke 10:17** And the seventy returned again with joy, saying, **Lord, even the devils are subject unto us through thy name.**

Remember what Jesus told them in Luke 10:18-21:

Luke 10:18-21   And Jesus said unto them, I beheld Satan as lightning fall from heaven. Behold, I give unto you power to tread on serpents and scorpions, and over all the power of the enemy: and nothing shall by any means hurt you. Notwithstanding in this rejoice not, that the spirits are subject unto you; but rather rejoice, because your names are written in heaven. In that hour Jesus rejoiced in spirit, and said, I thank thee, O Father, Lord of heaven and earth, that thou hast hid these things from the wise and prudent, and hast revealed them unto babes: even so, Father; for so it seemed good in thy sight.

I would like to ask a simple question; was the Holy Spirit of Jesus Christ in the apostles at the time of their missionary trip? At this point the apostles had lived with Jesus and walked with Jesus and witnessed the works of Jesus for about three years. The apostles studied the words of Jesus and heard the teachings of Jesus and Jesus had given to them and demonstrated to them the mystery of His Father's power and yet Jesus refers to them as 'babes'.

We read when the apostles returned they were all excited to tell Jesus about how His babes saw the power in His name and had used the power of His name and Father God worked His power at their command. Their missionary trip did bring glory to God. We believers can have missionary trips at work or to the store and gas station and these trips should bring glory to God every day.

Thinking about the way Jesus referred to the apostles and the effect His calling had on their life, I sometimes wonder how foolish they must have looked to their friends. Some of the apostles had good jobs and just walked away with a man who didn't have money or an education or a place to lay His head. And Jesus didn't do job interviews or tell them I can use your expertise to build my church and Jesus didn't ask them what can you offer to help me. Jesus just simply said come follow me and like children they did follow Him into true Christianity.

From what I read it seems the apostles were not prepared for their walk with Jesus but they could follow and they did. They probably asked themselves, "What are we doing?" They probably had a million questions going on in their head and yet the call to follow Jesus superseded their personal needs to speed down the normal road of life acquiring dung. For what is a man profited if he shall gain the whole world and lose his own soul? Or what shall a man give in exchange for his soul?

Yes, the first requirement for the apostles to follow Jesus Christ was for them to die to themselves and pick up their cross to follow Jesus. What cross did they pick up you might ask? I believe the cross never changed over all these years. The apostles were asked to lay down their needs – their life and we are still being asked to lay down our life. We simply must let the needs of others supersede our own needs. Dying to our self is putting the needs of others ahead of our own need thus our cross is to lay down our life and put aside our own personal needs. Jesus tells us about this three times in Matthew, Mark and Luke. I believe this must be important for us to understand.

Matthew 16:24-26 Then said Jesus unto his disciples, if any man will come after me, **let him deny himself, and take up his cross, and follow me.** For whosoever will save his life shall lose it: and whosoever will lose his life for my sake shall find it. For what is a man profited, if he shall gain the whole world, and lose his own soul? or what shall a man give in exchange for his soul?

In Matthew, Jesus is talking to the apostles and in Mark Jesus is talking to you and me.

Mark 8:34-37 And when he had called the people unto him with his disciples also, he said unto them, **whosoever will come after me, let him deny himself, and take up his cross, and follow me.** For whosoever will save his life shall lose it; but whosoever shall lose his life for my sake and the gospel's, the same shall save it. For what shall it profit a man, if he shall gain the whole world, and lose his own soul? Or what shall a man give in exchange for his soul?

In Luke, Jesus talked to everyone.

Luke 9:23-25   And he said to them all, **if any man will come after me, let him deny himself, and take up his cross daily, and follow me.** For whosoever will save his life shall lose it: but whosoever will lose his life for my sake, the same shall save it. For what is a man advantaged, if he gains the whole world, and lose himself, or be cast away

I hope you noticed in these scriptures that Jesus never told anyone to do anything but Jesus simply ask us to follow him. We must make the choice. My point here is this: the words of Jesus are discernment tools.   When we walk with Jesus we will have promptings to do some things but we will never be told to do anything. The devil tells us to speed up, to hate, to kill through unforgiveness, and to destroy your marriage and our loved ones. But Jesus only ask us follow Him into His loving forgiveness, peace and joy.

The preparation to follow Jesus is the same today – let him deny himself and take up his cross daily and follow Him. We must seek Jesus by giving Him your whole heart, mind and soul. To follow Him is to seek Him.   Dying to ourselves could be turning off the television and internet, sports, or whatever it is that is distracting you. I hope you realize that your distraction is your idol.

Matthew 6:31-33   Therefore take no thought, saying, what shall we eat? or, what shall we drink? or, Wherewithal shall we be clothed? (For after all these things do the Gentiles seek:) for your heavenly Father knoweth that ye have need of all these things. But **seek ye first the kingdom of God, and his righteousness**; and all these things shall be added unto you.

Earthly dung is so worthless compared to righteousness. Jesus is our example who to follow. His Word says we are to come after Him. I believe that means we are His apostles of today. When you do follow Him your life will begin a transformation process and your needs will be provided just like the apostles. The best part is your lust for idols will get washed away.

This is a story how idols deceive us:

I received a phone call the other night from a man who lost his wife a year ago. He told me how lonely he is and he thinks he would like to travel like I do. I sensed in our phone conversation he wanted joy back in his life. I told him my joyfulness doesn't come from traveling. My joyfulness comes from my intimacy with my Jesus. I know my life on the road probably looks adventurous to some. I know if the Lord was not directing my path I would be bored to tears if all I did is to travel full time to see tourist traps. Traveling can be an idol.

I pray for this man to, "seek ye first the kingdom of God," by becoming so close to God, the intimacy will fill his heart, mind and soul to over flowing. Traveling is not the answer. Ministry is not the answer and loneliness is not from God. I believe to follow Jesus is to lay down your life. I simply ask Jesus every day, "Dear Jesus, what are we going to do today? What I am saying is my life is, your life dear Jesus, please show me or led to who you want to see you today."

The man I talked to who is so lonely seems to be seeking happiness. I pray for him to become intimately connected to the Holy Spirit of God who is already in him. If I let myself think about how much I miss my Jenny I will be depressed in five seconds and as long as I stay in depression I am useless to the kingdom of God.

I simply make myself available to God and He rewards me with joy I cannot understand. The answer is to pray, knowing God has an answer and the Godly answer is on the way because you prayed. For this man the answer might be traveling but I cannot give him an answer only God can and God will give him an answer if he asks God. I believe we are to pray without an answer in mind and that frees up God to give us His answer.

Another short story about not being prepared:

One day I pulled onto a camping site and while I was hooking up my camper to the electric and water, I noticed the camper along side of me was pretty ragged out. A lady came out of that camper. She looked like a man to me. She had two big dogs and after the dogs did their business the lady turned and looked at me again. I greeted her, "Hi," but she just glared at me and went into her camper.

Then some wild music came on the outdoor speakers of her camper. I called it music but it was more like, "boom boom boom," and all noise. I shut the windows on my camper and turned on the air conditioning but the noise was still loud inside my camper. After about an hour I did what I should have done right away. I came to my senses and I ask my dear Jesus what you want me to say to that woman. God didn't give me any words but I knew in my heart Jesus wanted me to speak to her.

I went to her camper and knocked on her door. When she opened the door, I told her I am going to Wal-Mart in about a half hour and if she needed anything then I offer that I would pick it up for her. She turned her head back toward the inside of the camper and screamed at her husband, "Turn that damn music off, I cannot hear this man!" Then she looked at me and said, "What did you say?" I told her again and she replied, "I can't think of anything that I need right now." I said, "That is why I am giving you half-hour to think about it." Her hard demeanor changed and she pleasantly said, "Oh, okay." I said, "If you do think of anything just knock on my window or come around to my door with your list and I will gladly pick up your stuff." She replied with an okay with a smile.

I camped next to her and her husband for two weeks and they never turned on their outdoor speakers again while I was there. Thank you Jesus for being my best friend and thank you Jesus for giving me your words of peace. I didn't hear from Jesus before I went to her camper that day but I trusted in Jesus to give me the words and Jesus did.

My point is I had no idea what God would have me do that day. I guess talking to her was all He needed dune. Plant a little mustard seed of His love and my Jesus will turn it into a tree bearing fruit. My Jesus always makes my day. I didn't need money or a trip to some foreign country or a big tent to do the work of God. I simply needed to be available. If you are going on a missionary trip to a foreign country or preaching in a big tent tonight, then that is what God has for you to do today and may God bless you for being available. We are all part of the body of

Jesus Christ and if we all make our self-available God will use us for His glory.

The preparation to follow Jesus in the physical is to be available, to be teachable and most of all is to turn your hearing to Jesus and away from the things of this world. The preparation to follow Jesus spiritually is to die to yourself, pick up your cross and follow Jesus by seeking Him with your whole heart, mind and soul and allow Jesus to teach you like He taught the apostles.

Prayer is Very Important

How we pray to our Lord is very important. I have been taught by Jesus to pray without an answer. That is, I pray knowing God has an answer and so I don't spend my time trying to figure out what His answer is to all my prayers. I think when we try to answer our own problem as we pray to God we are saying to Him 'I have this problem figured out for you Lord so all I need from you God is do what I have figured out for you to do.'

The story about the lady with the loud music noise is a prime example of praying without an answer. I had no idea what to say to that woman until she opened her door. Then Jesus gave me the words.

The absolute worst thing we believers do when we pray is to give up our profession of faith because of what we only see physically. What do we believers do if we pray and nothing seems to happen? Do we find a loophole in the Word of Jesus to define our result? How much faith does it take to say, "It must not be His will or you know it is all in God's timing." Faith is to stand firm. When we stand firm in our profession of faith that the miracle will happen no matter what we see with our physical eyes. I believe that by standing firm in our faith we have pleased God and the miracle will happen.

When we pray, we are actually commissioning a battle in the spirit realm and God does the battle and God always wins so we always win. Our part is to stand firm in our profession of faith.

I believe it takes almost no faith to believe in a miracle that happens right in front of you but it takes great faith to stand firm knowing the battle is the Lords and knowing we just commissioned a battle and the Lord will always win the battle. Read how my Jesus spoke through Paul to tell us how faith works.

Galatians 5:6   For in Jesus Christ neither circumcision availed anything, nor uncircumcision; **but faith which worked by love.**

This might sound stupid but back then if you were not circumcised you would not be allowed inside the synagogue. I ask you, what is the difference between a person of circumcision and a person of uncircumcision except the physical removal of some skin? My point is the physical act of removing some skin does not change your heart, but faith which worked by love does change your heart.

I am thankful I live in the New Testament where Jesus tells us faith in our heart allows us to walk and have communion with God which is so much proof of belief than the physical sign of circumcision. In Hebrews 11:1 we see what faith is.

Hebrews 11:1 Now faith is the substance of things hoped for, and the evidence of things **not seen.**

I have actually told Jesus I like seeing the miracles but I like not seeing them even more. You see, when I pray for someone to be healed and I don't see the miracle happen in front of me, I believe Jesus is giving me an opportunity to stand firm in my faith no matter what I see. I believe Jesus trusts me to stand strong like Job and Abraham. You know the evidence of things that are not seen. I know in my heart that no prayer in faith goes unanswered. I know my Holy Spirit is bigger than what is in the world. I know my Holy Spirit loves me and I know faith works by love. Ask Jesus for His faith, His discernment, and His love and your heart will trust Him also.

I know Jesus has a great memory and sometimes He lets me know the person I prayed for was healed the next day or after I walked away and sometimes a year or two later. Standing firm in faith is a person who never wavers in his belief in the love of God. We read in our Holy Bible where Paul was beaten and left to die but Paul's faith in the love of God for him never wavered. Job in his trial never wavered. I think when we come to the realization by prayer in faith we are commissioning a battle and God always wins the battle and so we win and our faith will be strong.

We simply must stand firm in faith and then when you find out later that the person we prayed for was healed then your faith will sky rocket. Please never doubt the Word of God. God told us in His Word that He has elevated His Word above our circumstances and I believe God has truly elevated His word above our circumstances. Remember to seek God and not the answer to our circumstance, because God is and already has the answer to our circumstance.

Let us read on for we are talking about being prepared by seeking ye first the kingdom of God and His righteousness. I ask you, what good is prayer if we doubt God will answer. Here in Hebrews 10:35 Jesus tells us not to throw away our confidence, for standing in Faith has great reward.

Hebrews 10:35 Therefore do not throw away your confidence, which has a great reward.

How do we throw away our confidence? The answer is by simply looking at our circumstance. That is, we watch to see if the miracle happen in front of us and if so we believe and if not, then we shrink back. I have heard great preachers say words like 'come back tomorrow and we will pray again.' I just cannot find Jesus doing that. I was taught Jesus prayed for a blind man twice but I looked up the parable and it doesn't say Jesus prayed twice.

Mark 8:23-25 And He took the blind man by the hand and led him out of the town. And when He had spat on his eyes and had put His hands on him, He asked Him if he saw anything. And he looked up and said, I see men as trees, walking. And after that He put His hands again on his eyes and made him look up. And he was restored and saw all clearly.

Jesus laid hands on the blind man twice but the scripture doesn't say Jesus prayed twice. I pray for the faith of Jesus and the wisdom of Jesus and the compassion of Jesus. I believe our great reward is in knowing and trusting by faith the prayer is answered no matter what we see.

In Hebrews 10:36, we read our reward for doing the will of God —such as casting out devils, healing the sick, raising the dead, forgiving sins is to receive from God what God has promised. No prayer will come back to us void. Please ask God to help you stand firm in your faith and you will find out some day the person you prayed for received the miracle you prayed for.

Hebrews 10:36   For you have need of endurance, so that when you have done the will of God you may receive what is promised.

Yes we just read and heard we have need of endurance in faith for I believe faith comes from our relationship with God. With faith in God we are told we will receive what is promised by God.Let us read the words of Isaiah 55:10:

Isaiah 55:10-11   For as the rain comes down, and the snow from heaven, And do not return there, But water the earth, And make it bring forth and bud, That it may give seed to the sower And bread to the eater, So shall My word be that goes forth from My mouth; It shall not return to Me void, But it shall accomplish what I please, And it shall prosper in the thing for which I sent it.

I wonder if you are thinking right now is why does God let the rain and the snow fall on the just and the unjust. I know it is the goodness of God that leads a man to repentance. I believe God wants everyone to come to know His love through us His believers. If God was impartial we believers would have a right to be impartial. We are to live as Jesus lived and not show partiality.

Matthew 5:45   That ye may be the children of your Father which is in heaven: for he maketh his sun to rise on the evil and on the good, and sendeth rain on the just and on the unjust.

I want to live as Jesus lived. I want to be a child of my Father in heaven and I want to live without partiality. I want to turn the other cheek and be the love of Jesus to all I meet.

Our reward for faith is not the rain and the snow on our fields neither is it the warming sun from heaven. Our reward is being able to speak the Word of God in faith and seeing the power in His name come into our realm. Our reward is living in the joy of the Lord and living in the peace of the Lord today. I know the unjust or the evil doers I have met live with the sun and rain on their fields, but they do not have the peace and joy of Jesus in their heart. I believe my job is to bring the contagiousness of joy and peace of God into their life.

Jesus tells us we are too sent to the lost sheep and we go with joy and peace.

Isaiah 55:12 For you shall go out with joy, And be led out with peace; The mountains and the hills Shall break forth into singing before you, And all the trees of the field shall clap their hands.

I know the joy of the Lord and the peace of the Lord so I must be living in the reward. I have been in the mountains and I have been in the presents of the Lord and I have seen the trees clap their hands. I believe these rewards are for everyone who asks God for His Holy Spirit to dwell in them. I want you to know I did not go to the mountains to see these things but I was led to the mountains and Jesus showed me these things and then Jesus led me in the scriptures to know these things.

Here is a different type of reward:

Hebrews 10:37 for, "Yet a little while, and the coming one will come and will not delay;

Believing by faith is living in righteousness but if we shrink back our faith with sayings that seem right to a man like it must be in God's timing or it might not be His will, I believe we are putting our circumstances above the word of God and above the love of Jesus Christ. Jesus tells us plainly in Hebrews 10:38 that God has no pleasure in us that shrink back our faith.

Hebrews 10:38 but my righteous one shall live by faith, and **if he shrinks back, my soul has no pleasure in him.**

Hebrews 10:38 could say the very soul of Father God and Jesus have no pleasure in the one whose faith shrinks back and to the one who resorts to writing new doctrine, like miracles are all in God's timing or it might not be his will. It takes no faith to make up doctrine that sounds right to a man. I believe such doctrine put us in the unrighteous category but do not take my word on that. Instead take these thoughts to God and let Him teach you His truth from His word.

To believe God loves us does takes faith and we must stand firm, saying I have called on the name of Jesus and I know His will because I have read His book and I know what I pray will happen because my prayer aligns with the will of God. We must establish the will of God in our heart before we pray. If we don't have His will established in our heart we will look at the results of our prayers and if nothing seemed to happen in front of us we will shrink back, lose our confidence and sadly we will probably stop praying for people.

I believe the opposite of Hebrews 10:38 is also true. Standing firm in our faith in the word of God will put pleasure in the heavenly realm. I want with all my heart to be pleasing to God. I want to be righteous in His sight. I want to see God jump out of His mercy seat to hug me when I get there. I know how to make that happen because Jesus in His Word tells me how. I will not shrink back in faith, I will not write doctrine but I will simply believe Jesus and Father God love me and the miracles I see or don't see will not shake my faith. I also know by faith their love for me makes all things possible so if I don't see the miracle, I know God has great faith in me to stand firm in His Word.

Ask God to establish His will in your heart and spend time in His Word allowing Jesus to teach you, establish you, transform your heart and your faith will grow. The Holy Spirit of God will be establishing the miracle of God's love in us born again believers when we make being established in their love our priority. Believers in the Word of God who by faith in His love for us do not shrink back will never be referred to as hypocrites. Faith in the Word of Jesus and Father God will transform the world and the glory of God will be expanded. The righteous will see the Glory of God and God will rejoice in us being His glory here on earth.

Miracles will not just be a show of power in the name of Jesus but miracles will become the loving compassion of Jesus flowing through you by faith. You will know His compassion, you will know His will and you will know that miracles do happen and you will know the love of Jesus has given you the privilege to be an established miracle worker and with faith in God you will never shrink back.

Please let the love of God grow in your heart in abundance by simply making God your priority. Sometimes I start thinking about things that are not of God or sometimes my mind will drift by just looking around at the world and these earthly things can take my mind off from Jesus and His love for me. The distractions of the world are endless but they leave you empty. The love of God is joy beyond our understanding and is very fulfilling. Now I find myself asking God for everything. I even ask Him why I'm thinking about these distractions and my Holy Spirit puts me right on the narrow path again. Set your mind on the things above and the things below will stay under your feet and not in your mind.

Don't take my word on this but instead push yourself into quiet time reading His word looking for the heart of Jesus and you will find His heart everywhere in His word. Even if you have shrunk back in the past; please don't dwell on your past for the past will rob you of your future.

Look at Hebrews 10:39 and how the heart of God goes right on to say believers will become strong in their faith and as our faith grows by our knowledge of His truth we will not shrink back and we are not destroyed for lack of knowledge for we are those who have faith in God and with His faith rooted in us we know miracles happen when we stand firm in faith and we will preserve souls by the faith God has in us.

We simply must make intimacy with God our priority by listening and believing and not wavering. True intimacy will not happen by part time faith, you know, getting together on the first Friday night of the month and going out to pray for people as a group. These actions can be good stepping stones into more faith but faith literally has to become a lifestyle. Read Hebrews 10:38-39 again to see if there is any part time faith in them. Jesus and the apostles walked by faith 24/7. Faith is not a first Friday of the month event.

Hebrews 10:38-37   but my righteous one shall **live** by faith, and **if he shrinks back, my soul has no pleasure in him.** But we are not of those who shrink back and are destroyed, but of those who have faith and preserve their souls.

We just read in Hebrews 10:38 how Jesus has no pleasure in those who let their faith shrink from circumstances like when we don't see the results we want in our prayer. Sometimes I wonder if we even have faith when we pray. I mean listening to some of our prayers I think are we trying to talk God into our request? I think sometimes we pray to see if God works or to see if God answers our prayers. These faithless prayers come from not knowing we are loved by God. How on earth will we be the hope of God's glory if we don't understand and live in His loving covenant He died to give us?

So how does God deal with us when we allow the circumstances to shrink back our faith? I believe we will be relaying on the mercy of God to give us another chance like Jesus gave the apostles. The mercy of God is towards us. And if we struggle with faith, I believe Jesus through His love for us will forgive us. Jesus teaches us and helps us learn and become stronger if we willingly die to our self and take time to listen for His voice and allow Him to teach us and grows us up in faith.

In Hebrews 10:39 we read that the righteous are those who do not shrink back and we are not destroyed because if our prayer and circumstances don't seem to line up with the word of God at the moment we pray; the righteous will stand in faith knowing and not doubting the circumstances will line up with the word of God. Our prayers will be transformed from a request to a prayer that is a profession of faith. *Thank you Jesus for loving this person and thank you for healing this person.* Our prayer will be His loving words going back to Him and we will have faith our prayer will not return to us void of His power.

If you have ever shrunk back your faith by watching the circumstances please don't beat yourself up over your shortcomings. Instead, realize you may have been taught by the wisdom of man and you maybe praying from man's wisdom instead of a place of faith in God. Jesus teaches us He is full of mercy and compassion and Jesus demonstrated His mercy to the apostles so we believers will receive His divine mercy and compassion towards us also.

I believe what Jesus desires or values more than His own life while He was here on earth is for us to make knowing Him a priority in our life. Again, Jesus is our example of how we are to live, meaning Jesus made us His priority and we are to make living the life He modeled for us our priority. The life of Jesus brought a boat load of glory to His Father and our life will bring glory to God if we lay down the things of this world and seek God with our whole heart.

What Lack of Faith Looks Like

Reading the scriptures we also come to the realization the apostles got upset when the power in the name of Jesus didn't work for them. In this story I believe Jesus was teaching us believers a new teaching – that even when the power of God didn't seem to work for the apostles, what did the apostles do? The apostles went right to their source and ask Jesus why? You know we have the same source and Jesus is hearing our cries 24/7 so please turn on your hearing and start listening for when you do your faith will grow. Just in case you don't remember, Jesus told the apostles it was their lack of faith.

Matthew 17:19-21 Then came the disciples to Jesus apart, and said, Why could not we cast him out? And Jesus said unto them, **Because of your unbelief:** for verily I say unto you, If ye have faith as a grain of mustard seed, ye shall say unto this mountain, Remove hence to yonder place; and it shall remove; and nothing shall be impossible unto you. Howbeit this kind goeth not out but by prayer and fasting.

Reading how the apostles always went right to Jesus with there questions and how the apostles had full expectation in Jesus to answer their questions is a very, very strong teaching for us. Jesus let the apostles set a president for us to follow. When we have a question about God, we go to our source – the Holy Spirit of Jesus and Father God in us. We are not to go to the wisdom of man. We actually do not need to go fare to ask Jesus our questions because the Holy Spirit lives inside us now if we are born again of the Holy Spirit and believe the Holy Spirit of God living in us by faith will answer our questions if we have the faith to believe.

Look at the compassion of Jesus to correct the apostles. Jesus answered them plainly – *because of your unbelief.* But notice Jesus didn't dwell and lecture them about their unbelief. Jesus just went right on to tell them what they could do with faith the size of a mustard seed. All we believers need is to stand firm in our faith in His name. Yes, the name above every name. Cancer will disappear, your bad back will straighten, those clogged arteries will flow freely again and we will see miracles happen if we stand firm in our faith and do not shrink back our faith with unbelief. Please read Mathew 17:19-21 again:

> **Matthew 17:19-21** Then came the disciples to Jesus apart, and said, Why could not we cast him out? And Jesus said unto them, **Because of your unbelief:** for verily I say unto you, If ye have faith as a grain of mustard seed, ye shall say unto this mountain, Remove hence to yonder place; and it shall remove; and nothing shall be impossible unto you. Howbeit this kind goeth not out but by prayer and fasting.

Most Christians who I talk too think fasting is staying away from food and I know our Holy Bible does talk about disciplining the body through fasting. I believe fasting can be in any form that you like to do. Personally, I believe Jesus has called me to fast from television, internet, video games and all the dung of this world. I believe fasting is between you and God personally and not for the world to know unless you hear form God to share a testimony about fasting. For Jesus said in Matthew 6:16-18:

> **Matthew 6:16-18** Moreover when ye fast, be not, as the hypocrites, of a sad countenance: for they disfigure their faces, that they may appear unto men to fast. Verily I say unto you, They have their reward. But thou, when thou fastest, anoint thine head, and wash thy face; That thou appear not unto men to fast, but unto thy Father which is in secret: and thy Father, which seeth in secret, shall reward thee openly.

Personally I believe Jesus is telling us in Matthew that your fasting should be personal and just between you and God. Jesus doesn't get specific about fasting like you need to fast from eggs every Thursday for about twenty-two and a half hours. Please ask God how to fast and what to fast from and your teacher Jesus will lead you to scriptures about growing your relationship with Him. Yes, I believe fasting should give us time to seek God with all your heart so please fast from wasting your time and start spending time with Him.

Our time together with our Teacher is so important to God and fasting from distractions should be important to us also. Jesus plainly tells us to guard our ear gates and our eye gates for what we see and hear will affect our life and so I believe these are the things Jesus has told me to fast from.

Here is an example of guarding our ears and eyes. I went to the laundromat yesterday. In this laundromat was a table with free magazines on it. One magazine was open and there's a picture of very pretty girl, but the picture was so provocative and immediately I wanted to see if there were more pictures of her. I am so blessed to know Jesus is with me! Before I had the chance to pick up the magazine, I heard in my heart how sad it is to see her beauty exploited this way.

Then I went to my camper and I have a hard time getting the picture of the pretty girl out of my mind. I started crying for the girl in the picture, to think she needed to have a picture like that to get men interested or desiring to be with her. I prayed for her to come to know God loves her and God desires is to receive His love for her. Knowing God is so much more then a bus ticket to heaven. Yes knowing God loves you gives you self worth and knowing God's love for you will fill your heart and remove the desire to have men or women desire you that way.

I think if I watch television my mind would become numb to God and His everlasting love for me and instead my mind will be full of provocative pictures like the one I just saw. Jesus tells us in His word to guard our mind and if I didn't guard my mind this picture would arouse me into momentary lustful sin and I would become unpleasing to God until I repented and turned away from the distractions.

The devil knows our weakness and will exploit them to his advantage. The moment I saw the picture I wanted to see if there were more pictures of this pretty young lady. No one else was in the laundromat and so I think it was safe to pick up the Cosmopolitan magazine but I believe the Holy Spirit checked my spirit and I love knowing my Jesus loves me and I love having His purity of heart toward me. I know if Jesus didn't love me I would – well, I will not even think where the trap would have taken me.

Thank you Jesus for your purity of love toward me and thank you Jesus for letting me see the snare of the devil to dwell on her picture instead of you God. I am so blessed to know Jesus loves me and I pray for the pretty girl in the picture to come to know the purity of God's love towards her also.

I pray and hope that pretty young girl in the picture comes to realize what the devil meant to be bad had shown God in His love to turned her picture into an opportunity for me to pray for her to come to know the Lord. And I hope she is saying to the Lord today, "You know someone lifted my heart up to you Lord and you heard their prayers and answered." Thank you Jesus for I know by faith in your love toward us, this will happen.

Jesus also tells us faith works by love.

Galatians 5:6 For in Jesus Christ neither circumcision availeth any thing, nor uncircumcision; but faith which worketh by love.

Jesus knew the secret to moving the mountains. Paul knew the secret to moving mountains, and now we know the secret is the love of God toward us and we can move mountains. The secret is faith worketh by love. With faith in God we will simply know we are the beloved of Jesus and Father God here on earth.

The great man of faith knew they were loved above there circumstances and God will reveal His love to you and hopefully you will respond by faith in the knowledge you are loved if you simply seek Him above the dung of this world. Jesus told the Samaritan woman at the well we must worship God in spirit and truth.

John 4:23-24 But the hour is coming, and is now here, when the true worshipers will worship the Father in spirit and truth, for the Father is seeking such people to worship him. God is spirit, and those who worship him must worship in spirit and truth.

We worship in spirit through believing in Jesus being the truth and proving our belief by our actions of love. Actions of belief become actions of love when we share or demonstrate our belief in Jesus being the truth. In James 2:26:

> **James 2:26**   For as the body without the spirit is dead, so faith without works is dead also.

Please read on in John 4 how the Samaritan woman became the spokesperson for Jesus. She did not proclaim her belief to Jesus by signing to Jesus about her belief or telling Jesus you are worthy or asking the Holy Spirit to come down here. The Samaritan woman proved her belief by her actions of love. She was so excited to share the truth she ran and told everyone in her town come see the man *"He told me all that I ever did."* And the town people went out to meet Jesus.

How much time did the woman spend preparing to be the spokesperson of Jesus? Notice she hadn't even repented at this point or at least she hadn't repented to my knowledge. Yet Jesus was able to preach the word to the town's people and they became believers, because the woman gave these people a desire to know Jesus. I believe the woman felt in her heart the love of Jesus for Jesus never condemned her for having five husbands and living with someone now. I believe Jesus knew in His heart the woman would respond to the true love of Jesus and turn away from her former selfish, sinful desires.

Man's wisdom tells us we need an education. In the world today we are taught to go to school and become educated and prepared before you go out into the *real world*. Actually the schools today have been inundated with everything but God to a point where I see schools even some Christian schools as a place where our children are led away from God and His truth and His love.

I have noticed man's wisdom is almost constantly putting down the truth of the word of God and replacing the truth of God with the lies of man's wisdom. Man's wisdom is actually putting down faith in Jesus by calling the world we live in the *real world* as if to say we Christians who are living in the loving truth of Jesus, live in an unreal world. The Samaritan woman didn't need years and years of man's reasoning and sociology to change her life, Jesus proved she only needed a few minutes of Jesus and His loving truth to be transformed.

I believe our preparation for service in the work of the kingdom starts with knowing we are loved. We will repent, we will become worthy, we will become knowledgeable and we will become teachable as we seek first our Father God through Jesus. Our desire to seek God with all our heart will come alive when we first know we are loved. I remember falling in love with my Jenny but my joy, my peace and my strength to endure came when I knew Jenny loved me. The wisdom of knowing I am loved by God gives me the will and the desire to be a vessel of His love for my loving God.

The Samaritan woman at the well simply gave the people of her town the desire to know God and God brought the increase. Jesus is still our teacher and by faith we can know we are His loved ones and with the knowledge of knowing we are loved we can be of service to help build the kingdom of God. Jesus tells us in His word we are to be in the world and not of the world. I believe I live in the REAL WORLD of knowing I am loved; for living in the REAL WORLD of being loved by God removes my fear of man's *real world*.

I have traveled around the United States for over seven years now and have been in some pretty rough spots, someone asks me the other day if I had a dog for protection. I told him I do not have a dog and added I don't need a dog for protection. He said a dog can save your life, to which, I answered I would rather be in heaven, meaning I believe God will determine when my time here on earth is spent. My faith for my protection is in God and not a dog. I refuse to put my faith for protection in a dog or in a locked door or in a gun and yes I live in the real world.

This man's wife then asked me if I eat healthy. I told her I sure do and I added, "I ask God to bless the food I eat so I don't spend time reading labels and health books. I read in my Holy Bible I am to seek first the kingdom of God and from the knowledge of God being my teacher I am taught to simply ask God to bless the food I eat to my body and I believe He does. I also read in my Holy Bible to guard my eyes and ears for what I see and hear will affect me so I turn off the distractions and that frees my mind to seek first the kingdom of God. I simply allow God to be God and I live without the fear of death. Jesus actually showed us there is no death, so why would I fear death."

The couple walked away.

Fear of death is such a big deal in man's world. In the real world of my Jesus we will live forever and I am loved by the creator of the forever, He personally breathed life into me and His Holy Spirit lives in me. He sent His only Son at that time to show me how to live fearlessly. I believe the Spirit of love lives in me so I have hope and peace to travel and live without fear.

Like I said I truly loved my wife Jenny and I could of sang to her about how much I loved her 24/7 and I could tell her 24/7 how much I worship her, '*I worship you, I worship you, I worship you.*' I could wave flags for hours on Sunday or every day of the year and none of these things would prove I love her. To show Jenny I truly loved her I need to do unselfish works of love. An unselfish work of love could be simply having quiet time with Jenny which would prove I had made hearing her heart my priority.

You know looking back when Jenny and I were dating, I must say I had no peace about loving Jenny, I had no comfort but I had a lot of anxiety. I believe our peace, our joy, our hope, our trust, didn't come until I knew Jenny loved me. I believe a relationship with God is the same way. All these gifts of joy, peace, comfort and trust come from knowing God loves us. I love you too Jesus and I love knowing you love me.

Believing the Holy Spirit of God lives in you and believing you are loved by God will help you come into the wisdom you are one of His chosen one's and this belief will remove your fear of death and your need for protection from outside sources. I mean can a dog keep you from getting cancer, or something as simple as just falling down? How could we put our faith in God if His son needed a dog to protect Him? A dog can be a great companion and a dog can warn you of some kinds of danger but our faith has to be in God for our protection.

Why Do Bad Things Happen to Christians?

I have met some Christians and non-Christians that ask if Jesus Christ dwells in us and loves us and we are His hope of glory then why do bad things happen to believers while living in this world.

Please think about this for a moment. Jesus is the ultimate believer of all time. Jesus was filled with faith and had the greatest relationship with His Father in the history of mankind. Did anything bad happen to Jesus? Was the life of Jesus full of candy and spice and everything nice?

Jesus had faith in the protection of His Father and there are stories in our Holy Bible where His Father did whisk Him away from manmade trouble. This protection from our Father is for us too. Read about the numerous stories in our Holy Bible like Daniel in the lion's den for example and you will see how we are protected by God.

I believe that by putting my faith in God when trouble comes my way God will either protect me or be glorified in the trouble that I endure in His name. I understand the trouble that came to Jesus by the way of the unbelievers – the beating, the humiliation and the cross brought glory to God. Yes I pray to be steadfast in my faith like the faith that Jesus had when trouble comes my way.

We believers can easily see the glory of God in the life lived of Jesus Christ. I pray for the strength of Jesus Christ when the trouble from nonbelievers comes my way. I pray to bring glory to God by being rooted in His love for me so I may withstand the pain of persecution and finish well.

Peter told Jesus to His face that he will lay down his life to follow Jesus and within hours Peter denied Jesus three times. Remember the answer Jesus gave as the apostles slept.

Matthew 26:41 Watch and pray, lest you enter into temptation. The spirit indeed is willing, but the flesh is weak.

I know my statements of faith are just words like the words of Peter until I am given the opportunity to prove my words of faith are true. This is why I tell everybody I want my test. I want my night in the lions den and I want my Abba Father and Jesus to be glorified by another testimony that helps others in their walk on the narrow path gain faith in my loving God.

I believe and I know the Holy Scripture of God tells us every good thing and every bad thing we encounter here on earth is brought about through our belief or unbelief. I believe I am being transformed daily by listening to and living with the Holy Spirit of my Father God and Jesus dwelling in me. I have willingly ask my Jesus to make me the new me that he created me to be. I have willingly accepted Jesus into my heart through baptism of water and by choosing to have His Holy Spirit dwell in me.

I read in the scriptures this new life is not only possible but it is a requirement to a joyful eternal life. I read how we will have the Joy of the Lord in our heart now and we are to walk in the Joy of the Lord now. When we receive Jesus into our heart, all Jesus asks us to do is to stand firm in our faith in His name and don't shrink back our faith. The love of God toward us, the peace that surpasses our understanding, the joy that will entice others to desire what they see in us, our blind trust in our Father no matter what the circumstances look like, and faith that delights the heavens is in us *now*. These are the good gifts from Abba Father God and Jesus Christ through childlike faith in believing the Holy Spirit dwells in us believers.

Think about the effects of belief and unbelief has in our life. Belief in God brings faith in God, everlasting joy, power, authority, love and the capability to show people the loving compassion of Jesus and Father God. Faith in God brings hope, security and knowledge that truth is the person of JESUS CHRIST and the Holy Spirit of Jesus will live in us now by faith.

John 14:17   Even the Spirit of truth; whom the world cannot receive, because it seeth him not, neither knoweth him: but ye know him; for he dwelleth with you, and shall be in you.

I really love how clear Jesus makes the truth of where His Holy Spirit lives and dwells and who knows Him and who doesn't know Him.

Let us take a moment to contrast belief in God with unbelief or faith in the devil. With unbelief, we *feel* a need for security, we *feel* a need to lock our doors, and we *feel* a need for prisons, boundaries and laws. With unbelief we receive fear to the max along with *feelings* of sadness, depression, hopelessness and momentary life ups and downs. Unbelief drives us with *feelings* and not truth. Unbelief is momentary happiness and unbelief never has an answer. Unbelief is a search for security that will limit you to where you go and what time of day or night you go.

Unbelief brings a never ending search for truth because in unbelief truth becomes an answer to a question and truth becomes the knowledge that puffeth up oneself and man's truth usually does not edify the Spirit of truth. Unbelief leads people down a complicated wide path fueled by a need to know, a need to understand, a need for happiness or a need to look smart in your own findings, a need to have more dung than your neighbor. Contrast that to the simplicity of a simple life with faith in God being the answer and the truth.

By seeking the kingdom of God we are saying to God that we will live by faith in God and we know we have the truthful answer to life in our heart. Seeking God is a journey to freedom from the world. You know we are told we live in the world and we are told to be in the world but not of the world. These scriptures are discernment tools for us and will help us know who is of the world and who is not of the world. The scriptures will also show us where we need to improve and how God Himself through the Holy Spirit is sprinkling our evil conscience clean by the renewing of our mind if we receive God into our heart. Please read 1 John 4:4-8:

1 John 4:4-8 You are of God, little children, and have overcome them, because He who is in you is greater than he who is in the world. **They are of the world. Therefore they speak as of the world, and the world hears them**. We are of God. He who knows God hears us; he who is not of God does not hear us. By this we know the spirit of truth and the spirit of error. Beloved, let us love one another, for love is of God; and everyone who loves is born of God and knows God. He who does not love does not know God, for God is love.

When we seek ye first the kingdom of God and His righteousness we are choosing to allow God to transform our heart into His image and likeness.

He who does not love does not know God, for God is love. Jesus makes everything simple. If you meet someone who does not walk and speak in love we know immediately that they are not of God. We are told to love one another for God is love. If you would like to be pleasing to God, then simply become His love.

1 John 4:9-13 In this the love of God was manifested toward us, that God has sent His only begotten Son into the world, **that we might live through Him. In this is love, not that we loved God, but that He loved us** and sent His Son to be the propitiation for our sins. Beloved, if God so loved us, we also ought to love one another. No one has seen God at any time. If we love one another, God abides in us, and His love has been perfected in us. By this we know that we abide in Him, and He in us, because He has given us of His Spirit.

John is describing the supernatural transformation that we can only receive through belief. Oh how my heart yearns for and lives for this transformation and by faith in God to seek Him above all else! I will receive the love of God and become the love of God for I know once I was of the world and yet my Jesus was waiting patiently for me to turn off the world and turn my heart toward Him. Thank you Jesus for loving me so much and thank you for being so patient with me! Jesus, You prove to me every day that your love for me is beyond real and your love is supernatural.

Let us look at how Jesus does these supernatural transformations so willingly and what is required of us:

Ephesians 4:20-24 But you have not so learned Christ, if indeed **you have heard Him** and **have been taught by Him**, as **the truth is in Jesus**: that you put off, concerning your former conduct, the old man which grows corrupt according to the deceitful lusts, and be renewed in the spirit of your mind, and that you put on the new man which was created according to God, in true righteousness and holiness.

To become the new man Paul is talking about we need to spend time listening to our Jesus. We need to be teachable and reachable to Jesus for the knowledge of the truth we search for truly is in the Spirit of Jesus. I seek God with all my heart and His righteousness because I want to hear and be taught and live in the truth of Jesus. The truth of Jesus is in our Holy Bible but we must do more than know His truth in scripture. We must allow by faith for Jesus to teach us and talk to us. And be willing to listen and we will receive His Holy Spirit of truth in us and we will be transformed into His love.

If all you want from Jesus is a bus ticket to heaven then I am afraid someone has misled you. I believe you have missed the reason Jesus came. You probably have a relationship with the Bible and not with Jesus Himself. Jesus will personally teach you about His love and He will back up everything He says with scripture that's why we must know our Holy Bible. But we will only become Christ-like when we receive His Holy Spirit and allow His Holy Spirit to direct our path.

I know people who have been taught to say the sinner's prayer and they believe they are saved. The sinner's prayer is a powerful prayer and it is necessary but the sinner's prayer is only the beginning of our relationship with Jesus. If all you ever do is say the prayer then I ask you does simply saying the sinner's prayer help you hear from God and be taught of God and come to know God as truth. The sinner's prayer is not a prayer for intimacy with God. The sinner's prayer does not teach you to hear from God and the sinner's prayer is void of the love God has for us. Actually the sinner's prayer seems very selfish to me.

Jesus is in the transforming business here and now. Transforming comes through hearing from God and being taught by God and understanding the truth is the person of God. Paul says in Ephesians 4:21, *if indeed you have heard Him and have been taught by Him as the truth is in Jesus.* Notice that we are to hear from God not just to know God. We will know of God from reading our Holy Bible and we will know we can hear from God from reading our Holy Bible. But intimacy with God comes from spending quiet time with God not just reading His book.

The relationship I am talking about is not a relationship with your Holy Bible. Please read your Holy Bible to become acquainted with Jesus and His teachings. Read the scriptures to hear and have His compassion. Read for wisdom to see His love for you revealed. Read to know His will so you can become His will here on earth.

Please read the scriptures to have the discernment of Jesus and as you read listen for His voice and you too will become so close to Jesus the two of you will become one. Ask Jesus for these gifts and you will come to know God not as a book of Scriptures but as a source of truth, trust, faith and best of all to come into an awareness of His love for you. I can safely tell you with full assurance that being dependent on God is the best place you will ever be.

Talking about depending on God being a great place to be brings me to tell you about the gas gauge in my car that hasn't worked for years. I simply depend on God to tell me when I need gas and He does. I have lived this way for years and I never run out of gas. Jesus always prompts me when I need gas.

When I talk about hearing from God, I literally discern the voices I hear by the discernment Jesus is teaching me through the Word of God in His Holy Bible. Jesus is truth, love, compassion, and these are the gifts that led to discernment. I hope you will seek these gifts through your intimate relationship with God. Today, people seem to have their life centered on money and some even think of money as a gift from God. If money is a gift from God then why do Christians work long hours to get money? Why do Christians go to school to learn how to make money and at the end of the day it seems most Christians who are seeking money become broke, empty, wore out and tired?

The gifts I am talking about are hearing form God, peace beyond our understanding, faith that is supernatural and the Love of God towards you will bring everlasting joy and strength. These gifts encourage us and they come to us gift wrapped in the true love of God. Godly gifts will overflow to our heart and we are able to give these gifts freely to others. Godly gifts have nothing to do with momentary money but they will change your life forever. You don't work for these gifts and you cannot earn them but God gives us His gifts freely when we seek God above all else. I believe God tells us in His Word that He is always calling us. But sadly it seems a lot of us are too busy making money to listen for the loving voice of my God.

My discernment comes from knowing God through the Holy Bible. My relationship, my trust in God and my belief in God comes from knowing God through my Holy Bible. The Holy Bible is the rock of foundation that we stand on and discern from. The Holy Bible is the knowledge we need to *be renewed in the spirit of your mind.* But the Holy Bible is a book and I simply cannot fall in love with a book. The person of Jesus Christ, the truth of Jesus, the wisdom of Jesus and the love Jesus has for us comes to us by allowing the Holy Spirit of Jesus into our heart and through us willingly being baptized by the Holy Spirit into a supernatural faith in God's love for us.

Please think about this for a moment. Suppose you don't know me but one of your friends gave you this book and ask you to read it. As you read this book you are forming an opinion about me. You are deciding whether or not to believe what you are reading in this book. You could go to others that have read this book and ask them their opinion of me but the person with the final say as to what this book says is the author. Without access to the author all the other opinions are hearsay. I believe Father God sent His Son to remove hearsay from His book and give us the truth in a personal way. I believe I can talk to God 24/7 and I believe God is talking to me through His book. I believe Jesus calls this process *the renewing of your mind.*

This renewing comes through baptism, which is usually close to the starting point of our relation with God. Through baptism, we make a choice to seek God with our whole heart, mind and soul. We are baptized by water physically but spiritually we are accepting the Holy Spirit of Jesus and Father God into our heart. Please study the Word of Jesus and you will see I am talking from His truth. We Christians are so blessed because we have the freedom to study the Word to see if what we are hearing is true or not. Remember the things of this world are temporary and yet we are given favor from God to turn our thoughts toward God and for doing so we receive joy eternal.

The Word of God is written for us to study and show our self-approved. The heart of God is revealed in His Word along with His will. Relationship with God is receiving His truth into your heart so His truth becomes you and you live in His will. We become one with God by choice and through accepting His Holy Spirit into your heart and in doing so we can become one with His truth. When these beliefs are in place we will hear from God and be able to discern His voice and prove the voice we hear is from God because His words will always line up with His Holy Bible. Yes we will hear from our teacher, by listening for His word in what we hear.

John 4:40-42   So when the Samaritans came to him, they asked him to stay with them, and he stayed there two days. And many more believed because of his word. They said to the woman, **"It is no longer because of what you said that we believe, for we have heard for ourselves, and we know that this is indeed the Savior of the world."**

I hope and pray I am making myself clear. Don't believe because of what I say in this book but please do as the Samaritans did and ask God to stay with you and forever God will be your teacher. Then you will have heard for yourself and you will have no doubt Jesus is indeed the Savior of the world.

The voice of God will become distinguishable and recognizable and you will always be able to verify what you are hearing from God with His words in the scripture. Discernment is so very important and Jesus taught discernment all through His life. Jesus lived His life without fear and so should we. Walking in the knowledge of His love for us will enable you to walk without fear. Being fearless is not a concept to ponder – it is a gift of faith from seeking God with your whole heart and soul. Life without worry is life in the image and likeness of God and you receive true life by receiving their Holy Spirit into your heart.

The Scripture tells us the Holy Spirit comes into you and talks to you and the two of you become one. We receive the Holy Spirit by faith and we hear Him by faith and by faith we discern the compassion in His voice and then we are transformed into teachable and useable and Jesus our teacher will lead us into all truth for in Jesus is the whole truth. When we recognize the voice of Jesus and listen to His teachings, please do not doubt Him. We will prove our faith by accepting blindly the truth of Jesus. I believe this is the process of putting off the old man and being renewed in the Spirit of your mind. Then we will accept the new man with true righteousness and holiness into our heart and with the Holy Spirit in us we will attain the goal. We will be transformed into the hope of glory for Jesus Christ and Father God.

Guess what? When you choose to allow the love of God into your heart the Holy Spirit will come into your heart and fill your heart with the gifts of the Holy Spirit. You will be given choices every day. We must recognize in ourselves the old man with his deceitful lust doesn't give up easy. That is the old man doesn't say 'I give up on this one for he belongs to God now.' Actually I think the opposite is true. Just as Jesus was tempted in all manners after He was baptized – the devil wanted to see if Jesus believed He was the Son of God. We too will be tempted to see if we believe that we are now the Son of God. As soon as Jesus was baptized, Father God proclaimed to the world *'This is my beloved Son in whom I am well pleased.'*

Matthew 3:16-17 And when Jesus was baptized, immediately he went up from the water, and behold, the heavens were opened to him, and he saw the Spirit of God descending like a dove and coming to rest on him; and behold, a voice from heaven said, "This is my beloved Son, with whom I am well pleased."

You just read that Jesus was baptized with water and filled with the Holy Spirit and we know Jesus was still tempted and we are still tempted too so don't be discouraged by the temptation to not believe but steadfast to your confession of faith as Jesus did. Jesus was tempted by the devil to choose earthly gratification – the things of this world, or choose the eternal love of his Father. We have the exact same temptation as Jesus. So what do you choose? Is it the faith in God through His love for us or the lifestyle of the devil and live worldly?

This is an example of living worldly: I remember before I gave my heart to the Lord if I felt I needed some worldly possessions I would go into debt for it. Looking back, I realize I lived to make payments and had this mindset of when I get my debts paid off then I will be happy. Jenny and I always thought whatever went into debt is paid off then we will have extra dollars every month. It seemed when the payment was gone so was the extra money. I mean the money just disappeared.

My life and your life will have a big difference now that we have accepted the Holy Spirit into our heart. We now have the Spirit of truth in us and the Holy Spirit will be with us every step of our life. Yes, by our simple choice to believe we have the Holy Spirit in us we will enable the Holy Spirit of God to make the things of the world less attractive to us. The things of this world will not have the same draw on us as before. Slowly, we will see the joy of the Lord replace the momentary happiness of the things of this world. Our goals will be transformed into becoming Godlike in all manner of life and this transformation will send the devil and his lusts packing. I hope you understand the choice to have God in your heart is one we must make every day and right now is a good time to give your heart to the Lord.

Removing the Worldly and Becoming Godlike

I believe chasing worldly things and living in debt is perhaps what Jesus referred to as seeing through a glass darkly. Living in debt is chasing happiness. We believers all want to see Jesus clearly and yet until we get to heaven we will not know for sure what Jesus and Father God look like. Debt is the same way. We set our mind on the thing we think we need and it clouds our mind and we think it is worth going into debt for but when we buy it then we clearly see that paying it become bothersome. Set your mind on the things above and see clearly the joy of the Lord in your heart without payments.

1 Corinthians 13:10-13   But when that which is perfect is come, then that which is in part shall be done away. When I was a child, I spake as a child, I understood as a child, I thought as a child: but when I became a man, I put away childish things. For now we see through a glass, darkly; but then face to face: now I know in part; but then shall I know even as also I am known. And now abideth faith, hope, charity, these three; but the greatest of these is charity.

In our Holy Bible we are told to come to God with the faith of a child but in 1 Corinthians 13:10-13 we see when we invite Jesus into our heart we are to put away our childish ways. Faith of a child actually believes in the love of God towards us which brings everlasting joy and strength. The childish ways talked about in 1 Corinthians 13:10-13 that we are to put away are looking for the things of this world to bring us self-worth and happiness.

With child-like faith, we choose to believe in Jesus. We are choosing to abide in faith, hope and charity. We are told in the word that charity is the greatest of these three.

I pray for all Christians to put off the childish desires of this world and put on the gifts of our Holy Spirit – faith, hope and charity. For it is the gifts of the Holy Spirit that will remove the darkness of this world and open our eyes to belief that God does love us and our self-worth will be measured in our giving of His love rather then our earning of worldly positions. Our time will be spent doing for others instead of living to buy junk and making payments. Our joy will be complete and the devil with his lust will be under our feet. This is living with Christ in you and being the hope of His glory.

Jesus and the Spirit of truth will help you put down the things of this world and by your choice you will willingly let Jesus renew the spirit of our mind. I know this transformation will happen but do you realize we also control the speed of our transformation. Our renewing of our mind will take a lot longer if we continue to be distracted by the things of the world.

I am so blessed when some circumstances came into my life over 14 years ago where I had to remove the television from our house. Thinking back, I realize I was blessed for a couple years before the removal of our television because I had become totally board with television and would find myself searching all the channels looking for something I might want to watch and all the time I was thinking to myself, 'Why am I wasting my time like this?'

I now realize Jesus was gently removing my desire to watch television. Jesus is so gentle with me. So by the time I decided to remove the television from our house and my life, I didn't even miss it. I believe Jesus removed my desire for television before I actually removed our television, thus Jesus made the removal so painless.

Now, I cannot stand to be in the same room with a television on. I see it as a source of confusion, frustration and worse, I see it as stealing away the time I could be spending with my Jesus. Now, I think about the hours I wasted and I have repented and I thank God for showing me a more excellent way to live free of the television and from its distraction. I thank you again Jesus for your gentleness towards me and for giving of your time Jesus to transform me so gently.

I see the internet the same way. It is full of confusion, frustration, and the worse thing about the internet is some people even Christians see it as a source of truth. No one seems able to tell me who is responsible for the answers or definitions that you read from the internet. Yet, everyone seems to accept the internet as an authority and as truth. Accepting the internet as truth is really a dangerous place to be. I pray for people who are using the internet as a source of truth to become transformed by Jesus, for I am concerned they will wake up some day and see they have been deceived beyond belief. I pray that their wake up day is not also their judgment day. I pray today is the day they turn to my Lord and Savior for truth.

Here is a case in point. If you read a Webster's dictionary from the 1950's and then read one from the 2000's, you will notice the difference. You will recognize how the definitions changed. I believe in ten to twenty years the answers that will be on Google will not resemble the truth of anything that we know today.

Think about Jesus being tempted in the desert for just another moment. The devil quoted the Scriptures at Jesus and did so with 99% of his quote being truth but the cunning devil wove in 1% of his lies. Everyone I talk to about the internet will tell you there is a lot more than 1% bad on it. I am told every game played on the internet has some bad in it. People, please stop and think about what you are allowing into your house, worse into your heart and worse yet into the hearts of our loved ones. Our children look to their parents to for guidance and discernment. I wonder if they will find it.

I am blessed to know we have only one source of truth and Jesus proved His words true and Jesus even died for me. No one on the internet died to give me truth. I know this sounds extreme to some people but I beg you to please think about how much time you spend on the internet and try to spend that much time or equal time listening, learning and being loved by Jesus. I know if you take this challenge you won't regret it. Jesus tells us to guard our eye gates and our ear gates because what we let in through our eyes and ears will affect us. There is only one source of truth and the one source is my Jesus and He lives in me. Jesus is in my heart so I don't have an internet bill every month and yet I have a great trustworthy source of truth.

Here is a short story: A couple years ago, a friend gave me a book to read. My friend highly recommends this book. I didn't know the author and for some reason, I didn't have peace when I was reading it. I didn't Google if I should read the book but I did ask God if I should read the book. I felt a desire to see if the author quoted Scriptures and as I paged through the book I saw a Scripture quote with the address. I read the scripture quoted and it was about the apostles and Jesus passing by a blind man and how Jesus asks the apostles, "Who sinned? This man or his parents?" I immediately closed the book for I knew the book was full of lies. Jesus never asks the apostles who sinned. It was the apostles who asked Jesus who sinned.

The author of that book had a direct Scripture quote and seemed to very cunningly misquote the Scripture. I destroyed the book so no one else would read it. I couldn't help but wonder how many quotes on Google are actually misquoted. Again, go to Jesus for truth and you will receive truth.

John 9:2   And His disciples asked Him, saying, "Rabbi, who sinned, this man or his parents, that he was born blind?"

The other day while traveling in my car to see my friends I stopped in a rest area to use the bathroom. There was big sign out front that read 'Six million years ago, this area...' and that is all I would read of that sign. I knew the words on that sign were words of man's knowledge and they don't line up with the Word of God so I stopped reading it because I didn't want them to go into my mind or heart.

You might not agree with me right now and you might be thinking, 'Ron, no one knows for sure how old the world is.' So I ask you if I spend the next two years trying to figure out who is right – man's knowledge or my Holy Bible, do I have faith in God being the truth or a need for man's knowledge? I choose faith and in the six day creation. I believe in my Holy Bible and I have the joy of knowing who truth is and the truth lives inside of me. Also, I know if I need to know how old the earth is, my loving Jesus will tell me in that very hour.

I believe with the help of the Holy Spirit we will willingly and totally get rid of deceitful lust, unforgiveness, and all the sin of unbelief Jesus talked about in His Holy Bible. I believe all the sins of mankind come under one sin that is the sin of unbelief. Read what John 1:29 says:

John 1:29 The next day John seeth Jesus coming unto him, and saith, Behold the Lamb of God, which taketh away the **sin** of the world.

Yes, there is only one sin in the world and the sin of the world is unbelief. Believing in Jesus and his truth makes my life simple. I simply believe in the Lamb of God which takes away the sin of the world. Man's wisdom is still trying to prove that the six day creation of the world God talks about in the Holy Bible is a lie. Discernment is simple – man's wisdom six billion years or the word of God six days.

Jesus tells us to live by faith and man's wisdom tells us we can explain everything through knowledge. Jesus tells us to heal the sick and man says go to the doctor. Jesus tells us to be His loving ambassadors and man says don't be a fool. I believe Jesus is truth and love and He lives in me. I believe in His Word and so I live eternally. If man's wisdom confirms the word of God then fine, but I already believed in God. If man's wisdom contradicts the Word of God I still believe the Word of God over man's wisdom and I refuse to debate in my mind something I already know as truth.

The Transformation Process

Transformations usually will not happen overnight but by faith in God they will happen. The apostles who were with Jesus for three years and even after being baptized in the Holy Spirit still had some personal issues to deal with. So how does the transformation process happen?

Start by inviting the Holy Spirit of truth into your heart. Jesus tells us to seek ye first the kingdom of God. Prove that you want the Holy Spirit in your heart by declaring a time every day to sit quietly and listen for His voice. Set your priorities. Ask God for discernment. I find sitting quietly is very hard for me but if I write down my thoughts in my quiet time so I can ponder them then I will have a great time with my Lord. And because my thoughts are written down, I have our quiet time thoughts to ponder all day. You have to decide what is more important. I hope you realize or willingly let God gently convict you. Are you trading video games, internet, television and momentary lust for the joy of knowing God really loves you?

In my quiet time with Jesus, I find that I always have a desire to look something up in the Scriptures. As I look in the scriptures, I find that I am being prompted to look further into the scriptures and as I do, the heart of God becomes clearer to me. I find discernment, truth and peace comes into me and I don't want to stop talking with my Jesus. I have literally gotten out of my seat and started jumping for joy as Jesus talks to me.

If you decide to turn off the distractions and turn on our Godly hearing, I know you will never regret it. I see people every day seeking the emptiness of momentary pleasure and I'm saddened in my heart for I know they are missing the joy of the Lord. Yes, I have found the fullness of joy from knowing God has replaced the emptiness of momentary earthy dung with His love.

A while back when I was visiting some friends I met this man who loves God and does street ministry, prison ministry and has been a pastor of a church. He is getting up in years and has started with Parkinson's disease. His daughter came to visit and she has some disease that in a few years will be life-threatening. They are both on special diets and adhere to their diets very strongly. At dinner time, they asked me to pray the blessing on the meal. Without thinking, I said, "Dearest heavenly Father, I thank you for blessing this food to be a blessing to my body and I thank you I have faith to believe you for the rest of us here tonight I am not sure they have your faith so I guess they are on their own." Everyone laughed but I was totally surprised by the words I spoke. I had never even had a thought like that before.

On the way back to my camper, I was talking to my Jesus when I suddenly realized I needed to pray for that man and his daughter. Jesus showed me how they had their faith in food to solve their health problems. I cannot speak for God but I wonder if we grieve the Holy Spirit when we do all the things God commanded us to do – heal the sick, cast out devils and raise the dead, but when it comes to our own health we sometimes put our faith in our food. I believe this lack of faith comes from our lack of truly knowing God loves us. I know that man has seen miracles happen right in front of him so that is not the problem. If we truly believe Jesus loves us then we will know our circumstances should never dictate our faith.

I hope you understand me on this one. I know if I eat too much sugar I feel my body will react badly so I watch how much sugar I take. But I don't make my lack of eating sugar a big deal. If someone wants to buy me an ice cream then I will eat it. I love cookies and make desserts with sugar and I enjoy them very much. I was diagnosed with diabetes while in the navy. This is not the topic of my day and probably 99% of the people who know me never knew this about me. I have my faith in my Jesus and Jesus is taking care of me. My life is pretty simple.

I believe that having faith in God will make us more childlike. I know earlier in this book I quoted a scripture that tells us to put away the things of a child and become a man. But please don't confuse these two scriptures.

1 Corinthians 13:11 When I was a child, I spake as a child, I understood as a child, I thought as a child: but when I became a man, I put away childish things.

Matthew 18:3-5 And Jesus said, Verily I say unto you, Except ye be converted, and become as little children, ye shall not enter into the kingdom of heaven. Whosoever therefore shall humble himself as this little child, the same is greatest in the kingdom of heaven. And whoso shall receive one such little child in my name receives me.

In Matthew 18:4, Jesus qualifies it is the humbleness of a child that delights Him. I believe humbleness is being teachable, loveable, and someone who delights in making others joyful.

A child has to be taught what foods are good for him. A child will not look to food to heal himself but a child will look to mommy or daddy to heal him. We read in Matthew 18:3 Jesus telling us *"Except ye be converted, and become as little children."* I believe Jesus is talking about the faith of a child, being converted from nonbelief to belief. We are born into the sin of Adam which is nonbelief. We must be converted into belief in God and the tool used by God to convert us is His gift of faith. If you want more faith then ask God for it and childishly believe that God will give you more faith.

We are to have the faith of a child and therefore we will receive the Holy Spirit into our heart as a child receives truth from loving parents. We also read that we are to have the adultness of an adult to discern our every thought. As a child of God, we will look by faith to God to be healed but as an adult, some of us will turn away from Godly faith and turn to man's wisdom and doctors.

A child will not look to food to heal him unless he is taught man's wisdom from mom and dad. We simply must become childlike in faith and childlike teachable to hear from our Father God and Jesus who dwells in us for the Holy Spirit is closer then mom and dad.

We must be willing to be taught by our Jesus. I believe being teachable is a quality Jesus loves to see in us. I believe every one of us has some need to teach. Humans seem to love to tell people how to solve problems like that they should eat this and be well, and if the person takes our advice we rejoice and if the person doesn't then we might be saddened.

Can you imagine being God and watching His children so distracted by the things of this world that they do not have time to talk to the one who loves them and the one who is the answer. On my judgment day, I don't think Jesus will tell me, "If you had only eaten more organic food you would of made it Ron." I also pray that I don't hear these words from God, "I wished you would have spent more of your time with me, Ron."

We must recognize Jesus as truth and accept Him as truth by faith. Please make knowing Jesus and Father God a priority by being teachable, by setting quiet time aside to listen in your heart, read the life of Jesus to become Jesus and you will see a transformation happening and you will willingly put off the old man and accept the new man in the image and likeness of my Jesus by being renewed in the spirit of our mind.

Ephesians 4:22   That ye put off concerning the former conversation the old man, which is corrupt according to the deceitful lusts

Here we see the new man will put off the former conversations of the old man. Would you like an example? The old me used to tell dirty jokes and the old me loved making people laugh. I was good at telling jokes and because I was good at telling jokes people would invite me to parties. My jokes gave me self-worth, I saw people light up when I walked into the room because I brought laughter and my jokes took their pain of the day away momentarily. I joyfully report the old man is dying and the new man is coming to life because I have accepted Jesus into my heart.

In Titus 3:3 we see a picture of ourselves as the old man:

Titus 3:3   For we ourselves also were sometimes foolish, disobedient, deceived, serving divers lusts and pleasures, living in malice and envy, hateful, and hating one another.

Along the way or on our journey through life, we will meet the people of Titus 3:3. I was Titus 3:3 because I was spending my time finding jokes and foolishly telling jokes and seeking to be liked by others. We will recognize Titus 3:3 in us because we have all been there. We are born into these things through the fall of Adam but when we accept Jesus into your heart and we will no longer live in the foolishness of this world any more. Our hope for our land, in this world and our own future is for us Christians to be transformed by the love Jesus has shown us and feely gives us.

We read in Titus 3:4 a picture of Jesus. We must believe by faith that we are born again into the new life Jesus talked about. Jesus came to earth and with love and kindness, through His merciful grace for all of us that we are set free from Titus 3:3 and transformed right into Titus 3:4.

Titus 3:4 But after that the kindness and love of God our Saviour toward man appeared

Yes, Jesus came with kindness and the love of Father God flowing through Him like the world had never experienced. Jesus showed us His Father's love not just in words but in real life. Jesus showed us how to walk in kindness and in His love in everyday life. Jesus was tempted in all manners as we are tempted yet by His simple belief His Father loved Him. He rose above these temptations and by us simply keeping our focus on Our Father's love for us we too, will rise above our temptations and be transformed in to Our Father's love.

We can live life the way Jesus did. Jesus showed us it is possible. Jesus gives us supernatural help when we ask Him to let us be born again into the kingdom of having the Holy Spirit live and dwell in us so we can manifest the Holy Spirit of God to everyone we meet.

Yesterday starting at 6:00AM I had Coffee Time with Jesus and we continued writing on this book. About 3:30PM I decided to go to the pool here in the campground and swim. I was tired of sitting in the camper and felt a need to get off my backside. Arriving at the pool, I noticed I was the only one at the pool when two teenage girls walked in. In just a little while, I felt prompted and so I asked the girls if they were Christians. One girl said, "I go to church if that is what you mean," while the other girl said quite sternly, "No, I am not a Christian and I don't want to be one."

I felt they both had their guard up and are ready to argue. So I simply said okay and swam away. Shortly afterward, I felt prompted again so I ask them if they like to read. The girl that went to church replied yes while the other said no. "Do you like true stories?" I asked. She said yes so I told them just a little about Jenny and the book *Love Never Fails*. I told them the book is free and I will give them one if they will read it. The girl who didn't want to be a Christian said, "No, I don't want one." The other girl promised that she would read it so I went over to get my shoes on so I could walk to my camper. As I was leaving the pool area, the girl who doesn't want to be a Christian said that she would like one too.

On the way to my camper, I was rejoicing and thanking the Holy Spirit for His words and for giving me the privilege of knowing Him. I believe in the gentleness of Jesus and His gentleness will transform the hearts of those young girls. I thank you Jesus for your promptings and your answers being in my heart today. I know Jesus will bring the increase and now I know why I felt like going to the pool. Remember that it is Jesus Christ in us that will transform us into His hope of glory.

In Philippians 4:4-5 we read:

Philippians 4:4-5 Rejoice in the Lord always. Again I will say, rejoice! Let your gentleness be known to all men. The Lord is at hand.

Here in Philippians we read another reason to be born again, *'the Lord is at hand.'* If you believe the Word of God and think about His gentleness then there really is no reason to waste time thinking about being born again. You see the benefits, the blessings and the only thing you give up is your old sinful ways. I rejoice in the gentleness of God and we rejoice together.

There is another benefit of being born again. I am sure you heard of curses being handed down from generation to generation. Some people I know think they have received cruses or been deceived by circumstances that look like proof of curses being handed down in families. Do we have the ability to stop the curses dead in their tracts? Read Titus 3:5 and see what belief in God will bring into our world and how being born again will stop generational curses. The real power of generational curses is not the curse but the fact we spend our time fighting something that does not exist.

Titus 3:5-7 **Not by works of righteousness which we have done, but according to his mercy he saved us, by the washing of regeneration, and renewing of the Holy Ghost;** Which he shed on us abundantly through Jesus Christ our Saviour; That being justified by his grace, we should be made heirs according to the hope of eternal life.

May I ask you, will there be any generational curses handed down in heaven? If you said no then you are right. So ask the Holy Spirit of Father God and Jesus into your heart and become born again into your new blood line. They – Jesus and Father God through the Holy Spirit will teach you generational cruses are broken down and gone forever. They prove this in their word. Generational curses are broken the moment you simply believe you are born again and justified by grace *and by grace you are made heirs of the kingdom of God* for this is a promise in the Word of God. We cannot earn this blessing by works of righteousness but we will receive it by our belief in the gentleness and mercy of God towards us.

We read in Titus that we receive our new life by the washing of regeneration which is receiving the Holy Ghost in us. We are told this new life is shed on us abundantly through Jesus Christ. We, now being justified by grace, our sinful nature will actually flee. The more we set our minds on Jesus by seeking Him first for when you do set your mind on Jesus and His kingdom you will set you free of generational curses and the dung of this world.

In the word of God, Jesus spelled out how to be free of curses, dung and sin. Jesus tells us in John 8:32 *'And you shall know the truth, and the truth shall make you free.'* The truth is the Person of Jesus Christ wants to dwell in us and God truly has eternal love for us. I believe and I am free. Do you believe you are free? I am an heir to the kingdom of heaven so why on earth would I spend one moment striving to impress you with my earthly dung, worrying about my past or fight generational curses when the love of Jesus Christ broke and destroyed my old blood line?

2 Corinthians 5:17   Therefore, if anyone is in Christ, he is a new creation; old things have passed away; behold, all things have become new.

These are not just words in some old book. I hope you realize this was not possible in the old covenant. These words describe our new flesh, being in the image and likeness for Jesus when we believe. We are the word made flesh when we have the Holy Spirit of Jesus in us and this is how we become the hope of God's glory by believing and revealing Jesus is our Savior.

Paul tells us what to dwell on:

Philippians 4:8   Finally, brethren, whatever things are true, whatever things are noble, whatever things are just, whatever things are pure, whatever things are lovely, whatever things are of good report, if there is any virtue and if there is anything praiseworthy— meditate on these things.

We are not told to dwell on curses or our past in this scripture. Now, I wonder where those evil ideas come from. I believe those thoughts were needed in the old covenant because you had to make atonement for your sins every year. I believe Jesus removed the old system of sacrifice for forgiveness because it made you conscious about your sin all the time. You see, we live in a new covenant and we have a new blood line so fighting curses doesn't make sense to me because fighting curses makes you sin conscious instead of focusing on the kingdom of God being at hand.

Jesus is our example of how to fight curses and Jesus just told devils to leave and they went. Jesus did not dwell on the devil and Jesus never spent more the a few words casting out devils. We must understand we must be born again of water and the Holy Spirit for flesh will not enter the kingdom of God.

Finally, brethren think on the things of Philippians 4:8 we live in the new covenant and I thank God he sent His Son so I can choose to believe on the things that are true as explained in the Holy Bible.

John 3:5-6 Jesus answered, "Most assuredly, I say to you, unless one is born of water and the Spirit, he cannot enter the kingdom of God. That which is born of the flesh is flesh, and that which is born of the Spirit is spirit.

Please take these scriptures to our Lord and ask Jesus to give you revelation about them. In 1 John we read again that Jesus is our teacher and if we allow our self to become teachable then we will find that we are no longer of this world. Yes, we are in the world but not of this world. John tells us that there is an evil one who will seduce you back into the world by keeping some of God's laws physically and showing you generational cruses still exist.

I believe Jesus is giving us some simple discernment. I ask you, "Do the words people speak to you bring you into a desire to be intimately closer to God or do they bring you into a knowing of God?" I believe we need to ask God to help us discern the changes from the Old Covenant to the New Covenant. Are the words of Christians telling you what to do from the Old Covenant like you must fight and break this curse handed down to you even if it takes years off your life or do we now live in the New Covenant where seek ye first the kingdom of God and His righteous, with your **whole** heart, mind and soul. Please receive the freedom Jesus came to give us.

Jesus tells me I am being made into a new creation, adopted into a new blood line and I am born again and the Holy Spirit living in me. Jesus brought heaven to earth and destroyed curse. Please take these words to Jesus and let Him speak to you in your quiet time with Him.

1 John 2:26-27 These things have I written unto you concerning them that seduce you. But the anointing which ye have received of him abideth in you, and **ye need not that any man teach you**: but as the same anointing teacheth you of all things, and is truth, and is no lie, and even as it hath taught you, ye shall abide in him.

I have one teacher Jesus Christ and He abides in me. I know Jesus doesn't have generational curses and I know He abides in me. I focus on Jesus and He focuses on me. We are a team with His anointing in me.

Please come to God as a child. Come to him teachable and receive the anointing of God as His chosen one for you can be his chosen child by faith. The apostles were men of good age but read how the apostles ask Jesus questions like children – they ask Jesus which one of us will be the greatest in the kingdom of heaven. Some of their questions might sound stupid but yet Jesus simply answered them because they are His children.

I pray to be as teachable like a child of God. I pray to know my teacher on a first name basis and I pray you do too. I believe this is how understanding the wisdom of God comes.

1 John 2:28-29 And now, little children, abide in him; that, when he shall appear, **we may have confidence, and not be ashamed before him** at his coming. If ye know that he is righteous, ye know that every one that doeth righteousness is born of him.

The love of Jesus brings freedom and confidence in His love for us so we will never be ashamed. When Jesus comes back, I pray to stand in front of Him and see His face lights up. Think for a moment what the things of this world bring, captivity, rules, limits, hours and hours away from the ones we love. The dung of this world brings maintenance, up keep, they must be insured, and sometimes these things bring payments beyond the life of the thing we are paying off.

To my renewed mind, I saw these earthly things are holding me captive. Giving up the things of this world might seem hard at first but the freedom that comes from not being trapped in payments, not being trapped in needs and not being trapped in our own lust or fear is pure Godly freedom that goes beyond my understanding.

Please seek ye first the kingdom of God and His righteousness for when you set your mind on what Jesus has for us to do today, we will become His manifested love to someone. Again, in Romans 12:2 we read that we will be transformed by the renewing of our mind and we will become acceptable to God and live the perfect will of God.

Romans 12:2 And do not be conformed to this world, but be transformed by the renewing of your mind, that you may prove what is that good and acceptable and perfect will of God.

I pray for the good and acceptable and perfect will of God to manifest in me every day and everywhere I go. Please never waste more than one minute casting down or out generational cruses of any born again because you will be proving that you do not believe in the finished work of the cross or the power of the baptism and you will be missing the new you, Jesus came to give you.

Romans 12:2 could be read to do not be conformed by generational cruses of the old man. If you spend your time fighting generational curses, you are putting your mind on them and their evil power over you instead of focusing on God and His goodness in you. Jesus made this teaching so simple when He said to seek ye first the kingdom of God and His righteousness. I believe righteousness is *the renewing of your mind, that you may prove what is good, acceptable and perfect will of God.*

Jesus told us through Paul that we are His hope of glory here on earth. If you spend your life in Christian counseling trying to fight generational curses to get free of them then may I ask you to consider this – does your life bring glory to God by faith or is it a demonstration of belief in the devil and his power over you?

You cannot focus on God and generational curses at the same time. This is so easily understood especially when Jesus tells us so plainly to focus on God and His love for us. Is there any glory for God in us if we spend our time looking at what the devil has accomplished in our past? Jesus so plainly said you are forgiven? Jesus said anyone putting his hand to the plow and then looking back is not fit for the kingdom of God.

Luke 9:62 And Jesus said unto him, No man, having put his hand to the plough, and looking back, is fit for the kingdom of God.

Looking back is a problem because we are to please God by our faith in believing we are forgiven. Digging up the past and looking back is saying 'I am not sure I repented enough.' There is no faith in looking back. There is no faith in seeking signs before you move. There is no faith if all your ducks need to be in row before you serve the Lord. Jesus asks His apostles, "Will I find faith on the earth when I come back?" I believe by continually looking back we will become faithless and by looking back we might not be a joy to Jesus when He comes. Read what faith looks like to God.

1 John 2:28   And now, little children, **abide in him**; that, when he shall appear, **we may have confidence, and not be ashamed before him** at his coming.

1 John 2:28 could be read as now little children seek me, come to me, live with me, and spend time with me for it is my good pleasure to spend time with you. My children, when I come back I will have great joy in those who spend time with me intimately and my children will have great confidence of faith and my children will not be ashamed to stand before Me. Seek ye first the kingdom of God for God wants to transform us His believers into children of righteousness and we will be beaming children with our light shining.

After Jesus arose from the dead, did He lecture the apostles to deny Him? Did Jesus ask his apostles if they have repented? Jesus never asks them to check for generational curses to see if that was why they all ran and hid. My point here is Jesus didn't do background checks when He asked them to follow Him. So why do we fight all this stuff?

Please accept the love of Jesus who died to give us a new future and a new blood line with no generational curses. I know for some people to look to the future is scary. I talk to people who will not do anything unless they get a sign from God. I wonder if these same people are the ones I hear about fighting generational curses. I guess to some people it is easier to sit in your easy chair and dig up the past and fight some imagery curse then to look to the future. How much faith do you need to put your future on hold and wrap yourself up in the security of the past? Does God need you to be a shining light like His Word says or am I deceived?

I have actually heard people tell me excitedly, "I had such breakthrough this week and I feel so much better because the Lord showed me two more things to repent for and in a couple more years I will be free of my past." I pray for them to seek God for I know to some people looking to the future brings the uncertainty that requires faith and trust in God. Looking to the past just brings up things they can cry about while sitting in their easy chair. Please stop looking backwards and move forward knowing Jesus paid the price for us to have a future in Him.

Can you even imagine Jesus after being born again and coming out of the water and hearing His Father say, "This is my beloved son in whom I am well pleased?" Then after hearing His Father speak this blessing over His Son, Jesus says to His Father, "Hold on there, Father. This is a whole new future for me and I need a couple years to check for generational curses that might have come from Mary. Father let me do a background check to see if I am worthy of the praise you have given me. Another thing Father is I need you to give me a sign if I am doing the right thing before I go into that desert. Father are you sure I am ready? Father, do you want me to put out a fleece and if you want me to put out a fleece give me a sign for that too." I think this is why Jesus said it is a wicked and perverse generation that looks of a sign.

Jesus never said any of those things so why do we ask and say those things? Jesus never listened to the devil so why are we doing that? Every time we ask God for a sign I believe we are proving to Him that we have no faith. Think what you are asking God, "I might do it Lord if you give me a sign." Jesus asks us to follow Him and the apostles did and so will I. I know His will, I am reading His book and I have come to the greatest wisdom known to all of mankind – Jesus loves me. I don't pray for forgiveness anymore because I know by faith I am forgiven so when I sin I thank God for His forgiveness. I dwell on what Jesus needs to be done and we, Jesus and I are one and we are having fun being His love today.

Father God sent His son on a journey and we are on the same journey if we choose to follow God like Jesus did. Jesus said He came to set the captives free and I pray this book gives you a desire for the freedom Jesus came to give us. We believers are set free by our simple belief in Jesus Christ. Jesus told us in His Word how

His Father revealed things to His disciples even before they were born again. God loves us so much so please understand this.

Matthew 16:17 And Jesus answered and said unto him, Blessed art thou, Simon Barjona: for flesh and blood hath not revealed it unto thee, but my Father which is in heaven.

Jesus and Father God are still revealing their words to us if we just put down the things of this world and listen for their voice. Jesus chose the disciples and Jesus chose me and Jesus will choose you too if you choose to be His disciple. Just as Father God put His hope of glory in His son Jesus and equipped Jesus with everything He needed, we also have been given everything we need to be the Hope of glory for our Lord.

Jesus describes our new future in His spirit-filled word and how His joy is our strength. We bring glory to God by letting the wisdom of God overtake our knowledge of man and all we need is our simple belief in Jesus. We born again believers are the ones justified in Titus 3:7. Our hope is for eternal life with Jesus and His hope is for us to believe it is *Christ in you the hope of Glory.* Yes, this is so simple. Manifest His love and you will manifest His glory.

Repent your past and believe by faith God has forgiven you and get on with the future Jesus came to give you. True freedom is in intimate relationship with Jesus not just the knowledge of God from our Holy Bible but hearing His voice and proving what we hear is in our Holy Bible. The evidence of truth is in our Holy Bible but we must accept the person of truth Jesus Christ into our heart by listening to Him personally teaching us in our heart.

Titus 3:7 That being justified by his grace, we should be made heirs according to the hope of eternal life.

Do you see by our willingness to be transformed (justified by grace) into His love and by giving the Holy Spirit of God and Jesus permission to dwell in us by making them our priority of thought and our priority of our time here on earth we are actually allowing the Holy Spirit of Jesus and Father God to dwell in us. Granting our permission for God to overtake us with his love will transform us into their gentleness and their hope of Glory?

Please pray with me for a moment and ask God to let this become revelation to you. The reward for believing is so freeing and huge! We actually become heirs to the kingdom of God according to our hope and belief for eternal life with them. Allowing the Holy Spirit of Father God and Jesus to transform us is giving God the permission to transform us into the new man who will be in the image and likeness of God, full of belief and trusting in God the Father like Jesus did.

This is not something we go to college for and hope after years of schooling we will be good enough to get a job and work for some big impressive company with big benefits. In Titus 3:7 we see our reward comes through our belief. By our choice to believe in Jesus Christ we become Heirs of the Kingdom of God. I must admit the way I was raised I sought after a job and the prestige of a big house and earthly dung. I worked long hours for years for earthly dung and now I am proud to say Jesus and His transforming crew are transforming me into an Heir of His kingdom. I simply choose to believe He is real and rejoice in my heart believing Jesus is teaching me His ways.

We actually have been given the right to choose God so we have to choose to allow this transformation of us into the new man or continue to live the self-centered life we are born into through the fall of man when Adam sinned.

If you are having a tough time with me putting down the wisdom of man please think about the condition of this world and then think about how it got this way. I mean, if we kept our focus on the Lord and lived by His two commandments would the world be killing babies to the tune of millions. Would prayer be in schools and would people actually go to church to become Christ-like? Man's wisdom has crept into our churches and we have more denominations than I can count.

Listen to the words of Jesus as Jesus tells us who spoke through Him and guided Him while on this earth. The words of Jesus are pure and undefiled wisdom of God. We have the same Father and His words of wisdom need a voice and I pray to be His voice and I pray you do too.

John 8:28-32 Then Jesus said to them, "When you lift up the Son of Man, then you will know that I am He, and that I do nothing of Myself; but as My Father taught Me, I speak these things. And He who sent Me is with Me. The Father has not left Me alone, for I always do those things that please Him." As He spoke these words, many believed in Him. Then Jesus said to those Jews who believed Him, "If you abide in My word, you are My disciples indeed. And you shall know the truth, and the truth shall make you free."

Jesus in His wisdom is transforming me with His voice in my heart and I love it. This transformation is painless. I felt no pain, just a gentle conviction every time I started telling a dirty joke or sinning in any kind. Now because of being born again I have the Holy Spirit of God and Jesus in me and they give me a gentle conviction every time I have an impure thought.

Jesus said the pure in heart will see Him and I have ask Jesus to make my heart pure. So I have chosen or made my choice and I know beyond any doubt that Jesus is making my heart pure. I know this because I have read in the word of Jesus the renewing of my mind is possible and I have faith that all things are possible.

Ephesians 4:23 And be renewed in the spirit of your mind

You see the new man will not be conformed to this world but become transformed by the Holy Spirit living in us willingly. Yes, willingly my Jesus will dwell in me to guide me, teach me, protect me and it all comes through His beautiful love for me.

I don't need hair on my head to feel beautiful. I don't need to work out or run a mile in ten seconds to feel good about myself. I am beautiful, maybe not by the mirror or what the world considers beautiful but I am beautiful because I believe what Jesus says about me. I am in good shape, not because I work out or can run some long distances. I am in good shape because I know Jesus said all things are possible for me and I simply believe Jesus.

I am becoming pure in my heart because Jesus is my best friend and the Lover of my soul is transforming me daily. I am in His presence 24/7 and I love being with my Jesus. But more than that I know Jesus loves being with me. I know Jesus loves how I simply accept His word as true and I know Jesus loves me being teachable. This might sound childish to you but I have more joy than humanly possible because I know the secret – *that God loves me.*

I know I have all this because I simply choose to allow Jesus to transform me by the renewing of the spirit of my mind. Yes, the Holy Spirit of God wants us to choose Him and in doing so I choose to be transformed into the love of my Jesus and the life of Jesus will manifest in me and the coolest part is the sacrifice Jesus chose in His life has already paid the price for me. Yes, Jesus wants me to believe in Him and trust in His love for me and He wants you also. I believe I have a pure heart not because of some great work I have done but because I have chosen to believe in Jesus and His truth, yes the truth that sets me free is Jesus loves me.

I want to clarify something about my transformation from being a dirty joke teller to becoming someone who is aware of the love of God has for me. My transformation didn't happen because I became aware of how offensive my dirty joke telling was to Jesus. My transformation didn't happen by me putting great effort on my part into stopping the telling of dirty jokes.

The transformation happened as I grew up in my relationship with Jesus; I noticed every time I started to tell a dirty joke I felt a slight discomfort in my spirit. This discomfort was like a check in my spirit and even if I ignored it and told the dirty joke the discomfort in my spirit made me want to sit quietly and ask myself what am I doing and what happened to me Jesus and praise God I didn't receive happiness from watching people laugh about my dirty jokes anymore because somewhere in time I wasn't telling them anymore. Thank You, Jesus.

I knew something had changed in me. You know I didn't war against my sin. I didn't cast it out every time I thought of a dirty joke. I found I didn't dwell on my sin and try to stop my sin in my own strength. I simply turned toward the Lord and listened for His voice and Jesus showed me His love for me would guide me. Jesus is transforming me daily and this transformation is so up lifting for I know their love for me is real and with the Holy Spirit of Jesus in me I am His hope of Glory because I have chosen to be His child.

Are we Jesus reps? The Holy Bible says so!

In 2009, I was reading my Holy Bible when I came to realize I was supposed to be a representative of God here on earth just like Jesus was the representative of His Father. You know Jesus said, "You see me, you have seen the Father." I asked my Jesus to let me be His representative here on earth. This simple prayer request gave the Holy Spirit permission to transform me. I cannot tell you how or give you an exact date when the transformation started but sometime later I started praying from a different place of faith. I didn't ask God for what I wanted anymore. I just started thanking God for transforming me. I thanked God for purifying my heart and for blessing me and purifying me by putting His pure heart in me.

I asked the Holy Spirit of God to come into me to teach me and transform me for I know I simply must have this pure heart for I desired to see God. I also wanted faith for I had read that without the faith of Jesus in my heart, my life and my heart would not please God and I desired to please Him. Jesus says in His word that I could do great acts of faith here on earth but if I did them without a heart of love I was a zero, so I ask for love and not just any love but I wanted to be the pure perfect love of Jesus and my Father God.

Seeking God became my priority and pleasing God became my goal. I wanted to know God so I could be His joy here on earth. For the Holy Spirit revealed to me that joy is strength and strength is contagious. I cannot think of anyone who gets up in the morning and says, "I hope I get weaker today," or "I love my depression," or "I hope I find out I have cancer today so I can be even more depressed and yet I talk to people who say these things are their cross in life." I found the joy of the Lord is contagious and if I could demonstrate the joy of the Lord well my Jesus wins and people will want to know Him.

Matthew 5:8 Blessed are the pure in heart, For they shall see God.

Seek first the kingdom of God and then ask to be blessed with a pure heart and you shall see God.

Hebrews 11:6 But without faith it is impossible to please him: for he that cometh to God must believe that he is, and that he is a rewarder of them that diligently seek him.

Faith believes in God and believing has the reward of eternal life.

1 Corinthians 13:13 And now abideth faith, hope, charity, these three; but the greatest of these is charity.

With faith in the love God has for us we can draw near to God with a pure heart, clear conscience and full assurance we can be His ambassadors here on earth. Our part in this ambassadorship is to hold fast to the Word of God no matter what the circumstances of life look like. The word of God says *for He who promised is faithful.* I believe we are to stand in His faithfulness. God Himself said He is faithful and I believe it.

Hebrews 10:22 let us draw near with a true heart in full assurance of faith, having our hearts **sprinkled** from an evil conscience and our bodies washed with pure water.

I would like to bring attention to the word *'sprinkled'* in the scripture above. The Holy Spirit brought it to my attention. When we humans clean something like a car, a deck or our house we will use a hard spray or even a pressure washer to clean off the tuff dirt. Here we read Jesus sprinkles us clean and Jesus showed me that anything of His that grows enjoys being sprinkled. Flowers, plants, trees, etc will grow by being sprinkled and in Hebrews 10:22 we read that we are sprinkled clean with pure water so we can grow in the wisdom of Jesus Christ.

Think about the life of Jesus and His horrible last days and study the gentleness in those days to recognize His love for us.

Think again about His resurrection and the gentleness of His words toward the apostles who had deserted Him and recognize His forgiveness towards them and us. God is so gentle to us believers. Now we can see gentleness as a discerning tool for he who is not gentle is not of God.

When we Christians see evil we are taught to go to war against it, we will cast it out and demand it to go in the name of Jesus and all these things are good. You might say, "There is no gentleness in war, Ron." We are to only do the things we see Jesus do. Jesus spoke to the devil and cast him out. We must recognize our war is in the spirit world and there is no gentleness there. Our words commission a battle in the spirit world and our unwavering faith in God winning the battle gives us the victory. Jesus walked in a gentle victory and we can also.

By faith Jesus cast out devils and by faith we do the same. We do these things one time and then stand in faith they are done. Again, we are to only do what we read Jesus did. After we pray some people say, "I don't feel any different," and immediately the one praying, prays again which only proves his faith shrinks back by what he sees. Jesus said he has no pleasure in such. But if we cast out a devil and stand firm in our faith by seeking God with all our unwavering heart, we will see a difference in our life and theirs.

I believe Jesus is showing us in Hebrews 10:22 what standing firm in faith will accomplish. I am being taught by my teacher, Jesus Christ and I am witnessing in my heart a difference between an evil conscience in us and an evil spirit of the devil in us. The devil has to flee in the name of Jesus when we call on Jesus in faith, so when we accept Jesus into our heart by faith we are actually given the devil his walking papers and the devil must flee; but I believe our evil conscience has to be cleaned of the residue or dirt left behind from the devil.

I believe that by faith at baptism we have made our choice and with the Holy Spirit of Jesus in us we have given God the right to also remove the devil and all the remembrance of the devil from us. Jesus in His wisdom used the word *sprinkled* to show us again His gentleness in how we are cleaned and transformed. I know for a fact I am being transformed daily and sometime, I think too slowly but I have come to the understanding that Jesus sets the pace. Therefore I, by faith, receive the peace of knowing I am being prepared for an eternal life with my Lord and therefore I have become teachable, loveable and I am useable to the Lord today.

My conscience is becoming clear as the Holy Spirit washes me with pure water and I will hold fast to this confession of hope for purity for I know the purifier lives in me. I am becoming the hope of glory daily for I know He who promised is faithful and my part is to stay faithful to the promise. I do not spend my time trying to help God clean me up by dwelling on my past and constant repeated repentance. I have repented one time and I have asked God into my life one time. I know by faith the Holy Spirit lives in me and His cleaning crew is at work right now. Accept Jesus into your heart and you will have His peaceful cleaning crew working for you right now.

One more thought about the word sprinkle and how it is used here in Hebrews 10:22. In life, if we have anything we want to grow like flowers, vegetables, grass, etc. we will water them by sprinkling, knowing that water by a hard spray will kill the plant. We sprinkle our grass and gardens and our flowers and they all respond to the loving sprinkling by growing into what God designed them to be. I desire to be who God designed me to be.

I believe Jesus is sprinkling away my evil conscience and transforming me ever so gently into His consciences of purity and into a pure heart. We will all live forever and with a simple request to allow God to have His way in our heart, we are choosing where our forever will be. Please give God permission to transform your heart, knowing by faith the sprinkling will begin the moment you do. *Let us hold fast the confession of our hope without wavering, for He who promised is faithful.* I want to read these scriptures again while asking God for a full understanding.

Hebrews 10:22-23   let us draw near with a true heart in full assurance of faith, having our hearts **sprinkled** from an evil conscience and our bodies washed with pure water. **Let us hold fast the confession of our hope without wavering**, for He who promised is faithful.

In Hebrews 10:22, Jesus tells us how he will clean us up and in Hebrews 10:23 we read our part in this cleanup is to hold fast to our confession of faith and Jesus reminds us or helps us hold fast to our confession by telling us again He who promised is faithful to His promises. As I read these scriptures, I hear the heart of God. I become aware of the will of God and I receive faith from their love toward me. I receive peace from these scriptures knowing the evil in my conscience will be removed. I received discernment to know the devil is not in me anymore. So any voice I hear telling me I need deliverance is not of God and that voice is trying to get my mind on the devil again. I see how Jesus makes all things simple for those who believe and receive His truth into their heart.

I hope you understand that I have been blessed with a relationship with the Holy Spirit of Father God and Jesus living and breathing in me now and I am aware of their love for me and toward me through this intimacy. I hope you understand I cannot fall in love with the Holy Bible but I am in love with the Author. His joy is mine for believing in Him. I'm not striving to get to heaven. I am not simply seeking heaven as a reward for obeying. I am seeking to become so close to God that the two of us become one. I am seeking to be transformed into His love so I can be a transformer of others into His love. This will happen when others see the gentleness of God's love manifesting in us. Yes with these gifts inside me and manifesting through me. I am an ambassador for Jesus.

We Are Told to Love One Another With A Pure Heart

1 Peter 1:22 Since you have purified your souls in obeying the truth through the Spirit in sincere love of the brethren, love one another fervently with a pure heart

Peter tells us as ambassadors for Jesus that we are actually being purified in our soul though obedience to the truth of Jesus. Jesus teaches His truth to us and if you accept His love toward you as truth then you will willingly obey in spirit and truth and pass on His love to others. I believe this is how you know Jesus and His cleanup crew is working in you. A true pure heart will no longer see boundaries of denominations. A true pure heart doesn't argue but the love of God coming from a true pure heart will start the transformation process in others and we know from scripture God brings the increase.

Our purity will manifest through our love to our brethren. Yes, the Holy Spirit will purify our soul and our part is to obey the truth – truth being the person of Jesus Christ, for then we will live the sincere love of Jesus to our brethren by loving our brethren with a pure heart. Being sprinkled clean and washed with pure water are word pictures of the gentleness of God and all we have to do is receive their love by faith that God promised and believe God is forever faithful to His Word.

The Holy Spirit of God lives in us. Jesus is our teacher, our purifier, our sprinkler and the lover of our soul. We read in 1 Peter 1:22 that purifying our soul come also through obedience to the person or spirit of Jesus Christ who is truth. We reverence Jesus Christ by becoming Christ like in our actions of sincere love of the brethren through loving one another fervently with our sprinkled clean pure heart. All these blessings come from God and we receive these blessings by our steadfast faith declaring God is faithful.

Want more blessings? We know Jesus is truth and with that blessing in our hearts we learn the truth that Jesus is our source of wisdom. Let us read what James says about our source.

James 3:17 But the wisdom that is from above is first pure, then peaceable, gentle, willing to yield, full of mercy and good fruits, without partiality and without hypocrisy.

Isn't it amazing how this description of wisdom could double as a great description of love? Our Love that we are to give away is from God above and is first pure, then peaceable, gentle, willing to yield, full of mercy and good fruits, without partiality and without hypocrisy. We read all through our Holy Bible how God is love and God is wisdom (*all knowing*) and God set the standard for loving the brethren.

James 3:17 could also describe Jesus. Jesus is *first pure, then peaceable, gentle, willing to yield, full of mercy and good fruits, without partiality and without hypocrisy.* I believe you could use the same description to describe the compassion of Jesus and when I go to my final reward and if there is a funeral for me someday, I would like for James 3:17 to be said of me. Ron's love was from above and was first pure, etc...

If we choose to live in the wisdom from God, we will bless others with these gifts from God, just as Jesus lived in then so should we too. And in doing so, we will bring glory to God. Think about the wisdom of man and how it puffs us up and brings glory to ourselves. There is another good discernment tool. When we speak words of wisdom to others who gets the glory? I can tell you God created me or I can tell you I am star dust that came together over millions of years. To me man's knowledge sounds pretty stupid but you can choose who to believe.

I believe when you ask Jesus into your heart you will receive wisdom from above and all of James 3:17. Then the loving compassion of Jesus will flow through you to edify His kingdom here on earth. I have asked my Jesus for James 3:17 to be in my heart and in all I do and say. I desire *the wisdom that is from above.* I desire to be *first pure, then peaceable, gentle, willing to yield, full of mercy and good fruits, without partiality and without hypocrisy.* Jesus said all things are possible and I believe Jesus is moving the mountains of evil. I had picked up through the wisdom of men and I believe Jesus is casting that evil into the sea for me because I believe Jesus loves me.

Being an ambassador for Jesus is bringing peace into uncertain situations through faith in God and listening to the voice of God. You will become a peacemaker with heavenly wisdom, gentleness and being willing to yield to the heart of God. By purposely listening for His heart in all situations you will see yourself sowing mercy and the fruits of the spirit without partiality and without hypocrisy. That is another discerning tool. If your words do not sow seeds of these fruits in truth, compassion and love; you need to ask your teacher, Jesus Christ to help you learn and trust in Him to help you be a better listener. Jesus will help by giving you a desire to remove the mountain of distractions we have here on earth.

James continues with righteousness and how we sow the seeds of righteous.

James 3:18   Now the fruit of righteousness is sown in peace by those who make peace

There in is more discernment. If your words sow discourse and hurt others they are definitely not of righteousness. James tells us the righteous sow words and actions of peace. We will know the righteous by their fruit of peace.

One morning years ago in my Coffee Time with Jesus, I ask Jesus for a personal prayer that would help me become more like Him, a prayer that everyone in heaven would rejoice when I said it. Jesus gave me this prayer. Jesus even made the prayer short so I could remember it better.

"Dearest heavenly Father in Jesus name I pray, as I walk down the street today, I pray the people I see along the way, when they get home tonight and start to pray, will say, *I think, I saw Jesus today.*"

This prayer is not arrogant. This prayer is my goal. Please ask Jesus for your personal prayer and listen for His voice. Your personal prayer from Jesus is in your heart already and the Holy

Spirit of God will let you hear it and you will notice you will no longer be conformed to this world but you will begin the transformation of the renewing of your mind and you will become of His world. Please remember this transformation is the perfect will of God for you.

Romans 12:2 And be not conformed to this world: but be ye transformed by the renewing of your mind, **that ye may prove what is that good, and acceptable, and perfect, will of God.**

You might be asking how does this happen? Romans 12:3 tells us this transformation comes through grace. Someone asked me, "Does the devil have grace?" I answered, "The devil has judgment, the devil has condemnation, and the devil has hate. You know, the perfect will of the devil is to kill, still and destroy the relationship we have with our loving Father and Jesus Christ. Some of the tools of the devil are unforgiveness, envy, jealousy, hate and foolishness such as telling dirty jokes. Yes, years ago I played right into the hands of the devil by telling dirty jokes. I had no discernment. I was in the world and of the world but Jesus changed all that by transforming me daily. And a simple prayer like 'Jesus, please make me who you want me to be,' will change your life too."

Like I said when I was younger that I didn't discern the telling of dirty jokes as a problem to God. Now I thank Jesus for growing me up and giving me His gifts of grace, love and discernment.

Discernment is very important. Without discernment then we are lost. Please ask Jesus for discernment before you read His Word. When you ask Jesus for discernment, His Word will jump off every page of your Holy Bible and the simplicity of discernment will come right into your heart.

Through discerning the Word I know I am loved by Jesus. Now when I think back to my dirty joke telling days and what I was really spreading, I mean I thought my words were simply spreading laughter and good times. I didn't kill, steal or destroy anybody with my words of laughter. Oh thank you Jesus for opening my eyes and leading me to You and into your truth that showed me what kind of seeds I was spreading back then.

I actually spent a lot of time looking for sources of dirty jokes so I had a new one to tell to anyone I met. I dwelled on the jokes I heard so I could add something that made them even funnier or dirtier. My friends would see me and ask me, "What is the joke of the day?" Looking back on those days I realize how empty my life was and how void of substance my life was. Oh, I was saved and went to mass every Sunday so I was good with God and never once thought how my actions and words were grieving my loving Father God and Jesus. Now I thank Jesus for His loving grace toward me.

Jesus is cleaning my mind daily and sometime Jesus brings things up from my past, not to dwell on my past but to help me avoid these pitfalls again. Looking back, I remember every Sunday the priest of the church I attended told a joke from the pulpit. I loved his jokes because they were what I called clean jokes. The jokes the priest told are so clean I could tell them to my mom and dad and we will all laughed.

I remember being so disappointed when that priest got transferred to a different church. Thinking back, I remember his jokes but I don't remember any of his sermons. Not remembering his sermons is not the fault of the priest. The blame rests on me and where my priorities are. Sadly, I focused on the joke and not the Word of God. When I started thinking on my past, I asked God, "Why am I thinking about my past now?" I believe Jesus was gently showing me how these things are being removed (*sprinkled clean*) from my conscience.

Jesus is growing me up and teaching me discernment at the same time. I remembered most of my jokes were dirty and that made them terrible and displeasing to Jesus and Father God. I wondered if clean jokes are okay with God. I wondered if I stumble onto a clean joke and if I repeat it, have I done anything wrong? If the joke made a sound moral point for us to think about, is it wrong for me to repeat it? I went right to my teacher and Jesus led me into Peter.

1 Peter 1:15-17 But as he which hath called you is holy, **so be ye holy in all manner of conversation;** Because it is written, Be ye holy; for I am holy. And if ye call on the Father, who without respect of persons judgeth according to every man's work, pass the time of your sojourning here in fear

The Holy Spirit in me is my guiding light and He has brought me to these scriptures. I know for a fact if Father God or Jesus is in front of me right now, I would not tell them a clean joke because I would not want to waste their time. I believe Peter has some really good advice for us, *"Be ye holy in all manner of conversation."* I don't think this scripture is a suggestion.

Now because Jesus is renewing my mind by the Holy Spirit, I believe even telling a clean joke is a problem especially if I spend time looking for the clean jokes. My mind simply cannot be renewed if my focus is looking for any clean jokes to tell. My priority has become to become Christ like and to let His righteousness shine through me. I believe the Holy Spirit brings me the scriptures so I can recognize His voice and have this intimacy that only comes from spending quiet time with my Jesus.

Now, I thank Jesus for renewing my mind and helping me see the era's in my thinking. My purpose now is to only think on things that will edify my Jesus and bring glory to Him and my Father God. The purpose of my life is to become as close to Jesus as possible. My purpose is to praise God for sending His only Son to show me how to live, how to worship and come into an understanding that my past is forgiven through His grace to me. I thank you God for giving me the faith to believe.

Romans 12:3 For I say, through the grace given to me, to everyone who is among you, not to think of himself more highly than he ought to think, but to think soberly, as **God has dealt to each one a measure of faith.**

We read in Romans 12:3 that we all have a measure of faith. It is given to us through grace and I will never try to figure out how God does all these things. But by the grace given to me through faith, I receive His loving heart, his single eye and most of all the transforming love of God is coming by request into my heart so I can allow God to make me who He created me to be. Jesus said it and I believe it. I will never backslide into self-pity, unforgiveness and doubt. I will never try to figure how the Holy Spirit does this in me but I will, by faith accept the perfect will of God has for me so I can build His kingdom by following Jesus Christ and living His way. Yes, we can all become kingdom builders for Jesus and watch the love of God flow through us to help others. We will all grow into the understanding of His love by listening for His Holy Spirit in us.

The Word says, '*Christ in you the hope of glory,*' manifesting the love of God toward others is our way of worshiping God and our manifesting His love brings glory to God. Because of my choice to have intimate time with Jesus, I will spend the rest of my life being loved by God. I will not receive the love of God from reading and memorizing my Holy Bible but I came into the knowledge of His love for me from reading and studying His Holy Bible. After learning about God in His Word, I began asking God to reveal Himself to me personally and God lovingly responded with Coffee Time with Jesus.

Please ask God for a personal time and make Him your priority. Put down the things of this world and set your mind on the things above. Do not fight in the physical but give the battle to God and watch Him work. Depend on God and not your own strength. Walk knowing by faith you are doing what Jesus wants you to do today and His peace, joy and love will overtake you.

The Light of the Body is The Eye

Have you ever wondered what Jesus meant when He Said?

Matthew 6:22 The **light of the body is the eye**: if therefore thine eye be single, thy whole body shall be full of light.

You know I have often read Matthew 6:22 and wondered about what Jesus meant when He said if thy eye be single. Today I believe that Jesus is giving me revelation on this scripture. I believe being single eyed means to only look forward. From the moment we give our heart to the Lord we are to look forward. We are not to dwell on our past anymore.

I know I just told you about my dirty joke telling days but I did so from the perspective of how much the decision to give my heart to the Lord has transformed me into a new life. I do not dwell on my past trying to improve myself or to make sure I have repented for every detail of it. Dwelling on my past makes absolutely no sense to my renewed mind. I refuse to dwell on my past because I know from the Scripture that dwelling on the past is a big no from God.

Luke 9:62 And Jesus said unto him, No man, having put his hand to the plough, **and looking back**, is fit for the kingdom of God.

We all know the story of Saul and how God transformed him into Paul. The only time Paul mentioned his past was to show that the goodness of God had transformed him. Paul never dwelled on his past nor did he allow his past to take his focus off the Lord and the Lord's work of today. I hear people talk about their past and say this is why I am the way I am. Actually I believe that is man's knowledge and nothing could be further from the truth of God.

Past is past and if you have repented for your past, then it is over. The Goodness of God has come into my heart and I am now singled-eyed and looking only to my future walk with the Lord and I will forever be grateful for His love for me. I have put my hand to the plow and I will never look back to my past, as my past is a snare of the devil and through faith given to me through the love of Father God and Jesus by allowing their Holy Spirit to dwell in me. My past is just a past of someone I can hardly remember. Thank you, Jesus!

> **Matthew 6:22** The light of the body is the eye: if therefore thine eye be single, thy whole body shall be full of light.

I talked earlier in this letter about how beautiful I am. I hope I explained that well-enough that I am talking about my heart being beautiful and not my old body being beautiful. I look to myself in the eye every morning and I see how God is purifying me daily. My single eye is looking forward every day for even more revelation of the love of God and I look forward to a bright future that will only be possible if we look or keep our single eye looking and focusing on the Holy Spirit of Jesus and Father God dwelling in us. Please allow yourself to wake up in their loving arms and allow them to give you a bright narrow path that totally removes your past. Luke confirms the word.

> **Luke 11:34-36** The light of the body is the eye: therefore when thine eye is single, thy whole body also is full of light; but when thine eye is evil, thy body also is full of darkness. Take heed therefore that the light which is in thee be not darkness. If thy whole body therefore be full of light, having no part dark, the whole shall be full of light, as when the bright shining of a candle doth give thee light.

I believe we can be single-eyed by simply keeping our mindset on knowing our loving Father and Jesus have a love for us that grows more daily. If we set our eye on becoming as Christ-like as possible and read the life of Jesus to love as Jesus loved, our eye will become single.

Do you want more proof that we are to keep our mind focused on Jesus and His love for us? We are to be single-eyed looking to the Word of God in our heart least we be deceived by our own eyes. Look what happened to Eve.

2 Corinthians 11:3   But I fear, lest somehow, as the serpent deceived Eve by his craftiness, so your minds may be corrupted from the **simplicity that is in Christ.**

Let us talk about the simplicity of God for a moment. Think back to the Garden of Eden. Think how simple God made life for us. Everything God created walked in love. The animals were in harmony and pure water was in abundance. There was no shame and even being naked was just fine. The temperature was perfect. Freedom to run and play and enjoy this perfect life was ours. Could God have made life any simpler for us? God only had one rule for us – *of the tree of the knowledge of good and evil you shall not eat.*

Genesis 2:16-17   And the LORD God commanded the man, saying, "Of every tree of the garden you may freely eat; **but of the tree of the knowledge of good and evil you shall not eat,** for in the day that you eat of it you shall surely die."

Life in the garden was surely simple. God gave us everything and he gave us only one rule to follow. It seems simple to me but let us look at how the devil deceived Eve. The Holy Bible tells us the tree of the knowledge of good and evil was a fruit tree.

I can hear your thoughts as you read this book saying, "Oh, to go back that kind of simplicity can you imagine telling your children to stay away from one tree, for if you stay away from the fruit of that tree your whole life will be fine?"

Genesis 3:6   So when the woman **saw** that the tree was good for food, that it was pleasant to the **eyes**, and a tree desirable to make one wise, she took of its **fruit** and ate. She also gave to her husband with her, and he ate.

Actually, the coming of Jesus brought us back to the simplicity of Adam and Eve. Jesus tells us that we can now enjoy the fruit of His Holy Spirit to guide us and protect us. In fact, we can have all the fruits of the Holy Spirit and we can have all this in one word – *belief*. Yes, our life can be as simple as Adam and Eve if we believe. You know, we still have only one sin to stay away from. John said that Jesus came to take away the *sin* of the world. Notice that he didn't say *sins* of the world. John said *sin* (singular) of the world.

John 1:29   The next day John seeth Jesus coming unto him, and saith, Behold the Lamb of God, which taketh away the **sin** of the world.

The sin of the world is the same sin that Adam and Eve committed in the garden. That is **they did not believe.** They only had a simple command. God told them not to eat of the tree of good and evil. We are being tempted the same way as Eve. We look at a girl and see she is pretty and would like to be with her. We know Jesus said that it is wrong but do we believe God or the devil? Or some of us we take drugs and think we are not hurting anyone else but the whole time we are on drugs we deceive our selves and we are useless to God. Are we going to believe or not? My point here is the simplicity of the word of Jesus. There is only one sin today just as in the day of Adam and Eve. The sin of unbelief is the sin you commit every time you commit any sin.

Look at what God promised us if we only believe. We can walk in all these fruits if we only believe. Again, the simplicity of Jesus to the apostles and us is to believe or not to believe.

Galatians 5:22-23   But the fruit of the Spirit is love, joy, peace, longsuffering, kindness, goodness, faithfulness, gentleness, self-control. **Against such there is no law.**

These fruits are a description of the will of our Father God. I **believe** they actually describe Father God to us. I hope and pray you believe that Father God sent Jesus to bring us back to the simple life of Adam and Eve if we simply believe. We live in the simplicity of Jesus who narrowed our path to one word and that's *belief*. Yes, there is only one sin of the world today and forever. The sin of the world is *unbelief*. The coming of Jesus has put us back in the Garden of Eden if we simply believe. I continually praise God every day for Him to make my life simple. I have one tree I cannot eat of.

The word of God says if we simply believe we will walk in the fruits of the Spirit and then Jesus ended the Scriptures with the words *against such there is no law*. We Christians are to live our life in these fruits and bear these fruits to everyone we meet because like a fruit-bearing tree, the fruit of our tree is to share the abundance of the fruit God produces through us. The simplicity of the Gospel is we need no law if we walk in these fruits every day like Jesus did.

If I walk in the love of Father God as Jesus did then I will not commit murder, adultery, steal or break any of the laws of Moses. If I live as Jesus lived then I will live in the gifts of the Holy Spirit. My life has meaning. I love having hope for a bright future in America and the world. Jesus makes all things possible if I simply believe. The sin of my past is gone as far as the east is from the west and I will remember it no more.

Here in Matthew, we read that we will actually be recognized by our fruits. Yes, the world will recognize us as peculiar. They will see our glow and our joy and they will desire what we have. Remember, fruits are not works, denominations, or even how much time we spend in church or read our Bible. Fruits are the transformation of our heart into the manifestations of *love, joy, peace, longsuffering, kindness, goodness, faithfulness, gentleness, self-control*.

If you choose to live in man's wisdom then your purpose in life becomes acquiring more and more dung. You measure your worth by how much junk or dung you accumulate here on earth. Please don't be distracted by the things of this world for the things of this world are only momentary distractions that will lead us away form Jesus and the eternal fruits of God.

Let us compare for a moment. If you choose the world and are 'totally successful' then you can live in a new house with new cars, boats and campers and go to any trips anywhere you want, etc. If you choose to live with God then you will live in *the fruit of the Spirit of love, joy, peace, longsuffering, kindness, goodness, faithfulness, gentleness, self-control*. The contrast is very plain to see. The world has anxiety, depression and needs money, insurance, and tells you to work hard, get an education, for everything in life is about you and your accomplishments.

I believe true Godly wisdom is faith and trust in God. With Godly wisdom, our purpose in life becomes bringing glory to God by dying to ourselves to live the life Jesus modeled for us. This makes no sense to man's wisdom. In fact, man's wisdom tells us dying to ourselves make us worthless but with the wisdom of God in our heart we will become the love of God and our priority will be to share His love. Live for man's wisdom and the dung of this world and be worthless to the kingdom of God or live to give glory to God and become His beloved brethren. You choose!

Jesus tells us in Matthew 12:33:

Matthew 12:33 Either make the tree good and its fruit good, or else make the tree bad and its fruit bad; for a tree is known by its fruit.

To make the tree good and bear good fruit, we need to set our priority on the things above. If we choose to seek ye first the kingdom of God and His righteousness, Jesus tells us that all these things will be added which means that we will live in *the fruit of the Spirit of love, joy, peace, longsuffering, kindness, goodness, faithfulness, gentleness, self-control* and we will bear good fruit.

I believe one of the most powerful traps of the devil that will keep you from living in the fruits of the spirit is the devil will help you dwell on your past sins. I ask you what fruit you are bearing while searching your past. Please don't allow the devil to wrap yourself up in your past by telling you to dwell and trying to be forgiven.

Actually continually repenting is proving that we don't believe that we are forgiven. We show our belief in God by looking to our future and receiving by faith our forgiveness from God through His grace. Good fruits come from simply keeping our eye on Jesus, reading the word to become aware of how much God loves us will open your heart to receive the love of Jesus. This is such a simple plan and yet it is the plan God has given us and yet for some it might seem all too simple.

If you are hearing a voice in your head right now saying, "Oh, how I wish I could tell Ron my story and then he would understand my life is much more complex then his," and I am thinking, "I wish I could tell you to stop dwelling on your problem for Jesus has removed your problem by His forgiveness." When you start your day in faith knowing you are forgiven then you will be free to dwell on the *simplicity that is in Christ* which is you are forgiven. Please listen to Jesus in your heart for He needs us to dwell on Him and not our past.

If you could tell me your story right now, I wonder what your motive for telling me would be. I surely hope and pray your motive is not sympathy. For Jesus has revealed to me sympathy is the devil's counterfeit of the compassion of Jesus. Yes, sympathy takes you down into depression and depression takes you down into hopelessness and suicide. You can see sympathy is of the devil for it gives you a need for more sympathy which robs us of our future and your joy.

Contrast sympathy with the compassion of God. His compassion lifts us out of the problem and heals us to carry on the kingdom work and gives you a bright future. Compassion gives us the joy of the Lord and a desire to know Jesus even more. There is a Godly simplicity in knowing Jesus loves us and our belief in His love will bring us to a marriage feast in the heavenly realm. Do you believe you are to be the bride of Jesus Christ?

Is Worshiping Jesus a Good Fruit?

What is worshiping Jesus? Is it singing on a Sunday morning? To me, knowing the simplicity of Jesus and having Godly wisdom to seek God with all my heart and soul and knowing the Holy Spirit can manifest through me is worshiping God. As much as I have read about the life of Jesus, I haven't read about Him singing in the synagogue like *'break every chain, or you are worthy Father'* to worship His Father. Jesus worshipped His Father by living every second of His life to be the love of His Father to all. Read how Jesus boldly healed the hand of a man in the synagogue. To me, Jesus is worshiping His Father by believing in His Father.

I believe worshiping God is to live the life Jesus modeled to us! I know for some people there is a lift in their spirit when they sing so I will not try to put God in my box and say this is the way it is. I know God will use us if we make ourselves available and I guess for some that is through signing.

Here is an example. A friend asked me to go to a Friday night worship service a couple weeks ago. While we are there, the worship people sang a song over and over, singing, "You are worthy Lord, you are worthy Lord." The 'worship service' that Friday night was nothing but singing for four hours. The worship music was really loud and it seemed to me that a lot of the words didn't line up with scripture, so I went to the parking lot to get some relief.

My friend that took me there was really into the 'worship' and I didn't want to bother him. In the parking lot I hoped to have some quiet time and ask Jesus if I needed to have some adjustment in my thinking about these 'singing worship' services. I know Jesus said we overcome by the word of our testimony and loving our own life not unto death. In this singing service, there was no one giving testimony's so I wondered if there was any overcoming going on.

To my amazement there were people in the parking lot smoking and talking about everything but God. I just listened for a while and realized some of these men were from a teen challenge place nearby. I listened to some of there life situations and realized the pastor of this church was out here trying to talk to these men. The pastor had brought these young men here to worship the Lord but it seemed they were more interested in talking about their problems then singing.

At some point the pastor ask me who I was and how did I hear about the worship service. I told him that my friend brought me. I said I know my friend enjoys worshiping God this way. I guess the way I said it or maybe the words I chose led one of the men from teen challenge to say, "You know, I could sit in there and sing the words '*You are worthy Lord*' all night but it will not change me and I have the same problems when I leave." He said that singing '*You are worthy Lord*' is like going to a stupid movie and try to forget his problems for an hour our two. His friends agreed with him.

I asked him what would change him. He thought for a moment and replied that he doesn't know. I asked him why he came here. He looked at the ground as he said, "You know, it was just a way to get out of teen challenge for the night."

The pastor and I looked at each other. I think we both knew from his answer and body language that he was searching for something. I know I started asking the Lord what to say to this young man and I believe the pastor was also thinking the same way. The young man seemed so lost and he knew he wanted to change but finding the path he could stay on was not easy for him.

Suddenly I said, "You know, there is simplicity in Jesus that most people overlook. When I was in grade school, I thought the things my teacher was trying to teach me. It was so hard to learn but looking back I think how easy the lessons were. Looking back, I remember asking myself why I needed to memorize 2 plus 2 equals 4. I mean, I already knew how to count to four so I could just count and see I had four. I thought the teacher was just making my life harder." Surprisingly, everyone there laughed.

I added, "I believe a walk with Jesus is kind of the same way. I mean, everything I learned about God gives me a desire to know Him more." I said, "In our Holy Bible, there are some Scriptures which I call foundational. I believe in my search to find Jesus I was led by Jesus Himself to John 14: 26 which became my foundation. You know the foundation of all math is 1 plus 1 is equal to 2. If you don't understand the foundation then no math will make sense to you."

Jesus was telling the apostles He was leaving them and they naturally didn't want Him to leave, so Jesus gave His apostles what I call my foundation

John 14:26 But the Comforter, which is the Holy Ghost, whom the Father will send in my name, he shall teach you all things, and bring all things to your remembrance, whatsoever I have said unto you.

I asked them to imagine Jesus and Father God wanting to teach them. I mean Father God and Jesus are the Supreme Being so why would they care about me? I added during my childhood that I thought of myself as nothing. Why would the Supreme Being want to teach me? Jesus showed me in the Scriptures that I had value to Him and I could learn from Him and Jesus could actually use me to help build His kingdom here on Earth. There is simplicity to Jesus that the apostles needed. They already had jobs and self-worth but their jobs and self-worth will not build the kingdom of God. Jesus came to teach them what is important to God and Jesus is still teaching us today.

To me it seemed the apostles had learned to count and 2 + 2 equals to 4 but they didn't understand the need to trust God. They didn't understand Jesus math yet. Our math tells us that 1 + 1 = 2 but with Jesus math 1+1 is still one – *Ron plus Holy Spirit equals one.* The Holy Spirit and I become one but together I became transformed. The Holy Spirit asked me to open my heart to hear from Him. I thank God I was smart enough to listen and together the Holy Spirit started teaching my spirit how much God loves me.

You know the apostles trusted in Jesus the man who walked with them every day to have the answers for every situation of every day. Jesus told His apostles that He needed to leave them to fulfill the scriptures. The apostles didn't understand the limitations on Jesus as a man. Jesus knew as a man that He could only give them earthly knowledge or earthly understanding. Jesus the man could teach them 1 + 1 = 2 but the Holy Spirit could bring spiritual understanding of Jesus math 1 + 1 = 1.

Jesus told the apostles, "I need to send you and your descendents out to people that have never even heard of me. To do this I will equip you with all you need if you will trust me." Jesus continued by telling the apostles, he will even give you his peace as you go.

John 14:27 Peace I leave with you, my peace I give unto you: not as the world giveth, give I unto you. Let not your heart be troubled, neither let it be afraid.

I ask these young men if they would like to hear the voice of Jesus and to have Jesus give you the peace and comfort He promised to all men. One of them looked at me doubtfully but said yes. I said, "You just heard His promise, for these are His Words not mine and Jesus desire you to open your heart to let His peace and comfort in." Thanks to the pastor that they all had a Bible, so I ask them to memorize the address John 14:26-27. Please ask Jesus to help you be transformed in your heart and mind so you will see as He sees, think as He thinks and love as He loves and He will transform you into His image and likeness. Peace, understanding, wisdom and compassion are His gifts for those who earnestly seek Ye first the kingdom of God and His righteousness.

I went on to tell them about the book Jesus had me wrote *'A Precious Walk with My Jesus'* and I gave them each a copy. These men seemed to have a little more zip in their step as we parted and the pastor and I smiled at each other being pleased with what God had done for these young men. There were three men in the parking lot that night and even if only one got the message, we'll use God's math 1 + 1 = 1 and yet that is still one more then we had. I truly love watching how real math – God's math works.

I believe there will be plenty of time to sing to the Lord about how great He is when we get there. I believe our time here on earth is the time to be obedient to what Jesus asks and trained and equated us to do. I am so glad my friend asked me to go to that service and I am so joyful to know who lives in side me is always with me and always talking to me and through me. I must be truthful and admit I was not the least bit interested in going to a *singing worship service* but I knew my friend thought it was a great thing to do on Friday night and you know what, he was so right! Thank you Jesus!

I want to add this thought. In my quiet time I almost never listen to worship music. Actually, I only remember one time in the past three years where I by myself listened to worship music. If I am a little late for church service on Sunday morning and missed the music but I am not concerned. I just don't want to fill my life with music when I can fill my life with His voice. But I must admit a couple years ago I was the only person in a campground camping and one evening I decided to listen an old signing worship CD I found earlier that day.

I have a radio built into my camper with outdoor speakers so I was listening to worship music as I cooked some chili outside. Jesus and I danced and jumped off the picnic table as the words of the song said, "I'm not looking for a place to land; I'm looking for a place to fly." My joy in the Lord was exceedingly high and I look forward to singing and dancing with my Jesus again. I think my thoughts about worshiping God through signing were putting Jesus in a box, I know Jesus has no boundaries. In case you are wondering Jesus and I sing together a lot. We make good music together and I love the words Jesus gives me, we just never sing the same words over and over.

I believe Jesus and I are best friends because we spend quiet time together and I love so much to hear from Him. I really wish I could remember some of the songs we make up as we sing together because the words are so beautiful. When I asked God why I could not remember the words to write them down Jesus told me they were just for that moment. I don't consider these precious moments to be worshiping Jesus but I believe we both enjoy them.

I worship Jesus by listening to His prompting and doing what He prompts me to do. I worship Jesus by being a good listener. I worship Jesus by following Him and I worship Jesus by believing Jesus is the Son of God. I believe I worship Jesus more by seeing Him in the details of my life and being aware of His details in my life then if I sang to Him all day. I could sing I love you Jesus all day but I think Jesus would rather have me share a testimony that brings someone into a desire to know God intimately.

Here are some words Jesus and I sang the other day:

I have the joy of the Lord. Yes, put me in the lion's den and Jesus will make the lions my friends. I have the joy of the Lord. Yes, make the fire seven times hotter for Jesus and I and it doesn't matter. I have the joy of the Lord. Yes, Goliath looks like a big oak tree but I have the victory inside of me. I have the joy of the Lord. Yes, Noah built a big wood boat but only Jesus could make it float. I have the joy of the Lord.

This song went on for hours as Jesus and I drove down the highway...

Christ In You, The Hope of Glory

Colossians 1:27 To them God chose to make known how great among the Gentiles are the riches of the glory of this mystery, **which is Christ in you, the hope of glory.**

Jesus came and was the hope of glory for His Father. Everything I read about the life of Jesus tells me Jesus glorified His Father. We have the same opportunities to glorify our Father. If we study the day to day life of Jesus we will see how we too can bring glory to God daily.

Let us read about what is called the first miracle of Jesus from the prospective of faith and how Jesus had already died to Himself to bring glory to His Father through faith.

John 2:2-4 Now both Jesus and His disciples were invited to the wedding. And when they ran out of wine, the mother of Jesus said to Him, "They have no wine." Jesus said to her, "Woman, what does your concern have to do with Me? My hour has not yet come."

Jesus tells Mary my hour has not yet come and the wine problem is no concern to Jesus.

John 2:5 His mother said to the servants, "Whatever He says to you, do it."

Mary had not seen Jesus do a miracle at this point and yet she had to have great faith because she told the servants to do whatever Jesus tells them to do.

John 2:6-7 Now there were set there six waterpots of stone, according to the manner of purification of the Jews, containing twenty or thirty gallons apiece. Jesus said to them, "Fill the waterpots with water." And they filled them up to the brim.

What Jesus does then proves Jesus had died to himself and is a man of love. Jesus had already told Mary the lack of wine was no concern of his but Jesus laid down his life to please Mary and in doing so Jesus showed love and respect toward Mary.

John 2:8-11 And He said to them, "Draw some out now, and take it to the master of the feast." And they took it. When the master of the feast had tasted the water that was made wine, and did not know where it came from (but the servants who had drawn the water knew), the master of the feast called the bridegroom. And he said to him, "Every man at the beginning sets out the good wine, and when the guests have well drunk, then the inferior. You have kept the good wine until now!" This beginning of signs Jesus did in Cana of Galilee, and manifested His glory; and His disciples believed in Him.

Jesus told His mother that His hour has not yet come and yet Jesus did what His mother asks of Him. I believe Jesus had already died to himself to become helpful to others. Please notice the modesty in Jesus. Jesus did not make a big deal about His first miracle and say everybody come around and watch me change water into wine. Mary could have drawn a crowd and brought glory to herself and her son saying, "Look what MY son can do."

You know, in today's world we want glory for everything. I see bumper stickers that say *'My kid is an honor student.'* Mary's car would probably have bumper stickers from bumper to bumper. From what I read about Mary, she must have been a very modest person and I believe she had died to herself even before the conception and that fact alone made her available and useful to God.

We read in John how the miracle Jesus did at Cana helped the disciples believe. The whole life of Jesus was about helping us believe He is the Christ the living Lord. Our life will help others believe when we die to ourselves and become a vessel of our Abba Father's love. The more we die the more we can be used. Miracles will happen, hearts will be transformed and by living our life to be an example of the love of Jesus we will bring glory to God for we are His hope of glory.

Please ask Jesus to help you die to yourself. I read in Philippians where we can have the mind of Christ and we should ask for the mind of Christ.

Philippians 2:3-4 Let nothing be done through selfish ambition or conceit, but in lowliness of mind let each esteem others better than himself. Let each of you look out not only for his own interests, but also for the interests of others.

Here in Philippians 2:3-4, we see the perfect example of dying to self and looking at the life of Jesus we see the manifestation of and the outcome of dying to self. We also see we have the capability to let the Holy Spirit of Jesus into us to guide us, teach us and we will receive the heart of Jesus to have the compassion of Jesus. The Word of God says we can even have the mind of Jesus to speak like our Jesus spoke.

Philippians 2:5 Let this mind be in you which was also in Christ Jesus

Here we read we can have the mind of Jesus. When we receive the Holy Spirit of Jesus and Father God into our heart our life will no longer be about our self but we become transformed into who we ask into our heart. Hitler allowed the devil into his heart and the world saw how the devil transformed him. Ask Jesus into your heart and the world will see how God transforms people. Please ask for the mind of Jesus and ask to be His hope of glory for you know these request line up with His will and you know His will be done.

Philippians 2:5 Let this mind be in you which was also in Christ Jesus

1 Peter 3:8-9 Finally, all of you be of one mind, having compassion for one another; love as brothers, be tenderhearted, be courteous; not returning evil for evil or reviling for reviling, but on the contrary blessing, **knowing that you were called to this**, that you may inherit a blessing.

Peter wrote also that we can have the mind of Jesus, full of compassion for one another. With the mind of Christ we will love others as brothers. Peter tells us to be tenderhearted towards each other and to be courteous by not returning evil for evil. Peter says for us to return blessings, knowing Jesus calls us to do this and when we do we will inherit a blessing. I believe this is the '*Store up your treasures in heaven*' Jesus talks about where your treasure is so will your heart be also.

We are called to be a blessing. When someone steps on our toes or breaks our heart we are to respond in compassion, tenderness, by being courteous. These are the signs you are being transformed and that your conscience is being sprinkled cleaned. The best part is when someone *test you* is they are actually giving you an opportunity to show them the true love of God. The old Ron would probably returned evil for evil but the new transformed Ron will hear form my Jesus and allow my Jesus to give me the words to love on them. Yes I want the mind of Jesus and I want to be His glory.

I believe tests are a great way for us to measure our growth and transformation. I pray for my test to continue and as you grow you will actually thank God for the opportunity to demonstrate His love toward people that may not know of His love.

In 1 Peter 3:8-9, we read to return evil for evil is contrary to the word of God. When someone tempts us by being evil towards us we are to let the love of Jesus in us comes out of us toward them. I believe these test are opportunities that will actually help us discern the voices we are listening too. If you pass the test then thank God for being with you and helping you grow in His love. If you return evil for evil then go to your quiet place, repent and thank God for letting you see you need more time with Him.

I know our attitude toward the test will set the devil on his buns when the devil sees his test did not break us but rather his test give us an opportunity to prove we believe and we have come closer to the Lord. Actually these test are a good way to measure how fare we have been transformed and to measure how good we are discerning the voices we hear. Jesus tells us in Matthew 5:38-39:

Matthew 5:38-39 Ye have heard that it hath been said, An eye for an eye, and a tooth for a tooth: But I say unto you, That ye resist not evil: but whosoever shall smite thee on thy right cheek, turn to him the other also.

This teaching from God takes on a new twist when you think of someone being mean to you as an opportunity to show you are a Christian that takes the word of God seriously. When you turn your heart toward the Lord and ask the Holy Spirit to overtake your heart with His purity, His love and His compassion then you will see the world as a place of opportunity to demonstrate the love of God through you. I believe this is having the eyes of Christ, the heart of Christ and having the mind of Christ.

Luke 12:34 For where your treasure is, there your heart will be also.

Being transformed in to the image and likeness of Jesus Christ is to also see the things of this world as dung compared to intimacy with our Lord. You will notice you are fixing your mind on what Jesus needs done today instead of what would have been important to you before you ask the Lord into your heart. You will notice a conscience effort in your mind to discern the voices you are hearing. I believe this is the renewing of your mind Jesus talks about.

Here is an example of discernment:

Do you know anyone who has asked to be transformed into a need for sympathy or depression? I bet we all know someone who lives in depression and has a need for sympathy. Discerning our thoughts or whose voice we are listening to will determine our joy or lack of joy in our life. When we return evil for evil we feel good at first but then guilt and shame come into our life and compel us to take evil further, sometimes even into murder.

We just read in the scriptures where Jesus said *not returning evil for evil or reviling for reviling, but on the contrary blessing, knowing that you were called to this, that you may inherit a blessing.* The blessing for us is peace of knowing you are actually called to this Christ-like kindness. Jesus said my people die for a lack of knowledge. This is the knowledge His people are dying from by not knowing. The devil wants us to return evil for evil and miss our blessings. Then the devil will bless us with depression and a need for sympathy. If you live in the devils depression or sympathy you don't need drugs to help you cope, you need discernment and Godly knowledge that will only come by spending time with my Jesus.

Jesus said where your heart is your treasure is there also. Is your heart on going to the doctor and the drug store today or are you setting your mind on the things above. I know depression and sympathy are not from above so where is your heart today? Also depression and sympathy come with a voice so who are listening to? The voice of depression sounds like this: '*I don't know what to do*' or '*Oh well, what can one person do?*' or '*Maybe these drugs will help.*' That sounds like man's wisdom doesn't it? Please discern the voices you hear by asking God for help and with faith in God the help of God will come.

Please read Luke 12:34 again:

Luke 12:34   For where your treasure is, there your heart will be also. What is your treasure? Is your treasure good health?

I was with a couple the other day and as we walked into the grocery store they wiped off the grocery cart with sanitize wipes. They wash their hands with germicide stuff all the time. I ask wouldn't it be easier to trust God and they answered with man's wisdom, "Well God gave us a brain and he wants us to use it." I said, "You are right, God does want us to use our brain to trust Him. If your heart is into protecting yourself then why not take those wipes and sanitize everything you touch at the grocery store and everywhere you go? What about the gas pump handle or door handles, etc.?" After I made this comment I felt a gentle conviction form God.

I have praised God for the camper I live in. One of the nicest or best things about traveling in a motor home is that I have my own toilet. I hate using public toilets especially if I need to sit on one. After making the comment above, the Holy Spirit gently corrected me. Now if I need to use a public toilet I ask God to protect me as I sit down. I know for a fact God protected me my whole life, especially while in the navy for four years. Yes, I have been blessed to never have any kind of STD problem. Thank you Jesus and yes I will put my trust in you forever.

ARE WE STILL CALLED TO BE HIS HOPE OF GLORY?

Now there is something to ponder for a while. Jesus Christ, in You the hope of glory. We are the hope of glory to Jesus when we take on the responsibly of being an ambassador for Jesus. I know I am being transformed into the image and likeness of Jesus Christ. Just the thought of this was impossible for me to think about some years ago. Now because I have ask the Holy Spirit of Jesus and Father God into my heart I believe all things are possible and I see the transformation happening.

Could you ever imagine desiring to be transformed into the hopelessness of sympathy and self-pity? I don't know anybody who has gotten up in the morning and prayed, "Please Jesus give me a need for sympathy. Yes, Jesus I want people to feel sorry for me today so give me something to wine about. Please Jesus I love this self-pity I'm in and I want more of it. Please dear Jesus, help me have self-pity."

I bet you are laughing right now. I bet none of you know anyone who has said prayers like that. So where does self-pity come from and how does it get so routed in some of our lives? Where does the need for sympathy come from? Do you know there is even a condemning spirit called "cold heart" that accuses us day and night if we don't give sympathy? I think a lot of us Christians have confused sympathy with compassion.

I believe it is the compassion of Father God we see in the life of Jesus here on earth. There are a number of scriptures where Jesus had compassion on someone and He lifted their pain.

Mark 1:41-42 And Jesus, moved with compassion, put forth his hand, and touched him, and saith unto him, I will; be thou clean. And as soon as he had spoken, immediately the leprosy departed from him, and he was cleansed.

Matthew 14:14 And Jesus went forth, and saw a great multitude, and was moved with compassion toward them, and he healed their sick.

Compassion is powerful and up lifting. Self-pity and sympathy are draining our spirit of life right out of us. Those who desire self-pity and sympathy twist the Word of God or the Word of God has been twisted to them by the wisdom and teachings of man.

I believe there are teachings we Christians have listened to and taken into our heart that we need to take to the Lord and ask Him if these teachings are really about God. For example, where did sympathy come from? Did Jesus ever look for sympathy or give sympathy? I ask this because I believe Jesus is our example to model our life after. You know Jesus said "I only do the things I see my Father do." When Jesus saw people hurting He simply healed them from their hurt. Jesus had compassion not sympathy.

Look at these translations and compare, please ask Jesus to give you wisdom as you read.

Matthew 20:34 (KJV) So Jesus had **compassion** and touched their eyes. And immediately their eyes received sight, and they followed Him.

Matthew 20:34 (ESV) And Jesus in **pity** touched their eyes, and immediately they recovered their sight and followed him.

Matthew 20:34 (GWV) Jesus felt **sorry** for them, so he touched their eyes. Their sight was restored at once, and they followed him.

Mark 1:41 (KJV) And Jesus, moved with **compassion**, put forth his hand, and touched him, and saith unto him, I will; be thou clean.

Mark 1:41 (ESV) Moved with **pity**, he stretched out his hand and touched him and said to him, "I will; be clean."

Mark 1:41 (GWV) Jesus felt **sorry** for him, reached out, touched him, and said, "I'm willing. So be clean!"

I have been criticized for using the KJV while writing but I like the word compassion better than the word pity and sorry in these scriptures. I like the word Charity better than the word love in the scriptures also. To me, the word pity goes along with the words I don't know what to do so I will just pity you. I feel sorry about your luck. In my mind I have a hard time thinking of pity and sorry as being action words.

The word sympathy is not in the KJV but it is found in newer versions. I believe Jesus has taught me the word sympathy is the opposite of compassion – that is sympathy is the devils counterfeit to compassion. I know this because sympathy allows you to stay in your problem and pity them as you feel sorry for them but compassion lifts you out of the problem.

Look at the difference between sympathy and compassion in death. To most of us today, the loss or death of a loved one is a license for us to have years of sympathy and self-pity and we even dress in sorrow. We even give pity and sorrow a name – we say we need time to grieve.

To believe in Jesus and His truth *'there is no death'* replaces pity and sorrow with joy of knowing our loved one is in heaven. The simple truth that *there is no death* creates in us who believe in the compassion of Jesus to rejoice because we believe there really is no death. Believing Jesus removed death literally gives us no need for sympathy and pity and removes sorrow. I know I am to be His Glory here on Earth because I know the Holy Spirit lives in me and I know living a life of self-pity and sorrow makes me useless to the kingdom of God.

I declare having the compassion of Jesus does not mean I am hard in my heart. The compassion of Jesus is the opposite of a hard heart. I have cried over the loss of my precious wife Jenny. Jesus cried over Lazarus and Jesus said I only do the things I seen my Father do so I believe there are times when Father God cries. Compassion is not a harden heart. Compassion is a belief in the love of God to change things. When I cried because I missed my Jenny I actually heard from God and He reminded me where Jenny is and I rejoiced and thanked God for giving Jenny her precious place with Him. Yes, Jesus brought me right out of my pity and into a future of joy and strength. The Jesus plan sure beats pills and bills.

To me, pity and sorrow are the definition of a hard cold heart that starts with the word self like in self-pity and I feel sorry for myself. A hard cold heart is useless to God and man. Pity says I will help you be pitiful and self-pity says *I need, I need, I want* but I just cannot get out of bed. Sorrow is the same. How does it help for someone to be sorrowful with you? To me pity looks like 'let me buy myself some fatting comfort food; that will help me' while sorrow says 'I will buy you some fatting comfort food and maybe that will help you.'

I believe we are told in the word to feed the hungry because they are hungry and not because we feel sorry or pity toward them. We feed the hungry so they can hear the compassion of Jesus in the words you speak and in your actions. We feed the hungry in spirit to lift them out of pity and sorrow.

The loving compassion of Jesus will lift you up. Compassion is believing in the power we have been given through faith in God to transform death into life. Jesus called Lazarus's death to life, Jesus told people to be healed and Jesus told evil spirits to come out. These are words of compassion not pity and sorrow. Whatever translation of the Holy Bible you are reading, please asks Jesus to be your teacher and comforter he will be your teacher and comforter like He said He would be in John 14:25-28.

John 14:25-28 These things have I spoken unto you, being yet present with you. But the Comforter, which is the Holy Ghost, whom the Father will send in my name, he shall teach you all things, and bring all things to your remembrance, whatsoever I have said unto you. Peace I leave with you, my peace I give unto you: not as the world giveth, give I unto you. Let not your heart be troubled, neither let it be afraid. Ye have heard how I said unto you, I go away, and come again unto you. If ye loved me, ye would rejoice, because I said, I go unto the Father: for my Father is greater than I.

With faith in the words of Jesus we see *death* as a transition point. *If ye loved me, ye would rejoice, because I said, I go unto the Father: for my Father is greater than I.* I love knowing my little Jenny is with our Father in heaven. I love knowing Jenny is dancing with Jesus. I rejoice knowing Jenny is rewarded with life eternal. I love knowing Jesus is my best friend and I believe His words. *If ye loved me, ye would rejoice, because I said, I go unto the Father: for my Father is greater than I.*

Remember Jesus gave us a promise and Jesus is the great promise keeper. Remember it is Jesus Christ in you that is His hope of glory here on earth today. Yes, we are His hope of glory and knowing Jesus is in us is our hope to bring His glory to earth today. Simply ask Jesus, "Jesus what are we going to do today?" and I bet you will not hear "Go be pitiful and sorrowful and depressed so you can win some hearts to my kingdom today." Those spirits – self-pity and depression are not of the kingdom of God but they are real and they are building their own kingdom of hell and we are helping them if we are listening to them.

Here is another good reason to have a quiet time set aside for a faithful, personal relationship with my Jesus.

I have a friend who just started to read the Holy Bible and is trying to draw near to God. He asks me which Bible version to read. He started with the NIV and someone told him not to read that version. He has gotten information from different people and became confused about the differences in the different versions. I told him in my quiet time with Jesus that I had a conversation with Jesus about all these new versions of the word of God.

I assured him he too could do the same thing if he believes Jesus will answer him. I told him I take my questions to God because I know by faith God is my teacher and God is truth. I mentioned how I believe the word of God that says God is all knowing. I believe God knew years ago how people would translate His Holy Scriptures and make changes in these different versions. I said I believe Jesus made provision for these different versions even before they happened. My friend asked how Jesus did that.

I asked him to read John 14:26 and he did. I then assured him God would open up conversation with him also if he would read and allow John 14:26 into his heart through a simple believe Jesus is his teacher; his belief would open the door for Jesus to bring truth into His heart no matter what translation he is reading.

My friend asked me, "How does Jesus answer you?" I said, "Jesus brought me into Scriptures where He showed the word compassion and how the different Bibles translated the word compassion into pity and sorrow."

If you ask Jesus your questions in faith knowing God as truth and love and your teacher you will hear from Him also. Jesus will lead you into His Word and Jesus will lead you into His truthful answers in His Holy Bible. If for example your Bible version translates the word compassion as pity or sorrow Jesus will still bring His truth into your heart.

So if you are standing in front of someone and Jesus prompts you to pray for that person, I know for a fact you will hear the compassion of Jesus come out of your heart even if you have read a translation that says pity or sorrow.

I believe in John 14:26 and from that belief I have the peace of John 14:27 and I know even if the devil himself translated a Bible into his own teachings I believe Jesus will bring me into His loving truth that sets me free. I know Jesus asks us to seek Him with our whole heart and soul and I do so by faith for I know Jesus is seeking and protecting those that seek Him. To which my friend replied, "You really do trust God, don't you?" I said, "Yes, I do for I know God loves me. So why would I not trust someone who has already proved His love for me?"

You know I don't have an alarm clock in my camper so I trust God to get me up on time. My gas gauge in my car hasn't worked for years and yet Jesus always prompts me when I need gas. I don't use faith in Jesus for a better day and then get mad if my day doesn't go the way I want it to. I have my faith in Jesus to tell me what Jesus needs done today and Jesus handles the details so I don't have to worry.

My friend said I want faith like that. I said I just heard you ask Jesus for faith and I know Jesus heard you also. Continue in steadfast belief your prayers were heard and don't be swayed by circumstances. Jesus is real and he loves proving His realness to all that ask. Like what I said, I have never run out of gas in years because Jesus prompted me when I my gas was low; but if I ever do run out of Gas I know by faith Jesus still loves me and I know Jesus just wanted me to meet someone who I could bless with His words of love. Faith is so simple when we stay focused on Jesus.

Asking Jesus *What are we going to do today?'* is a simple decoration to give your day to Jesus. Jesus will open your heart to the compassion of Jesus and Jesus will use you for sure. Your life has purpose when we ask our Jesus and Father God to let us hear their voice and all they ask of us, is to make quiet time to hear their voice.

Jesus said we can have His heart and His eyes and His mind if we ask Him for these things and trust and believe it is His desire to make us in His image and likeness. I put my faith and my trust and belief that Jesus does want to be in me and live through me for Jesus says in His Word:

> **John 11:25-26** Jesus said unto her, I am the resurrection, and the life: he that believeth in me, though he were dead, yet shall he live: And whosoever liveth and believeth in me shall never die. Believest thou this?

I believe by faith in Jesus Christ that I have the resurrection life of Jesus Christ living in me today and by simply believing by faith God is making me singled-eyed, full of hope, living without fear, in need of nothing and never looking back condemning myself. I wake up with an expectation to continue to grow in the wisdom of God even more. My prayer is to give you a desire to know Him more and to trust Him more and by faith to know this intimacy is His desire for you.

Knowing the Holy Spirit of Jesus Christ is in you and knowing you are His hope of glory is not just wishful thinking or daydreaming it is real because He is real. This knowledge will become real as life itself is too you when you allow Father God to love you like He loved His Son Jesus! I hope you understand that our Father God desires to love us believers the same as He loves our teacher Jesus. Again, I ask you to allow the words of Jesus into your heart and let them become real to you. I know these words our true because Jesus said them and lived them.

> **John 15:13** Greater love hath no man than this, that a man lay down his life for his friends.

I pray the reality of Jesus becomes real to you. Your heart will never experience true love until you give Jesus permission to remove fear by giving Jesus permission to see you as you are. One of the big lies our enemy will tell us is we are unworthy. The enemy always mixes some truth into the lie to make the lie believable. When we trust and believe in the love of God toward us we receive the gift of discernment and with Godly discernment we will recognize the works of the devil. You see, to God we are worthy of His love and any voice in your heart that tells you different is not the voice of God.

Our past is usually a big stumbling block to receiving the love of God. There are a lot of stories in our Holy Bible about people with terrible past but these people overcame the lie of the enemy that they're not worthy by simply believing and dwelling on the forgiving love of Jesus and then allowing Jesus to transform them into His love.

I have purpose in my life and I purpose not to look back to my past failing even if the past failings were perpetrated on me and not from me. The hurt from the past is pain Jesus took to the cross. Repenting is to turn to the Lord and away from our past sins by simply focusing on our Jesus and His undying love for us. Our purpose is our future in Him and our purpose is to dwell on the life of Jesus so we can become His love to everyone we meet. I believe we will hear from God 24/7 and we are to follow His promptings forever.

I believe we receive boldness through hearing and through promptings from Father God. Jesus gives us power and authority to do the kingdom work by simply laying down our personal needs like a need for sympathy for when we lay down our need we will see the path to helpings others. We will become Christ-like and have our eyes opened to be comforters full of the compassion of Jesus. We will start our day asking the Holy Spirit of Father God and Jesus, "What are we going to do today?" and by faith their Holy Spirit will prompt us all day.

In my book '*A Precious Walk With Jesus*' I talk a lot about hearing from God. I talk about the joy of hearing Jesus call you by name, and knowing your name is written in the book of life in heaven. In my book '*A Precious Walk With Jesus,*' Jesus gave some really good examples of what heaven is like. Knowing Jesus knows you by name and hearing Jesus call you by name is truly heaven here on earth and part of the wisdom we are freely given from God to with stand the wiles of the devil. Would you please make hearing from God your priority for it is His communication with us that transforms us into a walking ambassador for God here on earth.

The Pure In Heart Will See God

Matthew 5:8 Blessed are the pure in heart for they shall see God.

To be pure in heart might sound impossible until we read and study the life of Jesus. Jesus has a pure heart for sure, so how did Jesus maintain a pure heart while living on the earth? It's simple – yes the answer is simple. What is Jesus? Jesus is pure love. If you want a pure heart ask Jesus to make you His love. I hear Christians tell other Christians, never pray for patients for you will have your patients tested. I think being tested is a good thing. We can measure our growth by passing the test. If you are not tested how will you know if God answered your prayer?

Don't worry if that makes no sense because you can go to God and He will help you with understanding also. When I asked God for patients, because I literally had none Jesus showed me a better way to pray. Now I pray and thank God for putting His pure love in me and God is giving me a pure heart that is full of His loving patients.

Think about this for a moment. I used to get so aggravated at traffic lights being red all the time. I mean, I would always hit them right as they turned red so I had the absolute longest wait. I would look in my mirror and see no one behind me and no one going through the light the other way and I would start boiling. I noticed while I was a passenger in a car with others they always hit the lights green and they never even thought about thanking God for green lights. These thoughts would play over and over in my mind as I sat boiling waiting for the stupid light to turn green.

As my Godly transformation began, I noticed I would be sitting at a red light with no one else even on the road and instead of boiling and asking God to turn the stupid light to green I started praising God I had time to sit and talk to Him. I found my mind going to Godly thoughts about how Jesus loves me. I have the Bible on CD and I play it in the car so I have more time to listen when I was sitting at red lights. Sometimes I shut my eyes as I listen for the word of God and people behind me had to blow there horn to get me to realize the light changed.

My point is I didn't wage war against my temper or my terrible temper tantrums when I saw the light turn red. I simply started focusing my thoughts on the love of God toward me and that allowed God to transform me. I used to be tormented with sleepless nights. Now when I can't sleep I get up and thank God I have time to be with Him and in a little while I go back to sleep in the sweetness of His peace and love for me.

The way to a pure heart is not some long battle with the devil. I would like to ask you this: If you are in some big war against the enemy, where is your mind? Is there any peace in your heart or just turmoil? Jesus tells us to set our minds on the things above and Jesus asks us to seek ye first the kingdom of God and His righteousness; do this by forsaking the things of this world. I mean, Jesus didn't have or own anything of this world. I know Jesus told me not to worry and yet in the past I found I was always worried about the things I owned.

Before hanging Jesus on the cross, the soldiers stripped Jesus of his clothes and then cast lots to see who would get them. I remember a saying from years ago that said *'He who dies with the most toy's wins'* which is man's knowledge. Now I know that saying came right from the devil. I believe Jesus proved to the world that he who lives and dies with nothing of the world is the winner and that is God's wisdom. I don't want anything holding me back, how about you?

I cannot think of a Scripture to back up what I just said 'he who lives and dies with nothing of the world is the winner' but I know the whole life Jesus lived is my back up. Yes, Jesus showed us how to be in the world and not of the world and in doing so Jesus was our living example how to live with a pure heart. My desire is to live as purely as Jesus lived. I hope I don't sound arrogant but I truly believe Jesus is sprinkling me clean of the evil conscience I used to walk around in. I believe we help the Jesus clean up committee and shorten the time they take to clean up our conscience by turning off the distractions of this world. When we turn off the distractions of this world we prove to God we are serious in our desire to seek the kingdom of God.

Jesus says only the pure in heart will see the kingdom of God. Jesus revealed to me things like television and internet and video games that are even one percent bad will not be found in heaven. So I ask you if you know something in your life is one percent bad, should it be allowed in your house or as Jesus referred to himself in your temple? What will come out of your heart if you are filling your heart with television sitcoms, news, internet and video games? Jesus said in Matthew 15:18-20:

> **Matthew 15:18-20** But those things which proceed out of the mouth come forth from the heart; and they defile the man. For out of the heart proceed evil thoughts, murders, adulteries, fornications, thefts, false witness, blasphemies: These are the things which defile a man: but to eat with unwashen hands defileth not a man.

Please hear what I am about to say with an open heart. I just don't know a better way to say this. I believe some of us have allowed our thoughts to turn into worry when Jesus tells us not to worry. Yet, some of us seem to worry more about what we eat then what goes into our heart. Jesus said to guard your eyes and ear gates for what you allow yourself to see and hear will affect you.

If you are filling your heart with useless television sitcoms, aggravating news, searching for something funny or interesting on the internet and or playing video games, you are probably one of those hopeless Christians who profess only God can straighten out this mess as you sit in front of your distraction every night. Remember these distractions tell us every day that there is no hope except through the government. That is man's knowledge.

Let us read in the word what we are missing by being distracted every day and night.

> **Romans 15:13** Now the God of hope fill you with all joy and peace in believing, that ye may abound in hope, through the power of the Holy Ghost.

If you are watching whatever is on television then you are missing the God of hope. You might have momentary happiness but you have no joy and no peace of believing and so you might not even pray. I ask you how we invoke the power of the Holy Spirit if we don't believe, for if we don't believe we will never pray. Every time I hear someone talk about how worried they are, I think how they need to ask God to help them understand Romans 15:13 and to let the God of hope come into their heart.

I pray and because I pray I know I am full of hope and I have the joy of the Lord and His peace abounding in me because thank you Jesus I am not sitting in front of distractions. I know Jesus gave me the power to change this hopelessness I see in others. I really believe the reason people worry so much is they feel hopeless to turn this world around. Jesus gave me a simple plan to turn this world around. The plan is spelled out in the book I wrote titled *One Heart at a Time*. I believe Jesus gave me this book to share with others. I call it the Jesus' simple plan to change the world. Jesus does have an answer and Jesus is a God of hope.

The distractions of the world are designed to keep you coming back to them as a source of knowledge. I believe all the distractions of today are designed to slowly and systematically steal your joy, steal your hope and they totally kill your communications even with loved ones. I see Christians sit, buy, watch television, or searching the internet for something interesting as our government is allowing the destruction of our babies in the womb. Our country is being destroyed right in front of our eyes while our very own families are coming unglued by a lack of hope that comes from a lack of commitment to spend time with God.

The Christians I know that do spend time in direct communication with God are full of hope for the future. They are not searching the internet for something interesting but instead they are talking to God about how they can be His ambassadors. Their lives are the difference America needs now and they have hope, joy and faith to trust in God that God will show them what He needs done today. Their life is a demonstration of life without worry and full of faith.

We can all sing *'You are worthy Lord'* in church on Sunday morning and leave feeling great. Some of us Christian's go to church like we are filling an obligation and while there we sometimes hear the pastor talk about foot ball stats from the pulpit, as if that will help you when your trial comes. None of these things – television, internet, sports, and useless vain conversations will give you a desire to have a pure heart of His love but they are by design interesting and interesting is steeling you hope, killing your future, and destroying our families. You choose!

If we do bring someone new into the church by giving them the feel good message about how good and worthy God is toward them and how God is there to bless them. I think we are setting them up for disappoint because the first time God doesn't perform for them; they now have a right or our teaching has taught them they have a right to be mad at God. If our preaching only brings people into a belief the message of Jesus is to bless us and to give us a wonderful day then we have truly missed hearing from God. Is it any wonder people think only God can straighten out this mess?

So much of what I hear in church today and so many people pray from a belief God is just here to bless us. To me that is like saying 'My God just blessed me this new car and with an extended warranty but all I am going to do is look at it and tell my new car how good it is and how worthy it is to be a car.' I just cannot imagine Jesus going through all He did for us. So we can sing how worthy He is and then have us watch our distractions while waiting for another blessing. I know Jesus didn't train the apostles to sing to Him while waiting for blessings. There is so much more to God's purpose for each one of us. Jesus' purpose is to give the apostles a pure heart of His love to share with everyone and He has the same purpose for us.

I just cannot believe Jesus came to earth and did all He did so we can sit in our air-conditioned church on Sunday morning as we plan where we are going out to eat and then we go home to watch hours upon hours of devil vision and we somehow believe our life brings glory to God. I tell you the devil is robbing us of our time with God. I hope you realize the devil has blessings for those who listen to him. I know what the devil will bless you with for listening to him. Where do you think hopelessness, fearfulness, forgetfulness, tiredness, unworthiness, lustfulness, sinfulness, depression etc, etc, come from? I know none of these things are of God but I see people sitting in front of their distraction and receive these devil blessings as if it is normal. You choose!

If you are living in any of these sins please discern where these sins are being feed from and who you are listening to. Please turn away from these wicked sources. I hope you know the devil vision and all the other time consuming distractions all come with a little button called OFF. Read these words of Jesus:

Matthew 18:8-9 If your hand or foot causes you to sin, cut it off and cast *it* from you. It is better for you to enter into life lame or maimed, rather than having two hands or two feet, to be cast into the everlasting fire. And if your eye causes you to sin, pluck it out and cast *it* from you. It is better for you to enter into life with one eye, rather than having two eyes, to be cast into hell fire.

I think Jesus is showing us with a very strong word picture, if something is making you sin, *turn it off!* I realize there was no television back when Jesus walked the earth but the message is the same today. If something is robbing you of your time to listen for the voice of God *turn it off!* If you are watching and listening to anything that is causing you to sin the sin of hopelessness *turn it off!* Jesus is telling us everlasting life will be better for us who to turn off our distractions and turn to the Lord, then for those who refuse to listen for the voice of God. Today is the day to make your decision. Please choose wisely!

I wonder if we Christians are being deceived with 'The God is good and God will bless us more then we deserve message that is taught in many churches today.' I believe the message we hear in some churches that 'God is going to pay your bills and give you a nice comfortable day' is an empty message because it is void of responsibility on our part. That message totally leaves out the fact Jesus taught us – that we are to die to our self, seek Him and turn away from sin and turn toward Him. How will we explain our life to Jesus on judgment day? Well, Jesus I tried to turn away from sin when we willingly watched sin for hours every week?

Our children see us watching hours upon hours of internet and then we show them what we found and call it interesting. I hope you realize every time you look for an answer on Google that you are training your children to trust something that is not of God. I have not read in my Holy Bible to go to Google for answers.

This is a short story about answers. My son Jason has a woodworking business. The most important machine in his shop is the CNC machine. It is a computerized router. Jason has owned and operated it for 8 years now. The other day the machine started acting up. Most of what Jason routes on this machine are 5 foot by 10 foot sheets of plywood with Formica glued to it. For some reason, the CNC machine will work perfect while routing plywood but the other day something changed and now the moment you put plywood with Formica glued to it, the machine suddenly has a mind of it's own and routs whatever.

Jason called the company that manufactured the machine and they told him they had never in the life of the company heard of such a problem. Jason called a person that sometimes works on the machine and the repairman had never heard of that type problem. Jason went on the internet and found no one has ever had this problem. That night Jason called me to tell me the problem with the CNC. I asked him when he would be in his shop again. Jason replied that he'll be at his shop by Monday morning. I said, "I will come over and in the mean time I will ask God to reveal what the problem is with your CNC machine."

Monday morning Jason showed me the problem. It is crazy. The CNC will work perfect with plywood but goes crazy if the plywood has Formica on it. I thought how the machine could even know the difference. Jason started routing some parts that were just plywood. I watched the machine for about three hours and kept thanking God for showing me the problem, but I wasn't seeing any problem.

Then all of a sudden as I was watching the machine, I started thinking about a story I read years ago. The story that came to my mind was about a recall General Motors (GM) had years ago on a lot of computerized cars. The problem was so simple. It seemed a man on the assembly line forgot to put a star washer between the ground strap that went from the engine to the frame of the car. Without the star washer the ground did not make good connection and the car would do funny things.

I walked into Jason's office and told him the GM story. Jason said, "Great, but what does that have to do with my CNC?" I told him, "I don't know but I believe I am hearing this from God so I am going to the hardware to buy some star washers. Jason looked at me like 'whatever dad.' When I came back with the star washers we put one on His ground connection and guess what? The machine worked perfect with the Formica on the plywood. Jason's face lit up and he started thanking me. I said, "You are thanking the wrong person. Please thank Jesus for it was Jesus that brought that GM story to my mind. I said all I did was trust upon the Lord for an answer."

We went into his office to talk. Jason knows I know nothing about the CNC machine. I told Jason, I am writing another book called 'Christ in You: The Hope of Glory.' In this book, Jesus and I are talking about man's knowledge verses God's wisdom. I mentioned if I had studied man's knowledge and was an electrical mechanical engineer I would have relied on my own experience and knowledge and would have been in your office looking at the owner's manual, instead of relying on God to tell me the problem.

I told Jason, "My Jesus is teaching me to separate man's knowledge form God's wisdom. If you put the words of man in the mouth of Father God toward His Son Jesus, the words take on a new view. For example, today if a dad tells his son to get a college education, everyone I know would agree with that dad by saying that is good fatherly advice. I said I believe Jesus is teaching me His wisdom and so I have come to realize some of the things we call good fatherly advice is what Jesus called man's knowledge that seems right to a man."

In the past I would not question the origin of man's knowledge and no one I know would question that dad's advice to his son. I then asked Jason, "Can you imagine Father God telling Jesus to go to school and get a college education and some Bible degrees before Jesus could go into the world to teach?" Jason started laughing. I told Jason, "Jesus is teaching me discernment this way. Now because I spend quiet time with Jesus I question if the words I hear from people are the words man's knowledge or Godly wisdom by putting them into the mouth of God to see if it sounds like something Father God would tell His Son."

I used to think we need to go to school to be taught the basics. Now I realize Jesus was taught by His parents (homeschooled). I believe we need certain basics and the basics we need are to trust Jesus to be your teacher and source of knowledge and wisdom for when you do trust Him and tell your children to trust Him they will have answers to questions that will astound others by going way beyond the basics.

Luke 2:45-47 They did not find him, so they went back to Jerusalem looking for him. On the third day they found him in the Temple, sitting with the Jewish teachers, listening to them and asking questions. **All who heard him were amazed at his intelligent answers.**

The really cool thing about letting Jesus become your teacher is you will have peace in knowing your children are learning truths that will protect them from man's knowledge the rest of their life. The Pharisees noted in the Holy Bible many times that the apostles were not educated like them and yet the Pharisees noted the apostles had been with Jesus and were out smarting the learned people of that day. I want to see bumper stickers that say *'My child is a Jesus student.'*

I have heard many parents tell me when their child go to college they stopped going to church and partied for years and did not live a God pleasing life. Yet these same parents will tell their children to go to college as if there is some change in college the children need. Man's knowledge is driving me crazy. One man I talked to said 98% of young Christians who go to college stop going to church for an average of ten years and some never come back to church. I told him that he just made my point. The information I just stated is common knowledge so I don't understand why it is still going on. What are we parents thinking?

Jesus plainly tells us to focus on Him and I do. I can tell you I have no knowledge of how the CNC machine works but I know Jesus personally and He does know how it works and I know Jesus told me how to fix the CNC. I truly believe when we put or trust in God all these things will be added and I don't mean financial blessing. In fact, I believe the biggest blessing God has given me is I have no need to be blessed financially.

Jason knows I have turned my whole heart, mind and soul toward seeking the Lord and I see my Lord as my source of all wisdom. The apostles learned to seek the Lord and they brought great glory to God. Jesus put His trust in His Father to speak through Him and Jesus brought great glory to His father, I believe to be a believer means we must put our trust in God for if our trust is in anyone or anything or rely on man's knowledge then we will be deceived.

I left Jason's shop praising God all the way back to my camper. The next morning, Jason called me and said the CNC machine is still running. Great! Thank you Jesus! Oh my goodness, I thank you Jesus my wisdom comes from you Jesus and I love being loved!

We Christian believers need to give people a desire to know God is good because God will give us the privilege to prove we believe. In my wildest dreams I could not have come up that set of circumstances to help my son come into a desire to know God. Yet the circumstances did happen and I believe they did give Jason a desire to know God. Notice I didn't have any bricks and mortar, I didn't need money, I didn't need to go to some far off country but God set all that up and all I needed was faith in God that God would show my children His love toward them. Thank you Jesus I love you too.

I realize how easy it was to praise God for what He did in my life. Sometimes our trials may be different. Sometimes our trials may require some suffering. I pray when my trials come to have the faith and wisdom to see the goodness and love of God in them also. My Holy Bible tells me the apostles counted it all joy when they were given the privilege to prove they believed and I want and pray for God to give me the privilege to prove I believe.

Every day I have a choice and I can tell you this. When God comes back; He will not find me watching a distraction called interesting. I thank God I have a choice between interesting and everlasting and I choose everlasting.

Now I think about the 'God is here to bless us' message. It is true Jesus will bless us as you just read in the CNC story. I believe we have a misconception that happens when we are taught by man's knowledge to live our life to be blessed by God instead of living to be a blessing to God. Jesus lived to bless others and Jesus is the one we are to follow. I think the way Godly blessings are taught today that God just wants to bless us is a message that has taken Christians off the narrow path and put many Christians on a path where they are allowed to question the wisdom of God if God doesn't bless them.

Jesus tells us in Matthew 23:15:

Matthew 23:15   How horrible it will be for you, scribes and Pharisees! You hypocrites! You cross land and sea to recruit a single follower, and when you do, you make that person twice as fit for hell as you are.

I ask my Jesus, "How did the Pharisees make the new believers 'twice as fit for hell as they are?'" I was prompted to read all of Matthew 23 and I did as prompted. I read it again and Jesus showed me all of Matthew 23 is a list of false Pharisees teachings. Jesus spelled it out for the Pharisees but they refused to listen. Yes, read Matthew 23 and you will see for yourself Jesus gave them a list of their false teachings. I believe these false teachings of the Pharisees made new believers twice as fit for hell as the Pharisees are.

Let us look at their teachings for a moment; Jesus tells the Pharisees:

Matthew 23:24   You blind guides, straining out a gnat and swallowing a camel!

A gnat is like a mosquito. It is something that got in their wine while fermenting that would be strained out before drinking. I asked Jesus what was the gnat the Pharisees were straining on. Jesus told me the Pharisees where always pointing out the sins of others to make themselves look good. Jesus led me into the Scriptures where the Pharisees were upset when his apostles ate bread without washing their hands first. They ask Jesus.

Matthew 15:2   Why do thy disciples transgress the tradition of the elders? for they wash not their hands when they eat bread.

Jesus showed me not washing your hands before eating was their gnat for it is not a big deal. So I ask my Jesus what was the camel the Pharisees swallowed so easily.

John 7:1   After these things Jesus walked in Galilee: for he would not walk in Jewry, because the Jews sought to kill him

Matthew 12:14 (KJV)   Then the Pharisees went out, and held a council against him, how they might destroy him.

Matthew 12:14 (GWV)   The Pharisees left and plotted to kill Jesus.

To Jesus, *swallowing the camel* is the Jews plotting to murder Jesus. The Jews plotted to kill Jesus for years. Jesus proved the Jews got mad if Jesus healed on the Sabbath or if Jesus and His disciples ate with unwashed hands (gnats) but the Pharisees were swallowing a camel when they plotted to kill Jesus for healing on your Sabbath. Jesus explained this to me another way:

Matthew 7:4   How can you say to another believer, 'Let me take the piece of sawdust out of your eye,' when you have a beam in your own eye?

The sawdust is commending people for not washing your hands and the beam is murder in your heart. Let each and every one of us examine our own hearts to see if we have been straining on a gnat while swallowing a camel.

I asked Jesus to show me the modern day gnats and the modern day camels we are swallowing today. Jesus showed me we are sanitizing our hands (gnats) while holding unforgiveness in our heart (camels)? Are we praying over our food asking God to bless it while wasting hour upon hours watching our favorite distraction? Are we focused on God and being His righteousness or focused on acquiring more dung? Do we wake up and ask God what are we going to do today or do we tell God how we need to be blessed with today?

I thank you dear Lord for helping me to examine my heart for I only want a pure heart and I thank you dear Lord for helping me remove the beam in my eye that is blinding me from seeing your needs today. Could the sawdust in our eye be not trusting God because of something a person here on earth did or didn't do. If a person broke your trust in them please remember Jesus told us to put your trust in Him and not man. I thank you dear Lord for opening my eyes to trust in you!

The end of Matthew 23 says Jesus wept for them for their hearts had waxed cold to the truth of Jesus Christ. I pray for the gentle conviction of Jesus to come into my heart and I pray for quiet intimate time to hear His words the first time He speaks.

The message of Jesus of seek ye first the kingdom of God and His righteousness and love not your own life unto death is so simple to me. I trust Jesus to be my teacher and all I have to do for Jesus is believe in Him and be available for Him to use me and allow Jesus to speak through me to give people a desire to know Him. I have total peace in my life for I know Jesus brings the increase.

The message in a lot of churches today is simply be baptized and you are saved so go live and do what you want; for the goodness and mercy of God will still bless you with salvation. This message goes along with (God knows my heart) which is man's wisdom. I hope you realize this message actually gives a man the right to get mad at God when anything goes wrong in his life. I pray for Christian leadership to ask God to help them refine their message because we are making that person twice as fit for hell as the scribes and Pharisees. I pray when Jesus reads these books He has given me to write, His face will shine upon them.

The Scribes and Pharisees plotted to kill Jesus because Jesus did not conform to their teachings. Do we Christian's of today do the same thing? If your wife doesn't live up to some standard we set in our mind, do we divorce her? If our parents get sick do we put them in a home because we don't have time for them? Are we protecting babies in the womb? Are we even telling our children about God? Who do you think is telling us to call His children baby goats (kids)? I don't know for sure but these might be some of the questions Jesus may ask us on judgment day. I pray you are not too distracted to think on these things today.

Look at the words Jesus chose in Matthew 23 and you will know modern man made messages like *once saved always saved* message or *don't worry Jesus knows my heart*, or *I'm just waiting to get ruptured out of here* and *only God can straighten out this mess*. I believe these messages are very offensive to my Jesus. Sitting home in your easy chair watching distractions while babies are being killed down the street is offensive to my Jesus.

Where do these messages come from? I know where they come from and I will call it *the devil*. I cannot find any of these teachings in the teachings of Jesus so why are they in our Christian churches? The message 'God is only here to bless you' is so misleading and by itself will produce faithless back sliders who will never see a need to serve God unless they are rewarded for doing a good deed.

I believe Jesus could add a lot of new verses to Matthew 23 today. Let us make sure our hearts are not waxed cold like the Pharisees of old. I pray for Christian's everywhere to put down the things of this world and stay focused on seeking Jesus for Jesus will tell you what needs to be done today. The cool part of walking with Jesus is you will not need anything except faith in Jesus. Your heart will change. Your world will change when Jesus is real to you. You will live to spend time with Jesus today.

Walking with Jesus is not some cake walk. Yes Jesus loves us and Jesus promised He will not let our trials be more then we can handle. Jesus tells us trials will come by way of offences.

Matthew 18:7 Woe unto the world because of offences! for it must needs be that offences come; but woe to that man by whom the offence cometh!

Jesus is telling us in Matthew 18:7 that we will see offences come our way. Jesus is also telling us woe to the man that teaches them or brings them. Jesus is good all the time and we need to know the goodness of God is what will help us and prepare us for the offences that will come. Jesus will walk with us through the offence if we simply believe by staying focused on Jesus and not the problem.

Think about this for a moment. If you wish to join a club, you must make a declaration of joining. For some clubs, the declaration is as simple as paying some dues. In some clubs, you take oaths or perform some act to prove you are serious about joining in the club. In some clubs or gangs, the entrance fee can be to kill someone.

I thank God I am a believer every day and I thank God His test for us believers is to simply show His love to someone today. There are evil forces that will test us to see if we believe God is good and I pray for Jesus to strengthen me with His strength as we have our quiet time together. I know I can read about having a pure heart in my Holy Bible but I will only receive a pure heart in intimate quiet time with my Jesus. My desire for you is to have this intimacy with my Jesus also. Come join His club and become a giver of His love. The only person you have to kill is your old selfish ways.

I talk all through this book about how important it is to know God loves you because His love for us is the true strength that will deliver us out of our trial. We need to pray for our trial so we can prove we believe. I don't think Father God sent His Son so we could talk about football statistics in church on Sunday morning. We have real work to do and it is not too late if we believe.

It seems most Christians today will tell you only God can straighten out this mess. I believe God has already sent His Son to show us how to straighten out our mess and now God is now sending you. The problem is some of us or way too many of us are sitting on our backside doing nothing while we wait on God. When we sing to God about how good God is on Sunday morning and then sit back and watch devil television all week, we are proving we have no commitment to God and we are proving we don't believe His love for us will change the world.

I beg you too turn off the distractions of this world. As you sit in your easy chair, please turn your thoughts toward God and ask God to help you come to know Him. Ask God to help you or lead you in proper prayers of faith. Spend your time thanking God for showing you what you can do to transform the world. Father God sent one person – Jesus and now Father God is sending you. You too will make a difference when you listen for the promptings of God and act on them in faith.

In my quiet time one morning, Jesus and I were talking about distractions of this world. Jesus asked me this question: If something is one percent bad, will it be in heaven? I said, "No, my Lord." Jesus asked, "If it is one percent bad, should it be in your camper Ron?" I said, "No, my Lord." Then I fell on my face and prayed and thanked God for revealing these things to me. Jesus led me into Revelation and what will be in heaven. I hope you see how simple my test was that day – the test was to get rid of my distractions. I thank you Jesus! I haven't watched television for 13 years and I never got started on the internet stuff and I never liked video games; so my distraction was my phone. I still have a slide phone but now I will not let it interrupt my quiet time with Jesus any more.

If you think your distraction is no big deal to God then read what will enter heaven and who will enter heaven? I believe it will be a lot easier to give up the distractions of this world now than to maybe pay some big price later.

Revelation 21:27   But there shall by no means enter it anything that defiles, or causes an abomination or a lie, but only those who are written in the Lamb's Book of Life.

When I read this, I fell on my face again knowing the Word of God just confirmed my heart. I cried and ask God to purify me more and more and more until I become a blessing to Him with a pure heart of His love. I hear Christians say, 'Well, Jesus knows my heart' and I know they are speaking truth for Jesus does know their heart. But are you asking Jesus to purify your heart or are you depending on His mercy on judgment day? Simply pray in faith thanking God for sprinkling clean your heart and you too will notice the transformation happening. Remember Revelation reads *'But there shall by no means enter it anything that defiles, or causes an abomination or a lie.'* I ask you again: What is in your heart?

Actually this is the formula for guarding your heart: *But there shall by no means enter it anything that defiles, or causes an abomination or a lie.* Please think about what you are looking at and watching on the devil vision and evil net and evil games you are playing. I know for a fact these things will not give you a desire to know God but they will surely show you a need for more dung. Give yourself the gift of desiring to know God and receive the worry free life God desires to give us believers. Ask God for a pure heart and focus on His righteousness and God will gladly partner up with you.

Are We Sheep or Goats?

Jesus said He will separate the sheep form the goats. Sheep are always being led, sheep need protection, sheep are harmless, loving, gentle, and have survived through the centuries without any self-defense. Goats on the other hand are hard headed, always into mischief and they never want to do what you need them to do. I think it is ironic that most people refer to children as kids today. In my Holy Bible, a kid is a baby goat. In the world today, a lot of children act like kids.

Today we set our children in front of the distractions which we work hard to buy for them and tell them to sit down and watch this distraction until we are done with our own distractions. We think we will have time for them when we are done with our distraction which usually doesn't happen because distractions are designed to make you watch more distractions. Distractions are traps used to louver us into staying tuned such stay tuned for the latest breakthrough or the latest update, or you need this app to help you save time, or collect all 4978 of these collector items and then you will be happy.

All these traps I mentioned are man's knowledge. I know you know what I am talking about. Think about McDonald's for a moment. They almost have some giveaway promotion for our children. You know, collect all ten items and you will have a whole set. So we set our mind on going to McDonald's every time we are out because we want our children to have all the ten items. Please make a decision now to lay down your distractions and seek ye first the kingdom of God and you will never regret it and neither will your children.

I just don't think collecting all ten will be as important on judgment day as we make it while we are here on earth. When we set our mind on collecting all ten we have just taken our mind off what the Lord has for us to do. This is such a simple example but I hope you see the devil in this distraction and how he starts us on these seemingly harmless journeys and how these seemingly harmless journeys will take our minds of Jesus. Please understand God can use you even while you collect all ten. I'm praying for us to be more aware of what God needs done rather than the junk we set on mind on collecting.

I believe we all know there will not be anything bad in heaven. I believe we are being asked by God to choose our priority's here on earth hour by hour. You know, heaven will be heaven because God made a choice as to who He lets in. We are choosing who we let into our mind and heart with every decision we make. I pray to have the strength to turn off or destroy my distractions so I have already purged my home but I thank God for His help for I know most distractions come from outside my home.

We all know sin and deceit are everywhere and these influences are not only affecting us but also they affect our children. Our only hope and defense is the knowledge that we have a protector. Our protector is with us and in us and in our children protecting them if we have accepted Him into our heart. I believe we all know there is a battle raging for our soul and for the souls of our children.

The good news is we win but not because you read the back of the book. We win by the choices we make every day. The formula is simple. Let us all put our hope in the man that came to give us hope. Jesus has asked us to lay down our life for others. What would happen in your house hold if you choose to put God first? My friends Will and Jamie have done this and they have the most respectful children and you feel the peace of God the moment you walk into their house. Their joy is contagious. They live on one income and home school their four children. I have actually cried when leaving their home after visiting with them because the peace in their home was so overjoying.

Anyone who puts their priority on quiet time with Jesus will experience the overjoying of the Lord. Remember we our His children and look what Jesus says about us.

Matthew 21:15-16 And when the chief priests and scribes saw the wonderful things that he did, and the children crying in the temple, and saying, Hosanna to the Son of David; they were sore displeased, And said unto Jesus, Hearest thou what these say? And Jesus saith unto them, **Yea; have ye never read, Out of the mouth of babes and sucklings thou hast perfected praise?**

Isn't that amazing? The children were not afraid to praise my Jesus even in front of the chief priest. I think how many times we shun our children because we are busy and maybe we are missing the perfected praise of the babes. Let us look at what Jesus called His apostles.

Luke 10:21   In that hour Jesus rejoiced in spirit, and said, I thank thee, O Father, Lord of heaven and earth, that thou hast hid these things from the wise and prudent, and hast revealed them unto **babes**: even so, Father; for so it seemed good in thy sight.

Jesus called the apostles babes. We believers are referred to as babes and children all through the Bible. Please accept these titles with joy and adoration for the one who calls us to be His children.

Is the Sinner's Prayer Enough?

I have asked God how to let people see this relationship they can have with Him is not only possible but also real. I believe the moment we try to figure out life on our own we have just made a choice to leave God out of our plans. Oh we might go to church on Sunday for an hour or two and maybe some Bible studies during the week but is God the center of our life.

Do we sit quietly with our spouse and talk about what God is doing in their life or do we sit with our children and have quiet time with them. Our children and our spouse are gifts from God. I talked to a youth pastor the other day who told me that children have no commitment to anything. I agreed with him for I believe there is a lack of commitment by what I see in the world today.

Children learn commitment from adults. If our life is about ourselves, their life will be about themselves. Look at the role models children have, it seems today marriage is not *'until till death do us part'* but *'until it is not fun anymore do us part.'* Coaches in sports tell the children to play hard and win for the team and for their school spirit. But if another school offers the coach a better salary, his school spirit probably went where the money is.

I see people so hyped up about their professional team. People wear sports on their clothes and the number of their favorite player on their back. I even see this in a church and I hear adults talk to these children about their favorite player in church. Yet if that player gets a better offer in some other town they are gone and then you will find there special expensive shirts in the Goodwill store. I believe we are teaching our children to seek money and don't get held back by commitment to your team, your school or even your marriage. I hear of children being abandoned by their parents because of lack of commitment. I met a woman that told me God wanted her to divorce her husband of 18 years because he was hindering her music ministry. This thinking is absurd.

Is there any wonder why adult children put their parents into homes when the parents get sick? I mean, the parents didn't have time for the children and now the children don't have time for the parents. The dung of this world is so enticing. The answer to the commitment problem is in our Holy Bible but the day-to-day life or living the answer is in our relationship with God.

God has told us we can have heaven on earth and most of us say really, I would like to see that. We all know heaven will be a place of trust, peace, and joy. We will not need hope in heaven because we will already be there. To me, heaven will be the perfect place where the love of God rules. I have witnessed heaven on earth in families who are in love with God. I have experienced heaven on earth by having quiet time with my Jesus.

I have a CD of a friend Dan Mohler talking about God and the CD is thirty minutes long. I asked people to take it home and give up one sitcom and listen to this 30-minute CD instead. I challenge people to see which half hour gives them a desire to know God more: the sitcom or the Dan Mohler CD? I tell them it is only half an hour of your life and yet a lot of people will not lay down a thirty minute sitcom to take this challenge. This is so sad because I know the choices we make have an everlasting value. I wonder if these people have any commitment to God.

I think some people are afraid of commitment because the devil has made commitment into works. I believe commitment is actually a way to show the love of God to others. Jesus modeled commitment in His life and we are to model commitment too. If we seek to be Christ-like by laying down our life for another we will show people this Christ-like love and we won't have to preach it because God will shine His love through us. If our children see commitment in us, our children will see the love of God in us and the joy of God in us will draw our children to want the commitment we have.

Is there any commitment in the sinner's prayer? Is there any relationship in the sinner's prayer? I think the preachers who preach the sinner's prayer are sincere in their belief but I think to most people the sinner's prayer is a bus ticket to heaven and they have their ticket so that is all they need God for. If all we need to do is say some prayer and we are guaranteed heaven, then why did Father God send His Son and write His Holy Bible?

I should be all for the sinner's prayer message. It is simple and I like simple. Repent and be baptized and go live life, how simple is that. Can you imagine what the world would be like if all Jesus actually taught us was to say the sinner's prayer and you are in? Yes, repent and be baptized and you are saved. My heart cries when I hear a message that is so void of truth, but the good news is my Teacher has brought me past this message and He will bring you past this message also if you let Him.

I spend quiet time with my Jesus and we talk about some really cool stuff. The apostles would never have been who they were transformed into without spending time with Jesus. Spending time with Jesus takes commitment and a desire to know what real love is. The apostles became the hope of glory for God the Father and Jesus and we can be their hope of glory also.

We have already read about faith and how faith pleases God. We know we are to live by faith and we are to transform the world by faith. I believe there are people who are saved the last moment of their life but they missed all the Joy of the Lord while here. That is the tragedy of the sinner's prayer.

The apostles modeled their life after Jesus and Jesus made the apostles ministers. Let Jesus make you into an instrument of His kingdom also. I don't know what your job will be or what part of the body of Christ you are but I know Jesus needs workers. Jesus told the apostles the workers are few and so I believe Jesus is still in need of workers today. Will you answer the call? Not the call to say the sinner's prayer but the call of Jesus to follow Him by faith?

Luke 10:2 Therefore said he unto them, The harvest truly is great, but the labourers are few: pray ye therefore the Lord of the harvest, that he would send forth labourers into his harvest.

We Christian's are *so blessed.* You know God could do it all himself without any of us but God is not seeking His own Glory. God is sharing His glory with us believers. The message of Jesus is love never fails and He has made His message our message. The gifts of the Spirit are great but they are nothing without love.

1 Corinthians 13:1-8 Though I speak with the tongues of men and of angels, but have not love, I have become sounding brass or a clanging cymbal. And though I have the gift of prophecy, and understand all mysteries and all knowledge, and though I have all faith, so that I could remove mountains, but have not love, I am nothing. And though I bestow all my goods to feed the poor, and though I give my body to be burned, but have not love, it profits me nothing. Love suffers long and is kind; love does not envy; love does not parade itself, is not puffed up; does not behave rudely, does not seek its own, is not provoked, thinks no evil; does not rejoice in iniquity, but rejoices in the truth; bears all things, believes all things, hopes all things, endures all things. **Love never fails**. But whether there are prophecies, they will fail; whether there are tongues, they will cease; whether there is knowledge, it will vanish away.

I believe the message of Jesus is the opposite of the sinner's prayer. I say this because we are only thinking of ourselves in the sinner's prayer. Compare it to the rapture message: 'Jesus, rapture me out of here.' If that is how you think, please think about your loved ones. Are they ready? These messages sure sound self-serving. I just cannot find these messages in 1 Corinthians 13, can you?

I beg you to consider the life of Jesus and read 1 Corinthians 13 over and over and asking Jesus every time you read these words for understanding to not only know what love is but how to become His perfect love.

So many people I meet put such pride in their accomplishments here on earth. From what I read in my Holy Bible and from what I understand, our physical accomplishments here on earth might not be so impressive when we arrive before Jesus on our judgment day.

1 Corinthians 13:3 And though I bestow all my goods to feed the poor, and though I give my body to be burned, but have not love, it profits me nothing.

I think the message is we need to focus on being the love of Jesus Christ if we want to be His hope of glory. Simplify your life by becoming the love of Jesus to everyone you meet and I believe we will have a great report card when we arrive on judgment day.

Our eternity rides on what we seek now today. Relationship with Jesus Christ living in you is becoming the hope of glory for Him by allowing the hope of glory in us. Why are we spending our time acquiring dung? In this world two things are for sure: the dung of this world will pass away and there will be a judgment day. Yes, we will stand before Jesus for judgment clothed in righteousness or we could be standing in a pile of dung. Now, you choose.

This goes for our heart also. Will our heart be a heart full of His love and wisdom or a heart of vain conversation from watching hours upon hours of internet, television and video games? I can tell you this: if you desire a relationship with God, the joy of the Lord will overtake you and giving up the things of this world will be easiest thing you have ever done.

I hear people say, "Well, God sees my heart," and I pray God will see His love in your heart. Jesus has already told us in Revelation 21:27 *'There shall by no means enter it anything that defiles, or causes an abomination or a lie to enter.'* So what will Jesus find in your heart? Useless sitcoms, hours of useless internet, sports statistics... No matter how interesting it is, I believe it is useless if our passing of time doesn't build a relationship with God. Please guard your eyes and ear gates for Jesus ask us too.

Jesus tells us all through the Holy Bible what to dwell on so I think we need to listen to the word of God.

2 Timothy 2:15 Study to shew thyself approved unto God, a workman that needeth not to be ashamed, rightly dividing the word of truth.

And Jesus tells what not to dwell on or listen too.

2 Timothy 2:16 But shun profane and vain babblings: for they will increase unto more ungodliness.

Can Jesus make His words any clearer then this? Please check your distractions and if they are vain babblings such as telling a dirty joke or even interesting vain babblings like sports scores or statistics. I tell you now that you need to let go of them. Remember you said Jesus sees your heart and I believe Jesus sees what you have been putting into your heart and we know that is what will come out of your heart. Remember also the Jesus clean up committee is gentle and this transformation is gentle.

These things might sound to harsh for you to hear or too hard for you but I beg you to set some quiet time aside and ask Jesus to talk to you, ask Jesus to teach you and guide you like He did the apostles. I hope this does not sound legalistic like God demands you to turn off your television, etc. On the contrary I believe we are simply trading our time of intimacy with God for these earthly things. Remember the choice is yours. If you allow God into your heart, you will gladly give up the earthly desires and you will gladly spend time with your loving God.

The people who say, "Well, God knows my heart" are saying it as if to justify the fact they are not seeking God and God is supposedly okay with them. Maybe these are the same people who said the sinner's prayer years ago.

If you were saved with the sinner's prayer and think you are living in the mercy of the sinners prayer which is once saved always saved. Please read what Jesus said about being saved.

Matthew 24:9   Then shall they deliver you up to be afflicted, and shall kill you: and ye shall be hated of all nations for my name's sake.

We all know Jesus was killed for declaring Himself the Son of God. Why should we believers be any different? If we have established Jesus is real in our heart we will know from reading His word we will be afflicted, hated and killed for our belief in His name. I want my test, I want my faith to be tested with fire so I know my faith is more than words. I never read where Jesus told His Father to rapture Him out of here. Instead, I have read the words of Jesus to His Father, "Not my will but thine be done."

Luke 22:42 Saying, Father, if thou be willing, remove this cup from me: nevertheless not my will, but thine, be done.

I pray for the faith and relationship Jesus had with His Father to be my faith and their relationship to be my relationship.

Matthew 24:10 And then shall many be offended, and shall betray one another, and shall hate one another.

We can expect to be betrayed and offended, see our own brothers hating us if our brother loves his own life not unto death. You probably will not think about these things while watching television tonight. But, oh well, Jesus knows my heart. This is true, but Jesus wants to be in you heart, in your thoughts and in your life.

Matthew 24:11 And many false prophets shall rise, and shall deceive many.

The false prophets will have an easy time deceiving those being distracted every night. I am afraid many people have chosen entertainment over relationship. Have you ever heard these words as you try to talk to someone about God: 'I'm good with God, I'm saved. Honey, get me another beer the game is about to start.' The deceiver doesn't make you choose between belief and unbelief. The deceiver will give you false comfort (*I'm saved*) and false happiness (*I must watch this game*) while robbing you of your true peace and joy.

Matthew 24:12 And because iniquity shall abound, the love of many shall wax cold.

Jesus says lawlessness, abortions and sins of all kings will become so common place we will just accept them as normal. Our heart will become indifferent as we sit in front of our distraction and ask. "God, how can you let this happen?" I believe God wants to ask us the same question, "Why are you letting this happen?" The deceiver says, "Don't worry God knows your heart."

Matthew 24:13 But he that shall endure unto the end, the same shall be saved.

I can guarantee that you will not find faith to endure unto the end on television and the net or in the sinner's prayer. The things of this world will seem so trite when our test comes. How we spend our time now will determine our determination to endure unto the end. Earthly knowledge, interesting knowledge, college knowledge and even Bible knowledge will fall short of having faith to love not our own life unto death. We simply must seek the kingdom of God and His righteousness or we will fall short of faith to endure to the end. The only way to know God is real is to give up your earthly pursuits and pursuit God with all your heart, mind and soul.

Christ in you the hope of Glory is our promise from God that our life can bring glory to God if we choose too. Jesus said all things are possible for those that believe. I believe and I declare what I believe all the time. If you hung around me, I am sure you will find a lot of things that need to improve in me. The good news is I am sure you will also see I am being transformed daily and my Teacher is able to work with me because I have opened my heart to hear and allow the Holy Spirit to live and speak through me. I am blessed; I have turned off my distractions.

Please allow Jesus to help you turn off the distractions and read His words of wisdom for when you do Jesus will remove worry and replace it with trust.

Luke 21:12 But before all these, they shall lay their hands on you, and persecute you, delivering you up to the synagogues, and into prisons, being brought before kings and rulers for my name's sake.

Sounds like bad news but Jesus goes right on to tell us the good news.

Luke 21:13 And it shall turn to you for a testimony.

I want my testimony. I want others to be desirous of knowing God this way and Jesus tells us we overcome by the word of our testimony. I don't want a bus ticket to heaven. I want to bring the peace of heaven to earth and Jesus tells me how.

Luke 21:14-15 Settle it therefore in your hearts, not to meditate before what ye shall answer: For I will give you a mouth and wisdom, which all your adversaries shall not be able to gainsay nor resist.

This is total peace. Jesus walked in total peace of knowing His Father was with Him in Spirit. Jesus didn't premeditate His words or His actions but He did model a life of living in the loving protection of His Father. We have the same protection if we believe.

There are areas in my life that Jesus is still transforming. Some of my old ways are still with me and I know I have areas that set off little alarms in my head. The cool thing is, the list of alarms is growing shorter and I know Jesus is proud of my efforts to put down entertain and seek Him first. Notice I am not seeking to shorten the list. I am seeking God with my whole heart and the list of things that need Godly transforming is becoming shorter.

Seeking God with all your heart is to make the things of this world dung. I live in a 21-year old camper and almost every day I see some big beautiful new motor home pull into the campground. If I am not careful, sometimes my thoughts will go to 'Wow I wish I could live in a fancy motor home like that one.'

Immediately, I realize how blessed I am to have this one. I mean, there are a lot of people in this world who would give their right arm to have a nice clean place like mine to lay their head every night. Jesus Himself didn't have a home as nice as mine to live in. I will forever be blessed that I don't seek after the things of this world and if I stay focused enough on the things above – Jesus Christ. I will not desire anything but a closer walk with my Jesus.

If your relationship with Jesus is based solely on the sinner's prayer I hope and pray for you to read John 14:26 and ask Jesus to be your personal teacher because He desires to be your teacher. Jesus will open up the Holy Bible to give you new thoughts of being sprinkled clean to receive the pure heart of Jesus. Your desires will grow for a relationship so intimate with Jesus that putting down the distractions of this world will be like eating cake every day.

Faith to endure to the end will come into your heart and replace the useless knowledge of man. Your eyes will be opened to see the need for relationship with Jesus and the joy of the Lord will replace the emptiness of earthly positions. Your faith will not shrink back and you will look for a place to lay down your life for another instead of hiding in fear when someone threatens your life. This is the wisdom from above that will make you fall in love with the Father of life and the Son who gave His life so you could know Him.

You choose - devil vision, right into hopelessness and depression or invite the Holy Spirit of God into your life and pray for discernment and a Godly transformation will start today? Read the Word of God to hear His heart come alive in your heart today. Read the Word of God with a desire to become so close to God the two of you will become one. I know God wants this for you but do you want this relationship for you?

Does Your Past Still Hurt You?

Only if you let it hurt you. Repent and move on. Isn't that simple? Did Jesus have a past? We know He did have a past but He never saw a need to talk about it. There is not much recorded about the childhood of Jesus and so not much is known about His young life. Not much is known about what His teenage years were like and His young adult life was like. Those years must not be too important because they are His past. It seems to me very evident and probably purposed not to have those years recorded.

I don't think Jesus wanted us dwelling on His past for once He was baptized and the Holy Spirit came into Him. A new life took over and He truly became in the image and likeness of His Father. The new life is what is important; yes I believe God is more concerned about your future with Him then your past without Him.

I was almost 60 years old before I truly started seeking God. My children were the first to tell me I am not the dad who raised them. My friends from my younger years will tell you I am not the same man that lived next door to them all those years. I believe my children could give no better complement than, "You are not the same dad who raised me."

I could repent the rest of my life for my past and I could dig up more and more things to repent for but how could dwelling on my past be beneficial to my Jesus, my children and my friends. Just as there is not much recorded about the first 30 years of the life of Jesus I will not worry about my past 60 years because I repented for those years one time and I believe in the freedom Jesus came to give me.

The Holy Spirit of Jesus and Father God dwell in me by my invitation and by my invitation they are transforming me every day and I love the transformation they are doing in me. While the Holy Spirit is doing His transformation in me, I have been prompted to make peace with some of my old friends and ask forgiveness of them. I have obeyed the promptings of the Holy Spirit and I prayed and ask Jesus for the words and He has given me the words and He has given me the right timing to ask for forgiveness. The Holy Spirit of love will flow through you too if you ask Him to. I know in my heart if there is anyone else in my past to forgive or to ask forgiveness from, Jesus will lead me to them and I will be obedient.

You see, I do not dwell on the past with all my shortcomings. I live by faith knowing that if there is anyone for me to forgive my Jesus will help me and guide me and bring me into His perfect timing. This is so important to trust God to be your conscience and live knowing if there is anything He wants you to deal with then He will bring the issue up to you with gentleness and when your heart is ready to receive His love of forgiveness. This purification process of God is done in total love for you.

Think about this: If you are digging up your past on your own and spending hours casting out demons and paying the price by fasting over and over and asking for breakthrough, it could be proof that you don't believe in the forgiveness of God. I ask you this, are you doing anything for the kingdom of God when you spend all your time warring against devils. Is your focus on devils or God? Is your focus on yourself or on God? Have you died to yourself to be the love of God to others or are you keeping your focus on yourself and your past.

If you are focused on your past, please go to God right now and ask Him to lead you into the scriptures Jesus wants you to dwell on. Ask Jesus who paid the price for you to be loved in to the kingdom. If you believe Jesus will answer, you will find your focus will shift from sorrow (*Oh my God, I am so sorry for doing that!*) to the joy of the Lord (*Oh my God, what are WE going to do today?*) You will be trading the hurt of the past for the joy of the Lord and living for His future in you.

Loving yourself as Jesus commanded us is really easy if you are walking in the presence of the Lord. Here is a simple test to see how you are doing in this regard. Can you look in the mirror and see Jesus looking back at you? I mean, stare at your own eyes in the mirror and when you smile at yourself and words like (*Good morning, Jesus!*) come out of your mouth, you will realize you are living in the presence of the Lord. Another great awaking of being in the presence of the Lord is to hear Jesus call you by name. You know, '*My sheep hear my voice and a stranger's voice they will not follow.*'

Hearing His voice and hearing Jesus call you by name is in the scriptures also. This is another sign of an intimate personal relationship with Jesus through knowing His word in the Holy Bible. Jesus proved in the Holy Bible that we can be deceived by what we see. But when we become used to hearing Jesus call us by name, we will not be deceived for Jesus said a stranger's voice we will not follow. The intimacy I am talking about is not a relationship with the Holy Bible but a relationship with Jesus Himself. I know God through the Holy Bible but I love God because I have spent time with Him intimately and I am in His presence 24/7.

Remember when Mary Magdalene went to the tomb and saw that it was empty. Mary saw a man she thought was the gardener there. She asked him if he could tell her where they had put '*my Lord.*' Mary had walked with Jesus and knew Him intimately but that day she didn't recognize Him. The gardener talked to Mary but she didn't recognize his voice until she heard Him call her by name.

John 20:11-16 But Mary stood without at the sepulchre weeping: and as she wept, she stooped down, and looked into the sepulchre, And seeth two angels in white sitting, the one at the head, and the other at the feet, where the body of Jesus had lain. And they say unto her, Woman, why weepest thou? She saith unto them, Because they have taken away my Lord, and I know not where they have laid him. And when she had thus said, she turned herself back, and saw Jesus standing, and knew not that it was Jesus. Jesus saith unto her, Woman, why weepest thou? whom seekest thou? She, supposing him to be the gardener, saith unto him, Sir, if thou have borne him hence, tell me where thou hast laid him, and I will take him away. Jesus saith unto her, Mary. She turned herself, and saith unto him, Rabboni; which is to say, Master.

The moment Jesus called Mary by name, Mary recognized Him. In a moment of time, her sadness left her, her weeping was over, her Joy returned, her strength was renewed, life for Mary would never be the same. I pray you fall in love with the one who loves you. I pray you seek to be the example of the Father's love. Jesus modeled this love for us in His Holy Bible and I pray as you read these words, your heart will come into a desire to have this intimate relationship with God in real life because God desires to live with you. Yes, God desires to talk to you, walk with you and God desires for you to listen in your heart to hear Him call you by name. Father God and Jesus are one with Ron Johnson, and I love having my best friends with me always.

Please ask God for discernment to know His voice and soon you will hear my Jesus call you by name. You will learn of His gifts in the Holy Bible but you will only receive them by living in the Spirit, seeking God in the Spirit and allowing God to solve your problems in the Spirit. As you seek the Lord you will come to know how much He loves you and the awareness of His love for you is the Spirit of truth coming alive in you. The Spirit of truth living in you is Christ in you the Hope of Glory and Christ in you is intimacy with Jesus and Father God.

Is Our Worship Music Really Worshipping God?

I want anyone who reads this book to know I sing to the Lord. We; Jesus and I have some very intimate time signing together. Jesus wakes me up some times with singing. Jesus tells us in His word He rejoices over us with singing.

Zephaniah 3:17   The LORD thy God in the midst of thee is mighty; he will save, he will rejoice over thee with joy; he will rest in his love, **he will joy over thee with singing**

Jesus even revealed the song He sings to Jenny and me. The story is in the Love Never Fails book. I know Jesus loves music. There are a lot of scriptures in the King James Version about singing and making joy with singing. Read these words of Isaiah and you will witness this as I have.

Isaiah 55:12   For ye shall go out with joy, and be led forth with peace: the mountains and the hills shall break forth before you into singing, and all the trees of the field shall clap *their* hands.

These are some of the real gifts God has for us to experience here on earth and in heaven. The singing I hear from God and the singing I sing to God have very intimate words of love, comfort and faith. The songs I hear from Jesus bring tears of joy to my face and in my heart.

Psalm 69:30   I will praise the name of God with a song, and will magnify him with thanksgiving.

Yes we are to magnify the Lord with a song from our heart and with thanksgiving. I believe Jesus will give you a personal song also if you have intimate time with Him. Our heart and our words magnify the Lord in our song.

I read where Moses sang a song to the Lord and so I know from the beginning God loves songs.

Exodus 15:1-18 Then sang Moses and the children of Israel this song unto the LORD, and spake, saying, I will sing unto the LORD, for he hath triumphed gloriously: the horse and his rider hath he thrown into the sea. The LORD *is* my strength and song, and he is become my salvation: he *is* my God, and I will prepare him an habitation; my father's God, and I will exalt him. The LORD *is* a man of war: the LORD *is* his name. Pharaoh's chariots and his host hath he cast into the sea: his chosen captains also are drowned in the Red sea. The depths have covered them: they sank into the bottom as a stone. Thy right hand, O LORD, is become glorious in power: thy right hand, O LORD, hath dashed in pieces the enemy. And in the greatness of thine excellency thou hast overthrown them that rose up against thee: thou sentest forth thy wrath, *which* consumed them as stubble. And with the blast of thy nostrils the waters were gathered together, the floods stood upright as an heap, *and* the depths were congealed in the heart of the sea. The enemy said, I will pursue, I will overtake, I will divide the spoil; my lust shall be satisfied upon them; I will draw my sword, my hand shall destroy them. Thou didst blow with thy wind, the sea covered them: they sank as lead in the mighty waters. Who *is* like unto thee, O LORD, among the gods? who *is* like thee, glorious in holiness, fearful *in* praises, doing wonders? Thou stretchedst out thy right hand, the earth swallowed them. Thou in thy mercy hast led forth the people which thou hast redeemed: thou hast guided *them* in thy strength unto thy holy habitation. The people shall hear, *and* be afraid: sorrow shall take hold on the inhabitants of Palestina. Then the dukes of Edom shall be amazed; the mighty men of Moab, trembling shall take hold upon them; all the inhabitants of Canaan shall melt away. Fear and dread shall fall upon them; by the greatness of thine arm they shall be *as* still as a stone; till thy people pass over, O LORD, till the people pass over, which thou hast purchased. Thou shalt bring them in, and plant them in the mountain of thine inheritance, *in* the place, O LORD, *which* thou hast made for thee to dwell in, *in* the Sanctuary, O Lord, *which* thy hands have established. The LORD shall reign for ever and ever.

Father God talks of singing and songs all through His Holy Bible. What I am about to say is not easy for me to say. I pray you give me grace on this topic. I have touched on it in some of my other books but the subject of praise and worship keeps coming up. I went to my Lord and ask Him why does worship music keep coming up? The answer might surprise you as it did me.

Jesus took my thoughts back to when Jenny was still with me. Towards the end of Jenny's life we sat in the camper a lot for Jenny just wanted to be held and song to. Jesus and I made words of love songs and I sang them to Jenny. During this stage of Jenny's life, the only human conversation I had was with people who walked by the camper.

Most of the people I talked to were retired. Then I asked them what they did today. Their answers were all similar. Some had been fishing and didn't care if they caught anything or not, their life was just about doing what they wanted to do. Some of the people told me they went to an antique town down the road and had a nice meal and the weather was nice so they had a nice day. They told me that they were just filling up a little time.

I asked Jesus why their answers made me sick to my stomach. Jesus told me those people are lukewarm and He will spew them out of His mouth.

Revelation 3:16 So then because thou art lukewarm, and neither cold nor hot, I will spue thee out of my mouth.

Jesus told me being lukewarm is worse then being murderers, adulterers and thieves. I asked Jesus why. I mean, the people I talked to seem like they are good people, they pay taxes, they don't break laws, they recycle, and they even use the right kind of laundry detergent. Jesus told me the problem is they don't even know they are sinning. They are positive they are saved and going to heaven so they think they can do whatever makes them happy while they wait for the bus to exit them out of here.

"What is their sin?" I asked Jesus. I heard Jesus say, "They are not seeking God. They have in no way died to themselves and they are seeking to fill up their time here on earth with happiness of their own desire." Jesus said a murder, an adulterer and a thief at least know they are sinning and they have an awareness of the sin they are in and their awareness of sin could give them a desire to repent. The people I talked to are not repenting for wasting their life because they don't see their lifestyle as a problem and have closed their heart to hearing from God.

I too am retired but I am blessed I have Jesus as my example of how to live. Jesus didn't retire and do his own thing. On the contrary, Jesus lived every second to show us the love of his Father and I want to follow Jesus. I am blessed to have a relationship with my Jesus and I am blessed to hear from God who gives me a minute by minute Godly purpose for my life.

So I asked my Jesus, "What do these retired people have in common with the singing Christian worshipers of today?" I wondered when we spend hours on hours signing how much we love God, have we accomplished anything for God? I wondered are we just filling up some time so we can check worship off from our to do list? Do we worship this way to brag? I hear Christians say, "I worshiped Jesus for 6 hours Friday night." Could worship music of today be entertainment or just a way to fill up a little time? Do we love God on our own terms and when we have time for Him?

I ask Jesus for an example of what we are talking about:

Let us say you are retired and you are bedridden. Your son comes every Saturday morning and cuts your grass. You have a big yard and so it takes your son about four hours to complete the cutting and trimming. Every time he comes you ask him to sit and talk awhile but he never has time to sit and talk to you. Your heart begins to grieve for you would like to know how his wife and your grandchildren are doing. You grieve to be part of his life but he is always so busy doing what he thinks will make you happy.

I wonder if we are just cutting God's grass when we go to the worship service of our choice and sing for hours. I wonder if Jesus would like to just sit quietly and talk to us about our lives. Every scripture I read about singing praise to the Lord came spontaneously and as a celebration of life and freedom to be with God in our quiet time. Read the song of Moses again and see how his song did glorify God. Moses did not sing over and over you are worthy Lord, but the song of Moses did prove he knew God was worthy of praise.

I am being forward here but I have been to a couple of these worship services and I felt no call to do anything for the Lord during or after the service. I had no growth in my spirit and I had not seen any miracles. I wasn't seeking God during the service because I was so distracted by the noise of the music that I could not have heard God if He was trying to talk to me. If you are thinking, "Ron, you just don't understand these worship services." You are right. I don't understand those worship services. Maybe I don't understand because I don't see any fruits from them.

I want to interject a thought for a moment. Yesterday, a pastor's wife named Jill was a little upset with me. It seems Jill is the worship leader in her church and when she heard me telling some of her congregation, "I don't think today's worship music is worshiping God at all." She gave me a challenge.

First Jill asks me what Christian artist I listen to. I told her I have gotten rid of all my Christian music and I only listen to the word of God on CD. Jill handed me a CD of worship songs and said I guarantee you will like listening to this worship music Ron.

That night I turned off my phone so I would not be interrupted and listened to 30 minutes of her worship music CD like I told her I would. Then I started listening to 30 minutes of the word of God from my Bible CD. I wish everyone would try this. I mean listening to someone singing *'Come Lord Jesus, fill my atmosphere over and over'* doesn't make sense to me, for I know I have the Holy Spirit in me already so I am the atmosphere. Another song said *'We wait, we wait, we wait'* over and over and then they sang, *'Even so Jesus come, even so Jesus come over and over.'* Truthfully, I was glad when the song was over and my 30 minutes were up.

I just cannot figure why so many people choose to listen to man's words when the inspired word of God is so readily available. I believe Jesus wants us to sing from our heart in the secret place for my Holy Bible says to sing a new song from your heart and the Holy Spirit will give you the words.

Well, guess what? I did the challenge and I still choose listening to the inspired word of God over Christian music seven days a week. I thank God I have a choice. I can spend time with

God or I can listen to man's music. When I see someone that needs prayer or someone asks me to pray for them. I am joyful I have a personal relationship with Jesus and I am joyful Jesus dwells in me. I am joyful because Jesus and I have spent time together and I am especially joyful because Jesus will flow through me and allow me to pray for that person.

My teacher is Jesus and He said He will bring to my remembrance whatever He has said to me. You see, the first step is listening. I have to be listening to hear from God. If I choose to listen to Christian music I might miss hearing from God. I don't believe Jesus will talk over or louder then what we personally choose to listen too.

Please my fellow Christians, turn off the distractions and listen for His voice so your heart will be full of his words. And if you see a person of need; you will be able to plant seeds of God's love from the reservoir of his word He has quietly given you in your heart as you were listening. I wonder what the person of need would think of Christians if they started singing *'Come Lord Jesus, fill my atmosphere and come Lord Jesus fill my atmosphere'* over and over. I wonder if we sing the right song if the person will be healed or delivered or raised from the dead?

Jesus tells us in John 10:27:

John 10:27   My sheep hear my voice, and I know them, and they follow me:

If Jesus wanted to talk to me during the 'worship services' I've been to, Jesus would have to scream really loud or wait until the service was over before I could hear Him. I realize a lot of people disagree with me on this Christian music thing and that is okay as long as I am not divisive. I just pray that you go directly to your Holy Spirit and ask him. I also pray you don't stop reading this book because the goal of the book is not to teach or condemn or to be divisive but to give the reader the desire to know God more and more.

Truthfully, some of the Christian music I hear in churches today makes me wonder if they are even singing to God or about God. I don't understand how the *'praise and worship'* songs I have heard bring anyone closer to God. Remember this is my opinion so if you don't agree, ask God for His discernment and then call me.

I believe a relationship with Jesus will grow and flourish in the atmosphere of knowing Jesus. If I just have a need to feel good or if I just have a list of needs for God, then I guess I can try to fill my needs with music and call it worship. I must admit there was one song on the CD Jill gave me called 'We Believe' and at least I liked the words of that song. I thank God I have a choice and I will still fill my heart with the Word of God and His thoughts over man's music.

Jesus told us to guard what we let into our heart because out of the heart a man speaks. I want the Holy Spirit of God in my heart and I want to hear from Him 24/7. Listening to the word of God on CD and reading the word of God gives me a desire to know God more and hearing more from God in your heart is intimacy with God.

For me the bottom line on this worshiping God through music is we are to recognize Christians by their fruits. I haven't read where Jesus told anyone to go to the singing worship service on Friday night and sit in some kind of trance for hours to be transformed. Jesus always taught by example and with His wonderful words of transformation. I believe Jesus is our example, I believe Jesus when He said come follow me into a whole new you. Yes, Jesus wants to make you into His image and likeness so simply start believing and let God transform you by having some quiet time to listen for his beautiful voice of love for when you hear His voice of love, you will receive His peace in your heart.

Here is an example of hearing from God:

I mentioned I took Jill's challenge. I listened to Christian music for 30 minutes and really had no Godly thought to ponder after the 30 minutes was over. Then I turned on the Word of God and in just minutes I turned off the word of God so I could talk to God about the scripture I heard. Here are some thoughts I had from talking to God about one scripture. The scripture was Mark 16:9:

Mark 16:9 Now when Jesus was risen early the first day of the week, he appeared first to Mary Magdalene, out of whom he had cast seven devils.

Apostle Mark recalls Jesus appearing to Mary. Mark tells us Mary Magdalene was the first person Jesus appeared to. In my earthly mind, this would be a really big honor and something to brag about. In the same scripture, Mark tells us seven devils were cast out of Mary. I guess the fact seven devils had to be cast out of her could make you question if Jesus should have chosen someone more worthy to receive this honor. I mean, Mary must have had a terrible past. My earthly mind could wonder if Mark was a little jealous of Mary being the first person Jesus appeared to. Do you think Mark's jealousy made Him remind us of the fact Mary had seven devils cast out of her?

I had never thought about the fact Mary Magdalene must have had a terrible past if she needed to have seven devils cast out of her until now. If Jesus would have asked Mary, "I want you to be the first I appear to when I arise from the dead." I wonder what Mary's response would have been. Should Mary say, "Oh Jesus, I am a just sinner saved by grace and I am not worthy for you to appear to me first so please dear Jesus, give this great honor to someone else." These were some of my thoughts and questions so I needed to take them to the Lord.

I talked to God about my thoughts and I believe the heart of Jesus was flowing through Mark in this scripture and Jesus used Mark's heart to tell us Mary had already repented for her terrible past and so her past and our repented for past has no bearing on our future and how God will honor us. Jesus came to give us His Holy Spirit and a new future. The love and thoughts of God are toward our future in Him and not our past without Him. God proved to me again in this scripture we are set free of our past when we repent and choose to follow Him.

If we listen to man's knowledge and put the price tag of worthiness on our self we will never become who Jesus asked us to be. My point is Mary Magdalene probably never had a choice to accept or decline the 'honor' of being the first Jesus appeared too. Jesus chose Mary Magdalene and Jesus is choosing you. I believe you will accept the place of honor Jesus has prepared for you when you believe in the loving forgiveness of God toward you and the fact Jesus paid the price to hear our simple words of repentance. Jesus gave His life to see our heart turn toward believing in Him.

Remember your evil conscience is being sprinkled clean and your unworthiness is being gently removed. Your past has been forgiven and your reward for believing in the love of God toward you is being prepared. Again, all these things are proved in the word of God but the truth of His word is in the spirit of truth whom you must accept by faith into your heart. Remember our relationship with God is birthed in the knowledge of Him we read about in His Holy Bible but the growth of our relationship is birthed in believing we will have intimacy with God Himself when we listen for His voice in our heart.

Jesus will elevate you and bring you into new truths about yourself if you will just humble yourself and allow Him to love you. I don't read anywhere in my Holy Bible about Mary Magdalene going around telling people "I am special, I am the first person Jesus appeared to." I believe Jesus knew this place of honor would not even enter her mind for Mary knew she was loved by Jesus already and her identity was secure in His love for her. She didn't need to pump up her own ego by making such claims. Remember Jesus sees our heart.

Jesus tells us in His Word that He will reward us openly for our humbleness. I believe Jesus is revealing a great reward for Mary Magdalene's repentive heart and for her strong conviction to turn away from sin. Jesus tells us He is preparing a mansion in heaven for us believers. I believe these rewards from God will come but I don't dwell on the fact God has these things for me. I believe and pray for the strength of God and the joy of God to enable me to build His kingdom here on earth.

I know what I hear in my heart from God and I know His love for me is real. His love is all I need. I have real security knowing I can talk to God all day and He is listening. I see Him in the details of my life like I have never seen before. I believe I bring great joy to the heavenly realm because I turned off the distractions and the noise of this world and allowed God to prove His love for me by having set aside quiet time to listen for His voice.

It seems impossible for me to put into words or to describe what a true relationship with God does to your heart. I can tell you the transformation God has for you will astound your heart into an awaking of His love for you. The best part is God will never leave you or forsake you – His Word says so. The love of God is more than some temporary feelings you get form the words of a song. His love is more real than feelings that come and go. The love of God is the Joy beyond our understanding that only comes through spending quiet time with my God.

Everyone who knows me knows I loved my little Jenny with all my heart and yet if I didn't spend quiet time with her in intimate conversion I know our love would have died. Our priority was to spend time together every day but I knew all my life I was Jenny's second love. I must admit at first I was a little put off by being second place in her heart but I soon learned without her first love then there is no love. Another thing I learned through loving Jenny was we didn't need to have any external signs of loving each other; our love just showed and people knew we loved each other.

I believe the love of God is the same way. I don't wear clothes with Bible messages or cleaver Godly words on them but I do expect God to make His presence known through me. I believe when Jesus said for us to come with full expectancy we should. I know the expectancy Jesus is talking to me about is not just for our earthly needs to be met but the expectancy Jesus is talking about is for us to become a new person with God living in us. We are to expect the Holy Spirit to transform us into His love, His peace, His kindness, His gentleness, His joy, His goodness, His Faith, His temperance and His longsuffering!

You can read about these gifts of the Holy Spirit in your Holy Bible 24/7 and if all you do is read about them, you will never attain them. You simply must do what Jesus asks us to do – die to the things of this world and seek ye first the kingdom of God and all these blessings will become you. Jesus said His blessing will overtake you. I desire to be the fruit of His Holy Spirit and I prove my desire by allowing the love of Jesus to overtake me.

Galatians 5:22-23 But the fruit of the Spirit is love, joy, peace, longsuffering, gentleness, goodness, faith, Meekness, temperance: against such there is no law.

When we ask God for His Holy Spirit to overtake us and when we by faith expect it to happen we will recognize Him as truth and knowing the truth is in us brings more Faith. We will put our trust in God and see Him as our source of truth which will enable Jesus to trust us. When we trust in the fact Jesus loves us we will not need to pump ourselves up with deeds nor seeking places of honor, nor seeking praises of man; for our honor will come through Jesus Christ Himself. The honor Jesus will give us is an honor that no one can deny for our honor actually lives in us. We are told in the word;

James 4:10 Humble yourselves in the sight of the Lord, **and he shall lift you up.**

1 Peter 5:4-6 And when the chief Shepherd shall appear, **ye shall receive a crown of glory that fadeth not away.** Likewise, ye younger, submit yourselves unto the elder. Yea, all of you be subject one to another, and be clothed with humility: **for God resisteth the proud, and giveth grace to the humble.** Humble yourselves therefore under the mighty hand of God, **that he may exalt you in due time**

I hope and pray I am explaining myself well-enough. My goal is not to be exalted by God. My goal is to have an intimate relationship with the one who I know loves me and wants to spend quiet time with me. If some kind of exalting comes from God like hearing God call me by name, I pray to be like Mary Magdalene. I will be honored but not boastful. I pray for the humbleness of Mary Magdalene.

I pray for the humility of Jesus to be in me 24/7. I don't remember Jesus ever pointing out to others 'You know I am the only Son of God' or 'My Father loved me first.' I know Jesus the man was probably tempted to have thoughts that would puff up His ego but Jesus the man had Godly discernment and took those thoughts captive and released them back to the devil by simply staying focused on His Father's love for Him. Jesus was humble. Jesus was loved by His father and I pray to be just like Jesus.

Yes, when the devil tells me I am worthless to the kingdom of God and the devil does try to tell me I am worthless and he tells me these books Jesus has me writing won't make any difference in the grand scheme of the world, I simply turn my focus to seeking the one true love of my life and I tell my true love Jesus I love being loved.

I know Jesus made a difference and the difference He made is still being manifested today by anyone that believes. I know I have Jesus in me so I am the difference Jesus has made me to be. That is not an arrogant statement – it is my goal and Jesus shows me how. Thank you Jesus, I love you too! Remember life is about receiving the love of Jesus and Father God have for you and when you let Jesus Christ love you then you become His love and His hope of glory.

I mentioned earlier in this chapter I want everyone who reads this book to know, Jesus and I sing to each other. Jesus and I have a very intimate time singing together. I sometimes I wake up to the sound of Jesus singing. I believe hearing form God is so very important and Jesus tells us in His word He rejoices over us with singing so hearing the voice of God singing is a priority of mine.

Zephaniah 3:17 The LORD thy God in the midst of thee is mighty; he will save, he will rejoice over thee with joy; he will rest in his love, **he will joy over thee with singing.**

Please my dear Christians, set quiet time aside to listen for His voice and you will be rewarded for dying to yourself with everlasting life. This reward comes from believing Jesus is the Son of God. I love hearing Jesus and I singing together and I love Jesus spending quiet time with me. I hope I don't sound arrogant but I am not driven by feelings and I am not into spending time listening to manmade music when I can have Jesus made music in my heart.

I believe the song Moses sang in Exodus 13 is a beautiful song of true praise. I hope the last 10 pages have allowed you to see how Jesus and I talk about scripture. Personally, I have drawn nearer to the Lord through intimate quiet time with Jesus than any other way. My prayer is for everyone to be drawn nearer to the Lord and if music brings revelation, answers to your questions, helps you pray for strangers, heal the sick and cast out devils raise people from the dead and have an intimate relationship with God; then by all means listen to your Christian music. But don't forget to have quiet time with Jesus and talk to Him about what He is telling us in His scriptures.

Like I said, I listened to Christian music for one half hour and had no thoughts to ponder. I listened to one scripture (Mark 16:9) and Jesus and I wrote seven pages of this book. Jesus does know our heart especially when He dwells there. I pray to be His hope of glory.

What is Truth?

Is truth something we can prove? Does truth become truth because we can prove it? Like a scientist proving the world is round or as some belief the world is round and flat like a pancake. If you believe the world is round and flat like a pancake then the truth to you is the earth is shaped like a pancake. It seems most people search for truth and think truth is what we believe it to be. Most people believe something to be truth when they can prove it true.

The truth of Jesus is something totally different. Most of what I read in my Holy Bible is not provable. To be a Christian we must accept the Holy Bible as the truth from God by faith. Think about Daniel for a moment. He is thorn into the lion's den and he lies down with the lions and spends the night with them. The next day the king has some other people thorn into the same lion's den and the same lions tear them up. Did the lions change overnight? Did Daniel have some mystical power no one else had? What is the truth and can you prove it?

The truth of the Holy Bible is we have no proof except to believe the Holy Bible is the inspirited word of God. Most of the stories in our Holy Bible are unbelievable. Jesus asks us Christians to believe by faith the incredible Bible stories are true. I believe in God and so I accept the Holy Bible as truth because Jesus asks me to.

A SIMPLE LIFE

Let us look how my simple belief makes my life simple. I believe in the forgiveness of sin Jesus talks about in His Holy Bible and I receive His loving forgiveness. Jesus tells us in His Word our past sins are forgiven if we repent for them by turning away from the things of this world and turning to a future with our focus on Jesus. Seek ye first the kingdom of God and His righteousness for their love will transform your life and restore you all knew and their truth will sanctify you to a new life through their Holy Spirit of truth who by our choice lives in us.

Jesus tells us how we are to be sanctified by His truth.

John 17:19 And for their sakes I sanctify Myself, that they also may be sanctified by the truth.

I asked Jesus to show me how His sanctifying by truth works. Let us say a big plane crashes and a lot of people die. There is an investigation and when the true problem is found and fixed then the planes are allowed to fly again. People will buy tickets to fly again because they have faith the true problem was resolved. So the problem was sanctified by the truth and truth gives us faith fly again.

We have a choice to be sanctified or not. Jesus said he sanctified himself for our sake and in doing so paved the way for us to choose to be sanctified by His truth. Believing in the truth of Jesus and by our purposing to have His Word in us we will be sanctified by His truth. Please read these scriptures together. Remember these are the words of Jesus praying to his Father. Please pray for your sanctification and believe Jesus will sanctify you with His truth. Remember these are the words Jesus prayed to Our Father.

John 17:16-19 They are not of the world, just as I am not of the world. Sanctify them in the truth; your word is truth. **As you sent me into the world, so I have sent them into the world.** And for their sake I sanctify Myself, that they also may be sanctified in truth.

When we allow Jesus to sanctify us by believing in His truth, we will see the world differently. We will want our minds to be renewed by an intimate relationship based on His truth. Is the earth round like a ball or flat like a pancake does not enter my mind? Instead my life will start to reflect the life of Jesus. We will be able to understand what seemed impossible in the past is now possible. Our earthly desires will change from vain conversations to meaningful, delightful to the Lord conversations about transformations. I believe Jesus Himself said all things are possible to those that believe and our part is to believe.

Mark 9:23 Jesus said unto him, If thou canst believe, all things are possible to him that believeth

I know to some of you I probably sound childish in my belief. I must admit when my life came down to a choice of believing the word of God I chose to become as a child. You see, I don't question anything in my Holy Bible even though I don't understand a lot of it. I just don't have a need to understand all of the word of God before I believe the Word of God. I know for sure I have the Holy Spirit of Jesus and Father God in me and therefore I know for sure if a situation comes up where I need understanding and truth I will have Godly understanding and Godly truth. I know to some people this sounds totally childish but I know my teacher personally and I trust in Him. I purposely and hopefully trust in God to the extent Jesus trusted His Dad. Yes, I want and I do ask for the same trust Jesus has.

I do remember stories in the Holy Bible where the apostles didn't have understanding until Jesus brought understanding to them. They never questioned Jesus as to the truth of the story, they just wanted understanding. Jesus was their teacher and He only brought truth to them. I love having a teacher who I know and trust is truth.

Actually our Holy Bible tells us that in some cases the apostles didn't understand the things Jesus told them until after Jesus arose from the grave. I don't think they were able to understand without the Holy Spirit in them and this is exactly why Jesus was excited to leave. I believe we receive understanding from the Holy Spirit and the Holy Spirit reveals to us what we need by faith.

Jesus in His Word said all things are possible with faith in Him. Let us look in Romans and see some of the all things possible Jesus talked about.

Romans 12:1 I beseech you therefore, brethren, by the mercies of God, that ye present your bodies a living sacrifice, holy, acceptable unto God, which is your reasonable service.

Without faith, I could never even dream to present my body a living sacrifice, holy and acceptable unto God. Yet, I read in the Word we are to do this and we are told this is a reasonable service. So to God this is not only possible for us believers but it is simply reasonable. I childishly believe I will present my body to my Jesus someday and I will, by faith, in my Jesus be holy and acceptable to God. I hope you understand that for me Jesus has made all things possible so it is simply reasonable for me to believe. Call me childish and I will thank you.

Romans 12:2 And be not conformed to this world: but be ye transformed by the renewing of your mind, that ye may prove what is that good, and acceptable, and perfect, will of God.

Again, I childishly believe I can live in the world but not be conformed to this world. I pray for and ask for the renewing of my mind to become the perfect will of my Father God and Jesus here on earth today and every day while I am on this minute by minute walk. Yes, I don't want to waste a minute. I purpose to be His good and acceptable perfect will in the flesh like Jesus was and I know if I fall short of His perfect will, I will not stop trying for I know I have the Holy Spirit in me and He makes all things possible for me. My faith has to be steadfast and I can never waiver. This may sound childish to you but I believe all things are possible to those that believe because Jesus gave me His word on it.

Romans 12:3 For I say, through the grace given unto me, to every man that is among you, not to think of himself more highly than he ought to think; but to think soberly, **according as God hath dealt to every man the measure of faith.**

I pray I don't sound or give the impression that I am puffed up by my belief in God. I do believe God when He said all things are possible. I basically have no understanding how that works except through belief. So I simply believe and I receive faith that is dealt to every man the measure of. Faith is possible because Jesus has given us all a measure of faith.

If you are living on the street right now and I gifted you a million dollars into your bank account but you didn't believe me, well the million dollars would not affect your life. But if you believed me the million dollars would change your life. I believe faith is like that in some ways. I believe by faith I have been given a measure of faith from God and because I believe the faith God has gifted me have totally changed my life. I tell everyone I meet that Jesus is so good to me because Jesus has given me a measure of faith. I hope you understand the measure of faith is useless to you if you don't believe you have it or draw on it.

THE PIER STORY

Is it faith or stupidity? You decide.

In the spring of 2016, I was in a church in Florida where I told a story about something that happened the summer of 2015 while I was up north. A person in the church told me that she feel guilty from the story because she doesn't have faith like what was demonstrated in the story. I wondered how many others have received guilt and maybe some shame from this story I told.

I believe God has me on a mission and while on the mission I seem to meet people who want to talk about the Lord. For some reason, our talks seem to end up with a story to tell. I haven't ever and will never start my day trying to make a story. I simply start my day by asking God what we are going to do today. God almost never answers me with 'Go, do this,' or 'Go, do that.' Instead, I just go about my day doing whatever needs to be done. But my priority is always to make myself available to do whatever God puts in my path.

After talking to my Jesus for hours, we have decided to tell the pier story that happened up north in 2015. I also want to share the talks Jesus and I have had concerning this story.

Last summer while I was up north on Sunday morning, I went to church with my friend Jay. After church, he introduced me to a friend of his. His friend (I'll call her Jane) and I talked for hours. She was a 45-year old girl. My daughter is 44 so to me she was still a girl. After talking that Sunday and a couple evenings that week Jane confided in me about her terrible childhood. And it was terrible, please just believe that. Jane told me because of her past, she would never see God as the loving, protecting God I portray Him to be. We talked in the evenings because she worked days in an insurance office.

On the falling Sunday in the early evening we walked out onto a concrete pier that creates a shipping lane for ships to have excess to the port in that town. We walked all the way to an old building on the pier. I thought the old building was the end of the pier. Jane was from that town, so she had me walk around the old building, for she knew there was about fifteen more feet of pier beyond it. We were all alone out there because most people think as I did that the old building was the end of the pier so most people walk to that point and turn around.

While out there alone, Jane told me again, she would never see God as a loving protecting God. She went on to tell me why. When she was in her mid-twenties, she had met a man she thought was going to ask her to marry. It turned out one night he decided he couldn't wait until marriage and so he drugged her and had his way with her. She told me the drugs made her muscles not work but she knew what was going on. So she begged God to get this man off of her. She said God didn't stop the man, God didn't protect her, and so she told me again she will never see God as a protector.

I mentioned to her again how God gave each of us a free will or a better way to say it would be we have been given the right to choose and God will not go against our will. So if someone chose to do harm to me right now, God would not go against the will of that person. But if we let God be God, He can and will still protect us. God could simply remove me from the evil person. If we try to protect ourselves, I believe we are limiting God. The scriptures tell us that there are times when Jesus departed from among the midst of an angry crowd and was protected. The Holy Bible doesn't tell us how Jesus departed but we read and understand Father God protected Jesus.

Luke 4:28-30   And all they in the synagogue, when they heard these things, were filled with wrath, And rose up, and thrust him out of the city, and led him unto the brow of the hill whereon their city was built, that they might cast him down headlong.   **But he passing through the midst of them went his way**

There are stories in the Holy Bible that show us the protection of God and how it works. I mean, sometimes what God asks us to do will sound totally stupid to us. Read Joshua and see if Joshua didn't need great faith to do as ask by God. What would the average person say today if God told you to walk around a massive wall seven times, blow some trumpets and the wall will fall down?

Joshua 6:1-5   Now Jericho was securely shut up because of the children of Israel; none went out, and none came in. And the LORD said to Joshua: "See! I have given Jericho into your hand, its king, and the mighty men of valor. You shall march around the city, all you men of war; you shall go all around the city once. This you shall do six days. And seven priests shall bear seven trumpets of rams' horns before the ark. But the seventh day you shall march around the city seven times, and the priests shall blow the trumpets. It shall come to pass, when they make a long blast with the ram's horn, and when you hear the sound of the trumpet, that all the people shall shout with a great shout; then the wall of the city will fall down flat. And the people shall go up every man straight before him."

This story is in my Holy Bible so I don't need any proof the story happened. By faith in Jesus name I just believe it happened. I don't believe this was the first time Joshua heard from God. My point is we must read and believe the Word of God to develop a relationship of listening to God before we can believe and have faith what we are hearing is from God.

In the eyes of Jane, God is not a protector. To her way of thinking God did not protect her during her childhood or from her boyfriend so she learned to protector herself. She became a martial arts instructor in kickboxing. She told me she is working in the insurance office because she has hurt her neck to the point the doctors told her if she continues kickboxing she will end up paralyzed from the neck down. As she told me these things I was asking God to please give me the words to help her understand His protective love for her.

I don't understand a lot of the things that go on in this world but I know Christians always win when we stay steadfast in faith being rooted in the knowledge Jesus loves us. If we let circumstances of our life dictate our faith in His love we will be driven by the wind, tossed to and fro and double minded. We will proclaim He loves us one moment and ask Jesus but asked "Why did this happen?" next.

Again, look at the life of Jesus. I mean, Jesus could have been mad at His Father for not protecting Him from the cross and all the suffering but look at the good that came from Jesus going through all He went through. I don't know why Jane went through such a terrible childhood and the boyfriend experience but to me she needs the love of God more than ever.

As we talked, we were both looking out at the lake so our backs where to the pier when I smelled the smoke from a cigarette. I turned around and noticed four men had come around the old building on the pier and they now had me surrounded. The man in front of me was blowing smoke from his cigarette right into my face. He was daring me to do something about it. He continued to blow smoke in my face as I didn't know what to do.

Then under my breath I ask my Jesus what he wanted me to say to these men. The words that came out of my mouth surprised me and them. I ask the man in front of me, "So how is your walk with the Lord?" He looked at me like I was stupid or something and I was about to get my butt beaten. Then I was prompted by Jesus to tell these men that I believe in Jesus and I believe He is with me right now. I said to them that Jesus lives in my heart and I know Him as my Protector and Savior and Jesus is here with me right now.

I ask these men, "Do you know Jesus like that? Do you know Jesus is real?" Again, they looked at me like I was stupid but I don't think they could figure me out. Then Jesus prompted me again. So I ask them if I could tell them a story about guns. They didn't say no so I just started telling the story.

I ask them, "What would you do if you were home right now and watching television? Let us say you had just finished cleaning your gun and your gun is setting on the couch right alongside of you with nice shiny bullets in it. All four of you are watching television. Then all of a sudden, the front door gets kicked in and a man is standing in front of you with his gun pointing right at you. What would you do?

They looked at me as if to say, "You really are stupid aren't you? We would blow him away in a heartbeat and it would be self-defense. I said, "You see, that is the difference between believers in Jesus and nonbelievers. You see, I just professed to you I am a believer in Jesus so if I did what you said you would do where I will blow the gunman away in self-defense, wouldn't I be calling myself a liar? I mean, with one breath I tell you I believe in Jesus Christ to be my protector and yet when confronted with a gunman in my face I pull out my gun and protect myself. To me, I would be saying to God, "I don't think you are big enough to handle this situation God, so I will."

I told these men that I have prayed and asked God if I ever found myself in a life threatened situation to have enough faith to trust God and let God be God. By letting God be God I would be allowing God to have His way. You see, if I get out of the way, God will have all the options. God could do anything He wants. God could let the bullets from the gunman go through me and my wife and my children and do us no harm; in that case I could lead the gunman to the Lord because the gunman just witnessed a great miracle.

The average person might think if the gunman kills my loved ones and I then I have lost the battle. To me, being killed is not a loss – *it is a gain.* You see the word of God says to be absent from the body is to be present before the Lord for judgment. You see to me the gunman would be given me the express ticket to heaven and I don't have a problem with that. Also in the word of God Jesus tells us there is no greater love then a man have then to lay down his life for another. So actually the gunman is not only giving us the express tickets to heaven but the gunman is allowing us or giving us the privilege to lay down our life for another which in my mind is like putting the get in heaven free card in my hand. I don't have a problem with that either.

I told them, "You know, if I did as you said you would do and killed the man in self-defense, I believe I would be doing the work of the devil. That is; if the gunman is going around killing people in cold blood then he probably is not right with the Lord and probably going to hell, I say probably because I am told by Jesus not to judge. But in my mind if I killed him in self-defense I am actually helping the devil put a soul in hell because by killing the gunman I might have removed his chance to repent.

I told the four men, "Truthfully, I hope I have time to pray for Him before he shot me so I could pray he would be caught and put in prison where some evangelist could get to Him and lead him to the Lord so he could repent and come to heaven and we could rejoice together some day. I would rejoice to God for the express tickets and he could rejoice to God that God gave him time to repent."

I believe we are here on earth to be the ambassadors for Jesus Christ. I pray my life brings glory to God and His kingdom. I believe laying down my life for another will bring glory to God and His kingdom. I believe laying down my life for another is proving to God I believe Him. I trust Him and I am proving my belief in the promise of eternal life by not being afraid to die.

I believe we bring glory to God by our life of believing in God. If I shot the gunman in self-defense like you said you would, do you think I am bringing glory to myself? You know, everyone would tell me what a good thing I had done if I take the gunman killer off the street. I would probably even receive praises from a lot of people, even Christians, and yet in my mind I would be thinking about the soul of that gunman.

I want to thank my friend Pastor Don for giving me new insight that God who can do all things could give the gunman time to repent even if I protected myself with a gun. I know my Jesus well-enough to know all things are possible and maybe in this situation even if my faith was not enough to let God be God and instead of faith in God I choose to defend myself by killing the gunman. I now know to pray for God to give the gunman the time, even a split second before the gunman died, to have time to repent and ask the Lord for forgiveness. So I would not be in guilt of shame for defending myself but I would be praying for God to have mercy on both of us and I will pray for God to help me grow in faith and trust in God.

After telling the four men on the pier the gun story, I felt prompted again so I told them I have written a book about my wife Jenny. I told them how the story about Jenny is not a sad story but a joyful story and how reading it might help them come to know the Lord. I asked them to walk with me to my car to get the books. I mentioned to them, "Even if you don't want to read the book now to please take one with you, for I believe someday you will find time to read it and hopefully it will give you a desire to know the Lord. The books are free so please come with me to my car and I will give you each one." They all looked at each other and the expression on there faces seemed to say we don't know what to do with this guy and as suddenly as they came, they all turned and walked away.

I looked over at Jane and she said, "I want to go home." I walked her to her car and she went home. Two days later she called me. She told me the event on the pier Sunday night was messing with her mind. She told me how even with her bad neck she thought she could have taken two of the men but she didn't know if I could have taken the other two. I told her, "I don't think I could have taken them because they seemed to be very street smart and I am not street smart so I believe they would have torn me up." I reminded her, "Isn't it cool how Jesus handled the situation and neither you nor I had to do anything?" She said, "Yes, it is hard to believe they just walked away."

The reactions to this story have been all across the board. A couple of people have asked me if it is true. I assured them it happened just the way I said it happened and I do have a witness. One person said I was putting guilt and shame on people because they would not have the faith to handle the situation the way God gave me the strength to handle it. I have assured the person, "I would not tell you or anyone this story if I thought for a moment I was putting guilt and shame on someone."

Actually, I believe Jesus gave me this story to help people build faith and not put guilt and shame on then. I believe faith in God makes my life simple. In this story it is easy to see how faith defiantly makes my life simple. I didn't have to spend time at self-defense classes, I didn't have to have a gun and a conceal carry permit and spend time going to shooting classes. There wasn't any need to have a police investigation and the best part is my Jesus gets the Glory. Faith in God gives me a simple life and removes fear. I pray you seek ye first the kingdom of God and not self defense by any means, other than faith in God.

Please read the stories in your Holy Bible and ask God to help you see them as faith builders; for the mission of the stories in our Holy Bible are to bring Glory to God and His faith into our heart. Please ask Jesus to be your teacher. And as you read the stories in your Holy Bible, these stories are no longer be stories of what God did but they will open doors in your heart to receive what God is still doing. Faith in God is letting God be your faith builder by simply letting God be God. Please spend your time seeking God and not self-defense.

Is Faith God's Will?

This morning in my Coffee Time with Jesus I ask Jesus to confirm His will on having me tell the pier story. I wanted to know if I was putting guilt or shame on people who don't have the faith to let Jesus handle the problem. Jesus led me into Genesis and Abraham.

Genesis 22:1-18 Now it came to pass after these things that God tested Abraham, and said to him, "Abraham!" And he said, "Here I am." Then He said, "Take now your son, your only son Isaac, whom you love, and go to the land of Moriah, and offer him there as a burnt offering on one of the mountains of which I shall tell you." So Abraham rose early in the morning and saddled his donkey, and took two of his young men with him, and Isaac his son; and he split the wood for the burnt offering, and arose and went to the place of which God had told him. Then on the third day Abraham lifted his eyes and saw the place afar off. And Abraham said to his young men, "Stay here with the donkey; the lad and I will go yonder and worship, and we will come back to you." So Abraham took the wood of the burnt offering and laid it on Isaac his son; and he took the fire in his hand, and a knife, and the two of them went together. But Isaac spoke to Abraham his father and said, "My father!" And he said, "Here I am, my son." Then he said, "Look, the fire and the wood, but where is the lamb for a burnt offering?" And Abraham said, "My son, God will provide for Himself the lamb for a burnt offering." So the two of them went together. Then they came to the place of which God had told him. And Abraham built an altar there and placed the wood in order; and he bound Isaac his son and laid him on the altar, upon the wood. And Abraham stretched out his hand and took the knife to slay his son. But the Angel of the LORD called to him from heaven and said, "Abraham, Abraham!" So he said, "Here I am." And He said, "Do not lay your hand on the lad, or do anything to him; for now I know that you fear God, since you have not withheld your son, your only son, from Me." Then Abraham lifted his eyes and looked, and there behind him was a ram caught in a thicket by its horns. So Abraham went and took the ram, and offered it up for a burnt offering instead of his son. And Abraham called the name of the place, The-LORD-Will-Provide; as it is said to this day, "In the Mount of the LORD it shall be provided." Then the Angel of the LORD called to Abraham a second time out of heaven, and said: "By Myself I have sworn, says the LORD, because you have done this thing, and have not withheld your son, your only son— blessing I will bless you, and multiplying I will multiply your descendants as the stars of the heaven and as the sand which is on the seashore; and your descendants shall possess the gate of their enemies. In your seed all the nations of the earth shall be blessed, because you have obeyed My voice."

I am not sure what I would do without going to Jesus first, but I think if someone walked into church today and told me, "God told me to sacrifice my *son* on an altar, and I'm going up on the mountain to sacrifice my son," my flesh would tell him he needs discernment and I might even call the police on him. If a girl walked up and told me the baby inside her was conceived by an angel, well, I probably would not believe her. What I am trying to say is I have faith the story of Abraham and Mary really happened because I read about them in my Holy Bible but at this moment in my walk of faith I don't have enough faith to believe you if you told me these stories happened to you.

I can assure you if God told me to do things like go sacrifice my son I would still have a problem believing I was hearing from God. My faith is not that strong yet but God promised He would not give us more then we can handle. If you are in a test right now please thank God for the faith God has in you. The apostles counted it all joy when tested because they knew the test would bring glory to God by their faith in God and so should we.

Hearing from God, listening for His voice, Godly discernment, and trusting in God are the key ingredients to walking in faith with God.

Romans 10:17 So then faith cometh by hearing, and hearing by the word of God.

In Romans 10:17, we see how faith comes to us by hearing. My point is God will establish his faith in you if you are quiet enough to listen. I don't know if I explained, God planted the gun story in my heart four years before being on the pier that Sunday evening.

Sometimes in our Holy Bible we actually read the history of faith. In the story of David we see David had confidence in God no one else had at that time and I believe his confidence came because David was a listener. David had quiet time while tending sheep to hear from God and we know God gave him the strength to kill the lion and the bear and those actions helped built his faith in God to enable him to kill Goliath. I believe God had prepared David for his challenge. I want you to know God did not just dump me out on the pier that evening and said, "Good luck with this one Ron." I believe God had prepared me for the four men on the pier.

When I read about the faith of the men in love with God in my Hoy Bible, I always react the same way. I ask God for faith similar to them. I want faith like the men in Hebrews 11. I read the stories of faith in the Holy Bible and I see them as faith builders and not a source of guilt and shame. I don't question the stories in my Holy Bible as to their truth. I know God well enough to know they are true and God will give us faith if we ask for faith and listen for His voice. In fact, with God we will receive faith in abundance, I know for the word of God says so. I pray for faith like Job, Abraham, Paul and Jesus. I pray to hear from Father God like Jesus heard from His Father. I pray for faith to face whatever the challenge is today.

I pray for my test. I want my test. I see where Peter failed his first test and yet Peter went on to be a great man of faith when he was baptized in the Holy Spirit. So I don't worry about or dwell on my past failings. I have faith Jesus is building up my faith even in my failings. Thinking about that Sunday evening on the pier, I cannot explain the peace I had while I was talking to those men. I cannot explain how fear left me the moment I asked God what to say to those men. I praise God for letting me know Him and trust in Him to handle the situation. All I can really say is when you ask God for His faith, His heart and His eyes and His mind and trust in Him to give you these precious gifts He will.

Peace, trust, faith and true love are not attainable by works or by keeping of the law but you will receive these gifts by faith and they will be as real to you as Jesus is real to you in your life. Please let Jesus show Himself real to you like He did to the men in the Holy Bible. I cannot explain the faith of Jesus or Abraham or David or any of the great men of faith in our Holy Bible, I just know they all heard from God and we will hear from God if we make listening for the voice of God a priority in our life.

Jesus told us to ask and we will receive. Jesus said He is no respecter of persons so what Jesus did for the great men of the Holy Bible He will do for you and me. Like I said, these gifts are not attainable by works or keeping the law but by faith you will receive these gifts from Jesus into your heart. You will be enabled to do great works and by faith you will keep all the law.

Law breakers are not walking in peace, trust, faith and the true love of Jesus Christ. They have no desire to do great works or to keep the law but we believers can choose to listen to God and God will give us the words to give the law breakers a desire to come to know God. I believe this is the peace on earth Jesus talked about in our Holy Bible.

I have asked the Holy Spirit into my life and I have watched Him transforming me daily. I have just told you a story about guns and when I was on the pier, Jesus reminded of that story. You see, Jesus and I had written the gun story four years ago. Another benefit of seeking God with your whole heart is you will receive faith from God and God will actually prepare you for the test.

The time to make a decision about whether or not to use a gun is not when a gunman is about to shoot you. If a gunman is about to shoot you and you are thinking, 'Did Jesus say to be absent or was it to be present or what did Jesus say?' then you are too late. You must seek God now and when the test comes you will be prepared and you will have the love of God in your heart and His love will flow out of your heart. How will God bring all things to your remembrance if we never took time to listen because you were to busy learning self-defense? In John 14:26 we see who our teacher is and who will bring all things to our remembrance.

John 14:26 But the Comforter, which is the Holy Ghost, whom the Father will send in my name, **he shall teach you all things**, and bring all things to your remembrance, whatsoever I have said unto you.

The gun story God brought to my remembrance that night on the pier is in the book God had me write and God titled the book the "Joy of the Lord." Guess what Jesus titled the gun story four years ago? It's titled *Freedom from self.*

I would like to share a few more thoughts about the pier story. Two years ago, my Jesus had me write a story about ices. You probably have heard of them before. They are some people who have a bad reputation or at least the news reports about ices lead us to believe the worst about them. I hear people ask, "Can you believe anything you hear on the news? What is amazing to me is most people I talk to will agree the news reporters lie and yet these same people will tell you the ices people need to die. My heart grieves for I know we will not transform the world by killing people. Jesus tells us our battle is not flesh and blood but our battle is spiritual.

Ephesians 6:12 For we wrestle not against flesh and blood, but against principalities, against powers, against the rulers of the darkness of this world, against spiritual wickedness in high places.

I don't know for sure why Jesus prompted me to write a story about ices, but I am sure I will find out someday. I am not sure why I am thinking about that story right now except to say maybe I will be in front of some ices people some day and by faith in my Jesus, I can talk to them and plant some seeds of His true love and God will use these seeds to transform their heart.

I pray my faith though being tested by fire will stand the fire and I will not smell of smoke. I pray if I am put in the lion's den I will not fear but I pray to be in the den and in the fire and by faith to be free of fear so I might bring glory to my Jesus and my Father God. The stories of faith in my Holy Bible are real to me and I have asked Jesus for the faith His hero have. I believe the words where inspired of Jesus when Paul said "Christ in you the hope of Glory."

Please put your name in that scripture. Christ in Ron Johnson, the hope of Glory. Please pray for listening with discernment and pray for the heart of Jesus, His mind, His ears and His eye. You will not be disappointed for faith comes from hearing and heart transformations come from having His heart and His mind, his ears and His eye in you. These are some of the precious gifts Jesus died to give us.

The pier story is the first story that I am aware of, where people have questioned the truth of it. My first reaction was hurt, that someone would question my integrity. I went right to my Jesus about my reaction. I was hurt and didn't really understand why. Jesus answered me saying, "Ron, you asked for my heart didn't you?" I pondered His question and then the answer came to me.

What happened on the pier was so minor to the things Jesus went through. Jesus proved himself to be the Son of God time and time again and yet sadly some people do not believe Him to this very day. Jesus is, was and will forever be the son of God made flesh. Now because I have ask Jesus for His heart I believe I have experienced a tiny, no a super tiny amount of His hurt when He sees His people not believe in Him. Jesus is so supernatural to me and yet He can and will let me feel His heart to the extent I can experience it.

I now see the hurt I was feeling was not for me but for those who could not see this story for what it is; a faith builder. Like I said, when I read about the men of faith in my Holy Bible I immediately ask Jesus for faith like these men have. Like when I read about discernment in my Holy Bible I ask Jesus for discernment like I read about in His book. I would really need good discernment to even think God would tell me to sacrifice my son.

When I read about the love Jesus has for us, I immediately ask for His love to flow through me. When I read about the compassion of Jesus in my Holy Bible immediately I ask Jesus for His compassion to flow through me. Yes I read about the relationship Jesus and Father God have and I want their intimacy. I believe these are the best gifts and I am told to earnestly desire them and I do.

1 Corinthians 12:31 But earnestly desire the best gifts. And yet I show you a more excellent way.

By faith I believe Jesus is showing me how to live the more excellent way. Like I said I love the words of Paul when he said I count the things of this world to be dung compared to intimacy with Jesus Christ.

You know this world we live in is actually God's world and we are the caretakers of it. Jesus gave us everything we need to take care of it. We lack nothing! I have never before heard of a ram getting his horns caught in a bush but I believe it. I have never before heard of paying taxes by taking money out of a fish mouth but I believe it happened. I have no idea how God could create the world in six days but I believe He did it. I believe we can have the steadfast faith of Job if we ask for it. I believe faith comes from asking for intimacy with the only one who guarantees us He will never leave us or forsake us; not even in a lion's den or in a fire.

Really, my life is simple because I simply seek first the kingdom of God and His righteousness for I know by faith God loves to spend time with those who seek Him. Please lay down the dung of this world and Listen for His voice. I believe the joy of the Lord is for Jesus to talk to His children who are listening. All the great men in the Holy Bible listened and from Listening came faith and from faith we receive strength to be the joy of the Lord here on earth. No one is strong without faith and no one has faith without listening for His voice.

So please do not spend time reading His Word without asking Jesus to be your Teacher because Jesus our Teacher transforms the knowledge of the word into the understanding and wisdom of the word, for the word is the truth of God that when we hear it we will believe it and belief gives us faith to understand the truth of it. If you don't understand His word, simply ask Him what He is telling you in His Word. I pray you realize Jesus taught the apostles and I pray you come to know Jesus is teaching you and Ron Johnson today.

Remember forever we are His children and we are all learning and being transformed daily and remember it is Jesus Christ in us the Hope of Glory. Jesus is my teacher and I am the teacher's pet but you can be the teacher's pet also. To be a teacher's pet, you simply have to LISTEN to the teacher – Jesus Christ. You know Jesus listened to His Father and look where listening brought Him. We believers have the same Father don't we.

Earlier in this letter I talked about praying for someone who was about to kill me so they would have time to repent before being killed. If you would like proof God is still turning killers into saints, please read the testimony of David Berkowitz. He was the killer known as the son of Sam and now he is known as the son of Hope. Christ in you the hope of Glory is real.

Thank you again for reading this story. My prayer for all Christians is for our life to be a testimony that brings glory to Jesus Christ and Father God. Remember the words of Luke 2:11-14:

> **Luke 2:11-14**   For unto **you** is born this day in the city of David a Saviour, which is Christ the Lord. And this shall be a sign unto you; Ye shall find the babe wrapped in swaddling clothes, lying in a manger. And suddenly there was with the angel a multitude of the heavenly host praising God, and saying, Glory to God in the highest, and on earth peace, good will toward men.

I believe in the words of Luke because they are in my Holy Bible and I know by faith the Holy Bible is the inspired Word of God. All it takes to believe is faith. I believe we bring Glory to God when we love as Jesus loved; having died to our self and in doing so we again bring to the earth the peaceful good will TOWARD men of Jesus Christ. Please simply let the love of Jesus flow and the world will know.

Remember guilt and shame come from the devil and not from stories of faith.

Sincerely in love with my Jesus and listening for is voice.

Jenny, Ron and my teacher Jesus Christ; will love you forever.

Faith and Compassion

I want to tell you a short story of faith and compassion. This is what happened one morning while praying for the compassion of Jesus Christ to come into my heart. What I am about to say is I have no proof of. I don't have any scripture to back it up. I just ask God a simple question and I believe I am supposed to share what I saw with you? Before I share the vision I want to make very clear there is no way I can back up what I am about to say with any kind of proof but I do believe it is important and a way to show the compassion of Jesus Christ and our Father God.

Here is the vision:

I have an awesome time talking to my Jesus every day. I have conversations with Jesus that sometimes seem hard for people to grasp. For example, I remember asking Jesus what was it like when Father God sent all the plagues on Egypt and parted the Red sea and let the Israelites walk across on dry land and then drowning the soldiers that were chasing them. After his chosen people watched and lived through these great miracles Father God did, I wondered how anyone could doubt His love for them.

I thought about the impact all these great miracles should have on our lives. I pondered what it must have been like to perform them and then watching His chosen people build a golden idol to worship it.

As I thought of these things, in my mind I saw a vision. I saw Father God and Jesus on big thrones. I cannot describe them but I knew who they were and where they were. They were looking down through the clouds watching everything that was happening here on earth. As Father God and Jesus saw the people worship the golden idol, Jesus looked over at His Father and saw His Father weep tears of sadness. Then I heard Jesus say, "Father, send me. I will personalize your love to them. Father, I will heal one heart at a time, I will cast devils out of one person at a time, and I will raise one person at a time from the dead, I will personalize your love to them Father and maybe then they will believe You love them." I could not see them but somehow I knew Father God smiled at His Son.

I cannot back up the vision of these last two paragraphs with scripture, I cannot say if that is the way it happened in heaven but I can tell you we are sent *'as Jesus was sent, so are we.'* We are to do the things we see our Jesus do. We are to talk to Jesus the way He talked to His Father. We are to live in the freedom of knowing there is no death. We can walk boldly knowing we are loved and protected. We are to know when we die here on earth our earthly death is the will and timing of Father God and our place is prepared.

You won't find love, peace, compassion or faith like that of the heroes in the Holy Bible on television or anywhere here on earth except in believers that seek first the kingdom of God and His righteousness. I pray you know you are loved as Jesus knew He was loved. I pray for the faith of Jesus and His followers to be mine so I too can be a blessing as the other great men of faith blessed my Father and my Jesus by their simple belief.

Yes, simple belief is a blessing form God and the faith that comes from choosing to believe in God will remove the mountains in your life.

One person called me after reading this and said they just find it hard to think of Father God weeping like I talked about in this vision. I thought Jesus plainly tells us in the scriptures He only did what He saw His Father do. I know the scriptures tell us *'Jesus wept.'*

John 11:35 Jesus wept.

The only reason I am writing about this vision is to tell you another way I believe I hear from God. I don't put faith in anything I cannot back up in the Word of God. Two years ago, Jesus had me write a book called One Heart at a Time. I believe the book is scripturally discerned and it is a good description of how one person can change the lives of the many. It is a simple plan. I know it will change the world because it is modeled after the life of Jesus. We know Father God had faith in one person changing the world back then and I believe we are commissioned to do the same. I believe the simple plan today is Jesus Christ in you the Hope of Glory.

A word of caution, before I shared this vision with anyone I took this vision to God in our quiet time. I didn't want to share it because I have no scripture to back up what I saw. I believe I am supposed to share what I saw and heard because it was a vision of compassion and hope and an example of the strong loving connections Jesus and Father God share together. As you know Jesus did come and Jesus taught us to listen for the compassionate voice of God in our heart. Jesus came and shared their hopes and dreams with us to give us the same capacity for love they have for each other.

Please allow the Holy Spirit of Jesus and Father God into your heart and watch the world around you transform by the power of the Holy Spirit flowing through you. All you need is simple faith and God does the rest.

When Bad Things Happen, Why Do We Look for Someone to Blame?

A while back I was visiting some friends when I noticed Bill, the husband of this family seemed totally bored while I was talking about my Lord. I was kind of surprised by his boredom because I have talked with him and his wife before and I had not noticed his boredom.

That evening, I told a couple stories about God when Bill interrupted me. Bill said, "Ron, I know you do not watch the news but not too long ago there was a big story about a family with little children that were severely tortured by their own parents." Bill gave some details of the torture and I don't think I need to repeat it in here. After Bill told me the news story he asked me, "How could a loving God allow that to happen to defendless children?" I started to answer him when he literally cut me off by telling me, "I don't want to hear it."

About a half hour later Bill brought the news story up a second time and made his comment again saying, "I just cannot believe a loving God would let little children suffer that way." I said, "You know Bill, Jesus doesn't." And again Bill abruptly cut me off and said, "I don't want to hear it; I just don't want to hear it." I thought to myself, "Why does Bill keep bringing this story up if he doesn't want to discuss it?"

Again about an hour later Bill brought the news story into the conversation with this question, "Why does a loving God allow little children to suffer so? Adding those children did nothing to deserve being tortured." Again Bill cut me off before I can even say anything to him.

I excused myself for a moment and went to the bathroom to have a little quiet time with my Jesus. I didn't hear from Jesus so I didn't say anything. It was getting late so I went back to my camper. Actually I was a little confused and needed to talk to my personal teacher and Savior Jesus Christ.

The next morning I started asking the Lord about the questions Bill was asking the night before. I found myself thinking about the faith I see in the Bible stories I have read, but Bill's questions didn't seem to be about faith. My thoughts then continued. Jesus tells us in His word that we are not to let the circumstances of life dictate our faith. My Teacher gave me an example. I am told it took years for Noah to build the ark. Read in the word about Noah in Genesis 6, 7 and 8 and ask God to let you see the great faith Noah had just to believe he could build an ark.

Noah built an ark by faith. With faith in God, we too can solve the problems of the world. Without faith, we will sit in our easy chair, watch the news and ask God, "Why did you let that happen?" I started thinking and asked God, "What is our responsibility in this?"

Try to think, how many times we are driven by our circumstances. For some reason, Bill seems to be finding ways to talk himself into believing God is not a loving God and his attitude was very confusing to me. Whenever I hear questions similar to Bill's question, I question the circumstances of the question.

Bill's question is, "How a loving God could let that happen?" needs an answer for sure. We are taught in church that God is love, God is all powerful, God is almighty, and God is in control and all that is true. God is all these things and more. So I believe I know where Bill's question came from. What puzzled me was Bill did not want an answer.

I totally agree that God is love, all powerful, all mighty, in control, a protector and to me God is the answer. I believe God lives inside me. So I have the answer already in me if I believe. We believers, you and me, have the power, the wisdom, the knowledge, and the love to change this world if we believe Jesus lives and dwells in us.

As I thought about the question, I was gently reminded of a story I heard a long time ago and think it will illustrate how stupid the question of 'Why did God let this happen?' really is.

The story is about a man that had a business worth millions of dollars. This man was getting up in years and decided to turn his business over to his son. Before he did the man bought land in the Virgin Islands. The man built a mansion for his wife and him to live in. Then he built a big hotel complex to supply himself a retirement income.

When those things were completed, he turned his business in the states over to his son. The day the son took full position of this big manufacturing business he walked into the office and told his employees, I am not interested in being here every day. My father has you in the position you are in because he knew you could do your job. I want x amount of dollars a week and as long as I get that amount I will not be here. You earn your money and you do the day by day running of my business.

The son built himself a mansion, joined some country clubs and bought a big boat to play on. About six months later, the son got a call. The doors to the factories were locked and the office was locked up also. The son had his limo driver take him to the office to find the IRS was there. He found out almost no bills were paid for six months and the money was gone and so was his business. The son became angry. He called his dad and started screaming saying, "Dad, how could you let this happen to me? I don't deserve this."

After the son calmed down the father asked his son, "Before I left, didn't I give you everything you needed to keep the business running?" The father told his son, "If you remember a couple of months ago I had gotten a call from some of the suppliers in your business about not being paid. I called you and ask if you would look into this matter and see what is happening. I gave you some gentle reminders but I guess you were to busy playing to run your business."

The father said, "Son, I gave you the power and authority to make decisions, you have freewill, don't you? And you had choices and it sounds like you made some bad ones." The father then added, "Please don't ask me how I let this happen to you when you were the one I left in charge. Where you just living for yourself? It seems you did nothing with all I gave you." I wondered, "Will Jesus ask us these same questions on judgment day?"

As I started thinking of the business story and how it related to Bill's questions about the tortured children I started seeing the similarities in the two stories. Our Father gave us all we need to take care of the affairs of this world. He gave us the power and authority to transform the world back into believers of Jesus Christ. I wondered if we are likened to the son in that we are only interested in our self and just building our own mansion and tending to our own needs and in doing so we are forgetting the needs of others.

Then I started thinking about the son and his reaction to losing his business. It appears in the story the son was spoiled and only thought of himself. Are we spoiled and only thinking about ourselves when we see the world Jesus gave us falling apart and we just go about our day as if someone else is supposed to fix the problem? Are we so spoiled in our own little world? We watch a story on television about some tortured children dying and we make God responsible as we ask God, "How can you let that happen to defendless children?" and then we go occupy our time by doing something we want to do.

My Teacher Jesus brought me to understand why Bill did not want an answer to his question. You see the answer puts the responsibility on us to fix the problem. God has given us the power and authority to transform this world one heart at a time, into a world of peace and love and good will toward men and we can achieve these Godly goals if we only believe. I think a lot of us are like Bill. We watch the news from our nice comfortable easy chair and then clear our conscience by blaming God for letting bad things happen. Blaming God takes the burden and the responsibility off us to do anything. We go to bed and sleep comfortable excusing our responsibility thinking these problems are so big only God can clean up the world we live in.

I don't know if Jesus had reminded me of this story while I was at Bill's house if Bill would have actually understood the business story related to his questions but I could not stop praising God for his wisdom. Years ago when I heard the million dollar story I never thought of it the way Jesus has brought it to light for me today.

In today's world of modern sociology we seem to need someone to blame for our shortcomings. Some call it blame-shifting. This need to have someone to blame relieves us of our responsibility and comes directly from earthly sociology of man. Jesus warned us, there is a way that seems right to a man but the end of those teachings is death.

Proverbs 16:25 There is a way that seems right to a man, But its end is the way of death.

According to what I read in my Holy Bible I simply must take responsibility for my decisions. I hear of so many people locked in their childhood or there past and it seems they go to sociologist who tell them to dwell on the past, as if dwelling on your past will somehow help. I pray for anyone locked in their past, to please make Jesus your new councilor and teacher and your best friend.

I find I am saddened by how many hours people spend at councilors seeking earthly wisdom and man's understanding. By seeking God I have learned the true answers are in your heart already. Are you seeking God or are you blaming God?

It appears to me in the business story above the father took no responsibility for his son. There were no details given as too how the boy was raised but a lot was implied. I wonder how many people reading this story thought the boy was a rich kid with a silver spoon in his mouth and I wonder if they actually felt a little joy when his life style led him into poverty.

Did anyone think about all the people who lost their jobs because of the lack of Godly morals in the son and the father and the business people that took the money. I believe we all have a responsibility to ask Jesus into our heart. Dream with me for a moment and think if a man of God had been around the father in this story and if the man of God planted some Godly seeds of love and Godly responsibility, then the conclusion of the story could be completely different.

In the tortured story above most people will automatically think badly of the parents involved. Again, we need to ask if everyone around those parents were not so busy and only thinking of them self the story could have had a completely different outcome. These two stories make real clear to me the need for us to do as Jesus ask to do – that is to die to ourselves so we can live to build the kingdom of God. How long do you think those parents could torture their children if Jesus lived next door to them? I wonder if a Christian lived next door to them what a different outcome that story would have? In the rich man's story, the outcome would have been completely different also if the father and the son had died to themselves and lived to supply jobs for their workers and families.

I don't know anyone involved in either of these two stories. I have purposed to be vague in the descriptions of these stories so no one can make accusations toward anyone. The whole purpose of telling the stories is to show how stupid the question, 'How did a loving God let that happen?' really is.

The world is a different place when you have the Holy Spirit of Abba Father and Jesus living in you. I tell people I really don't know what I am doing but I love knowing the one who does know what He is doing and He dwells in me. I have surrendered my life to allow Jesus to teach me and transform me into who Jesus needs me to be and I pray to be a blessing to God by not asking stupid questions like how did you let that happen Lord?

Remember Jesus tells us to guard our eyes and ears for what we see and hear will affect us. I firmly believe we are to know and be aware of what is going on in the world we live in. If however the news stories we see and hear on television bring us to a place where we our always defeated and if they rob us of our hope or if they make us question God then we need to step back and examine how we are spending our time.

Here is a simple discernment tool. If you find yourself blaming God or asking God to rapture you out of here, then you are not hearing the voice of God. Jesus tells us in His Word there is only one accuser in this world. Please ask God to help you discern the voice you are listening to.

We have an answer when we seek God with all our heart. Think about this for a minute please. If you are busy all the time, are you really enjoying life at all? Jesus promised us peace, joy, rest, and we have it all when we know we are loved by God. I know you are thinking 'I wish life could be that simple.' Well it is! Please ask Jesus to come into your life and watch answers come to you like the ones you just read about for they are true.

Noah was one man who laid down his life to do what Jesus ask him to do and the world can and should rejoice that Noah was not to busy living for himself to do what Jesus ask of Him. Noah is such a great example of dying to self and being prepared to do what God ask even when what God ask looked totally impossible. I praise Jesus and Abba Father for loving me so much they have given me their very own Holy Spirit to forever be my guide.

I hear His voice because I laid down my life to listen. I literally danced in my camper last night and went to bed excited to wake up and be who Jesus created me to be. I pray this love of God and His Holy Spirit is welcomed into your heart so your joy will be full also. 'Jesus loves Ron' this I know because Jesus wakes me up every morning to tell me so! Did you hear your wakeup call this morning? Jesus is there if you are listening. Happy are those who have ears to hear and eyes to see. I love my Jesus smiling at me. Yes, Jesus is in me and I am forever grateful He laid down His life for me. I pray I don't waste a minute of our time together for our time together is all I live for. My desire is to be His hope of glory today.

We have choices. We can blame God or we can receive God. We can sit in our easy chair, watch the news and ask God why did you let that happen or we can take responsibility and ask God to show you what you and I can do to transform the heart of the men of this world? We can spend our life watching funny sitcoms on television or we can seek God with all our heart by reading, listening and coming into intimate relationship with Jesus. Jesus will transform you into a vessel of His love so Jesus can flow His love through you. Again the choice we have is to stand by and do nothing while the world is going to hell or we can stand firm in our faith the Holy Spirit is in us and we will send hell right back to the devil.

You choose rightly and God will light your path. The Holy Spirit lives in you and will work through you if you make yourself available to Him. I hope you realize we have the same commission Jesus had and we can have the same relationship with our Abba Father as Jesus has. Remember all things are possible because Jesus said so. All we need to do is believe.

Pray By Faith

One Sunday, I met a man in church that had a testimony. If you were not a believer you would probably dismiss his testimony as stupid and maybe think he is in need some kind of professional help. I don't have any idea if his testimony is real or not but the event he describes did change his life. We are told to recognize the fruits and in his life he received a desire to know God so I know something great happened in him.

After this man described the event he went on to tell me he will only read the Bible and nothing else. He said, "I have ask Jesus to help me memorize the scriptures so I can quote them correctly to anyone he talks to and he wants to be able to tell people the scripture number and verse when he talks about scriptures."

I mentioned I don't have the scripture numbered or verse memorized. I call it the address. I simply know by faith when I am talking to people if I need the address the Holy Spirit will give it to me. I believe Jesus will manifest through me whatever He needs to help someone. I have asked my Jesus to reveal His faith, His hope, His discernment and most of all His love to me as I read my Holy Bible and I believe He does.

When I read about Jesus turning water into wine at the wedding, I ask Jesus, "What you are showing me in this story?" The Holy Spirit of Abba Father and Jesus talk to me. After asking the Holy Spirit about whatever scripture I am reading, I notice that understanding comes. Like when Mary told Jesus that they have no wine, I started thinking about how much faith Mary needed to even ask Jesus to do something about the wine. I noticed in the scripture passage this miracle is called the beginning of miracles so I think this was the first miracle Jesus did.

Think how much faith Mary needed to ask Jesus to do something about the fact they were out of wine. To my knowledge, at this point Mary had not seen a miracle. Jesus also brought to my attention that Mary simply told Jesus the problem. She didn't tell

Jesus what to do. She didn't pray and fast for breakthrough for three days prior to asking. She simply saw a need and asks Jesus to do something. I know I need more faith because I would not have the faith to ask Jesus to do something about a wedding party being out of wine.

Mary saw a need and simply talked to Jesus about it. Jesus could have said, "Mary, have you considered the teaching that will come out of this if I change water into wine." I mean, people will debate forever if Jesus is okay with drinking and maybe being drunk. For the scripture says Jesus turned the water into wine after the men were well drunk. Jesus could said, "This will be my first miracle and I want my first miracle to be a really big one and not something as trite as this.

John 2:3-4 And when they ran out of wine, the mother of Jesus said to Him, "They have no wine." Jesus said to her, "Woman, what does your concern have to do with Me? My hour has not yet come."

We see by the reply of Jesus that Jesus wasn't concerned about the wedding party being out of wine. Jesus could say to Mary, "Did you hear me? I said my hour has not yet come." Jesus basically said no to Mary for this is not my will and it is definitely not my timing and yet Mary was not the least bit defeated. Mary did not argue with Jesus but Mary showed great faith by what she said to the servants.

John 2:5 His mother said to the servants, "Whatever He says to you, do it."

I would like to ask a question. What do you think was the motive of Jesus to perform the miracle at Cana? I believe it was pure love. I believe Mary knew Jesus loved her and so His answer did not displease or distract her. Mary showed great faith and Jesus loves faith so much He honors the words of faith all through the Holy Bible.

Reading on we see faith at work:

John 2:5 His mother said to the servants, "Whatever He says to you, do it."

Listen to the words of faith Mary chose. I believe total faith is so beautiful to our Lord. To me, faith makes everything simple. Look at the problem (the wedding party was out of wine) look at the prayer (Jesus they are out of wine) and within seconds the problem is solved and look at the result (His disciples believed in Him).

Please notice the simplicity of Mary's prayer. Mary didn't pray with an answer for Jesus like 'Jesus please go down to Wal-Mart and buy some wine.' On the contrary, Mary's prayer simply mentioned to Jesus the problem but her prayer didn't pray the problem or give a solution she wanted. As we read our Holy Bible, we will see Jesus always has an answer. Our part is to pray one time, stand in faith, and realize Jesus is the answer.

Continuing on in John 2:6-11:

John 2:6-11 Now there were set there six waterpots of stone, according to the manner of purification of the Jews, containing twenty or thirty gallons apiece. Jesus said to them, "Fill the waterpots with water." And they filled them up to the brim. And He said to them, "Draw some out now, and take it to the master of the feast." And they took it. When the master of the feast had tasted the water that was made wine, and did not know where it came from (but the servants who had drawn the water knew), the master of the feast called the bridegroom. And he said to him, "Every man at the beginning sets out the good wine, and when the guests have well drunk, then the inferior. You have kept the good wine until now!" This beginning of signs Jesus did in Cana of Galilee, and **manifested His glory; and His disciples believed in Him.**

When we read our Holy Bible we need to ask Jesus to give us the lesson from His scripture teaching. While reading your Holy Bible please ask Jesus to bring to life the scriptures and Jesus will show you the faith in them, the hope in then, the discernment in them and the heart or love in them when we listen for the voice of God we will hear His voice of truth in them. Jesus always has me read the scripture over and over revealing more of His love toward me and His truth every time I read His scriptures. At the rate that we, Jesus and I read, I will need years and years to read the entire Holy Bible.

Read John 2:3-11 again. This time, ask Jesus to reveal the hope in them. Then read them again asking for His discernment in them and His timing in them and His love toward you in them. I believe when I stand before Jesus for judgment I will be judged on what I did with the gifts He gave me. I tell you these things because Jesus has become very real to me this way. I pray you too will ask Jesus for a personal relationship and Jesus will reveal Himself to you in a completely different way and I know He will come to you if you ask Him too.

I think the wedding story above is a good illustration for us about laying down our life for another. Jesus plainly tells Mary this problem is no concern of Him. Jesus had to have great faith in His Father to perform a miracle for Him. I mean, what if Father God decided not to turn water into wine for His son. The apostles might walk away saying, "What manner of man is this? He and His mother are crazy! Who can believe this Jesus guy, trying to turn water into wine? Who wants to follow a nut case like them?"

I know a lot of people in this world today who will way the circumstances of the situation before they ask God for a miracle. Some of us "believers" will ask ourselves under our breath before we say anything out loud, does our request line up with the word of God? I think a better question maybe is 'Does our request bring glory to God?'

I believe a prayer of faith is thanking God for His love for us. When we know we are loved we will become the Hope of Glory to God.

Who Will Be The Greatest In the Kingdom of Heaven?

I remember reading in Mathew what Jesus said about John the Baptist and asking Jesus to reveal to me why John would be the least in the kingdom of heaven.

Matthew 11:11 Verily I say unto you, Among them that are born of women there hath not risen a greater than John the Baptist: notwithstanding he that is least in the kingdom of heaven is greater than he.

I thought about the life of John and how John had laid down His life to prepare the way of the Lord. John had definitely laid down His life, living the way he did.

Mark 1:6 And John was clothed with camel's hair, and with a girdle of a skin about his loins; and he did eat locusts and wild honey.

I thought about how uncomfortable that must have been to where camel hair and to have his diet. I thought how I complain if my cotton clothes are not soft enough or too tight. I thought about how I want my hot food hot or my cold food cold and how spoiled I am. I thought about my soft bed and the clean camper I live in. How can I possibly be greater in the kingdom of heaven then John the Baptist after reading how John laid down his life the way he did? I am pondering this question because I believe John did something displeasing to God and I don't want to make the same mistake. I want my life to bring glory to God not disappointment to God.

So why did Jesus say that about John the Baptist? The question that came to mind was "Did John the Baptist follow Jesus?" Jesus in His word asks us to pick up our cross and follow

Him. Could it be the actions of John condemning Herod that displeased Jesus? Jesus tells us in His Word not to judge any one or we will be judged by the same judgment we judge by:

> **Matthew 7:1-2** Judge not, that ye be not judged. For with what judgment ye judge, ye shall be judged: and with what measure ye mete, it shall be measured to you again.

John condemned Herod for his lifestyle.

> **Mark 6:17-19** For Herod himself had sent forth and laid hold upon John, and bound him in prison for Herodias' sake, his brother Philip's wife: for he had married her. For John had said unto Herod, It is not lawful for thee to have thy brother's wife. Therefore Herodias had a quarrel against him, and would have killed him; but she could not

Look at the results of condemning people. Did John achieve any good for the kingdom of heaven by condemning Herod? Did John's actions open the heart of Herod or Herodias to a possible conversion to Christianity? Jesus plainly said to condemn no one for what measure you measure you will be measured by. Could this be why John will be the least in the kingdom of heaven?

I believe above all those things John did and didn't do; above all his suffering, there is one sin we all will be called to be judged on and that sin is the biggest sin possible. The sin is the sin of unbelief. Did John believe Jesus to be the son of God? Did John believe in the forgiveness of God?

> **Matthew 11:2-3** Now when John had heard in the prison the works of Christ, he sent two of his disciples, And said unto him, Art thou he that should come, or do we look for another?

To me, Mathew 11:3 is one of the saddest scriptures in the entire Holy Bible. John had baptized Jesus and saw Jesus come out of the water and John had heard the mighty voice of God proclaim Jesus to be His son. John saw the Holy Spirit descend on Jesus so how could John doubt. John was one of the first to recognize Jesus to be the Son of God. I hope and pray Jesus does not have to question my faith in Him? I believe Jesus has made himself this real to everyone who will open his heart toward the Lord.

I believe we teach our belief more by how we live then what we say. Look at the life of John and you will see boldness and Jesus loves boldness. I would think it would take a lot of boldness to speak out and call a king an adulterer the way John did. The problem is Jesus never asks us to condemn and John condemned Herod. John had followers so was John teaching his followers to condemn. Read in Mathew 5:19:

> **Matthew 5:19** Whosoever therefore shall break one of these least commandments, **and shall teach men so**, he shall be called the least in the kingdom of heaven: but whosoever shall do and teach them, the same shall be called great in the kingdom of heaven.

I believe by condemning king Herod, the life of John and the words of John were teaching his followers to condemn. Noticed Jesus never condemned John for condemning King Herod and Jesus never called John a doubter for doubting but Jesus did tell us John will be the least in the kingdom of heaven.

I pray and thank my Jesus for His gentle conviction of my sins. I thank God for forgiveness. I thank God I will be in heaven someday and for faith and guidance from God to build the kingdom of heaven while I am still here. I thank God for revealing to me His love through grace to me is sufficient. I pray for help from God to remove the plank in my eye so my life will become an example to others. The joy of the Lord will attract others to His joy if you open yourself to His joy.

Jesus has showed me through His life we should live and have our being in His love. Our desire to live like Jesus lived will transform us into a loving example of Jesus Christ. If we will accept and live with the Hoy Spirit in us we will not make the same mistakes over and over. Repentance to freedom from sin is really freedom to choose to seek God with all your heart. As we read in the life of John we can do great works and even die to our self, we can keep most of the commandments but our motive has to be to love one another into the kingdom of God. Jesus never condemned and neither should we. Jesus loved and so should we.

Who will be the greatest in the kingdom of heaven?

Matthew 18:1-4 At the same time came the disciples unto Jesus, saying, Who is the greatest in the kingdom of heaven? And Jesus called a little child unto him, and set him in the midst of them, And said, Verily I say unto you, Except ye be converted, and become as little children, ye shall not enter into the kingdom of heaven. **Whosoever therefore shall humble himself as this little child, the same is greatest in the kingdom of heaven.**

How do we humble our self like a child? I believe the humbleness of a child is the child-like faith Jesus talks about in His word. Being child like in faith is to expect God to honor His Word without us wavering and making excuses. We read in our Holy Bible how Jesus as a child marveled the people in the synagogues.

Today in most churches we take our children out of church the moment the preaching begins. I have been very blessed to meet families who have some really great children and I noticed the parents of these great children make their children there priority. I realized God has made His children His priority. I realized I am the priority of God and I realized how being the priority of God makes me oh so special.

Today we want our children to have self-esteem. We want them to be good in sports and sometimes we let these things replace our intimate time with them and Jesus. Our job as parents is to give our children a desire to know God. Sports and self-esteem will follow our priorities but they should never be our priority.

Making earthly esteem our priority or seeking self-esteem from manmade challenges like sports, could be a huge problem. We all know the winner only has the title for a short time or until the next game is over. I pray people realize earthly self-esteem is so momentary. Contrast earthly self-esteem to seeking God with all your heart and receiving your everlasting esteem by knowing you are the priority of God and unlike the praise of man; the praise of God will be forever on our lips.

To be the best at something or to desire the gold medal at the Olympics is a challenge for a momentary status that we humans will pour our hearts into and direct our children into if we see the possibility of their success. Yet we see in Mathew 18:4 the simplicity of Jesus Christ is to spread His loving kindness by simply being humble and the gold medal for being humble is Christianity at its best. Please give your children a desire to be the greatest in the kingdom of heaven by showing and living in the humbleness of a child who has his priority on seeking the kingdom of God and His righteousness.

Matthew 18:4 Whosoever therefore shall humble himself as this little child, the same is greatest in the kingdom of heaven.

Humbleness is defined all through our Holy Bible. Jesus lived it, Jesus displayed it and Jesus is the completion of humbleness. Before Jesus left to be killed Jesus humbly washed the feet of his apostles. Even when Jesus arose from the dead, Jesus never stood on a stage holding a big medal with everyone applauding him. Jesus came back as a gardener. Jesus cooked a fish dinner for his apostles. Jesus quietly appeared to hundreds of people to prove He arose and to give us peace of knowing death has forever been defeated. Oh how I pray and hope for the humbleness of Jesus Christ and my Father God to be on display in my life forever also.

When Is Love a Problem?

If you know God intimately, you will know that God is love. Jesus proved when people saw the love of His Father in Him. Most people fell in love with His Father's love. This phenomenon is still going on today. When you see two young people truly in love, their love is contagious. They walk in a joy that everyone can see and their countenance is inspiring. I want to share this with you, "How being in love with Jesus is the same way and yet so different?"

Anyone who falls in love with Jesus will know the difference that I am talking about. My first true love was my precious wife Jenny who became my wife for 40 years 6 months 16 days and 3hours. I didn't realize at the beginning of our relationship how much pressure I put on my Jenny to be a certain way. Thank God Jenny loved me or she probably would have walked away. I had a picture in my mind of what love looked like and how love worked. I think back about how narrow-minded I was and I am surprised Jenny stayed with me.

As our love for each other grew my picture of what love was supposed to be started changing and our love grew deeper. I now believe the love of Jesus is more like the love Jenny had for me at the beginning of our relationship. One of the differences of a Godly love we will become aware of is we come to God knowing we are sinners or we knowingly have crossed boundaries Jesus has set for His believers and yet Jesus never gives up on us and Jesus still loves us. You know in human love we have certain boundaries we will tolerate in each other but if our mate crosses those boundaries we give up on our mate and look for another.

Another aspect of human love verses Godly love that complicates our lives are the priorities that we set daily and the choices we make minute by minute. In human love our time is always divided between our spouse and our earthly possessions. While we are in love with our mate we almost always pursue earthly possessions. So many times we read about people working two or more jobs or super long hours away from their loved one to acquire earthly possessions, only to find their loved one having an affair because their mate was gone working all the time.

Contrast human love with the Godly love described in our Holy Bible and we see Jesus wants seeking Him to be our first priority and our only priority. Nothing is to come before our God. We are to seek God and nothing else. I thank you Jesus for your never ending love toward us. I know your heart is for us to seek you the way you seek us. I thank you Lord that your love is very patient, extremely patient and yet the simple task Jesus has given us is to seek Him first and above all else. Sometimes it is too hard for us to do. We seem so eager to seek earthly possessions and we seek earthly knowledge, like schools of higher learning. In seeking these things we are willingly setting aside quiet time with our real teacher Jesus Christ in exchange for dung.

Contrast earthly possessions with Godly gifts. Godly gifts last forever. We don't work for them, moths and rust will not eat them away and if we freely choose to live in His gifts we are rewarded by God with living in His gifts now. Godly gifts help us focus on Jesus and our mission here on earth. Godly gifts actually multiply over time and Godly gifts are described in Paul's letter to the Galatians. Read in the word how Jesus modeled the life style of living these gifts, yes Jesus is the perfect Galatians 5:22-26

Galatians 5:22-26 But the fruit of the Spirit is love, joy, peace, longsuffering, gentleness, goodness, faith, Meekness, temperance: against such there is no law. And they that are Christ's have crucified the flesh with the affections and lusts. If we live in the Spirit, let us also walk in the Spirit. Let us not be desirous of vain glory, provoking one another, envying one another.

I know if we set our heart on the goodness and righteousness of the Lord we will start living in the spirit of Jesus (Galatians 5:22-23). If we are distracted by the things of this world we will become earthly in our nature and separated from the love of Jesus until we ask Him back into our lives and learn to trust in Him alone in all aspects of our life. Trusting God in all aspects of our life is the dying to self our Holy Bible talks about.

You probably know friends who love the Lord. They also trust the Lord to be their provider and yet they don't seem to trust the Lord to be their teacher and protector. I have met people who think to seek the Lord is to study His word and receive knowledge or revelation about the word of God. Seeking the Lord through studying His word only works to a point.

I will not judge there pursuit of the Lord for I know I am not supposed too. I am simply stating we are told to seek ye first the kingdom of God and His righteousness for then great revelations will come to us about the scriptures. There might be a problem if we simply seek great revelations and are not really seeking the heart of God.

We are to read our Holy Bible and we will receive revelation from God about His Word. But if we don't apply the word and these revelations to our life of living the love of Jesus toward others, sadly we will become educated Christians who strive to be doers of the word. Yes, it is fun to tell others about revelations we receive but we must put these revelations into action or we will be viewed by others as Christian hypocrites.

Seeking knowledge and revelation is not necessarily seeking God. I have observed the people who are just seeking knowledge and revelation always have a lot of unanswered questions for our Lord. I have met some people who have even gone so far as to say Paul's writings are contradictory to the teachings of Jesus. It seems to me these people are spending their life trying to figure if Paul's writings are contradictory to the teachings of Jesus. This is sad to me because their focus seems to have been replaced with seeking knowledge of truth rather than on seeking the Lord with all your heart, mind and soul for Jesus is the truth.

I think to spend your life questioning the scriptures instead of allowing the scriptures to show you the narrow path and how to please the Lord is another snare of the devil. I believe the simplicity of Christ is to believe His word not question His Word. I believe we are here to help build the kingdom of God by being His loving ambassadors and if we miss this message in the scriptures; our life would be a tragedy.

Personally I have never read anywhere in the Holy Bible to question the word of God. On the contrary I have read I am supposed to accept His word as truth. I have read and heard Jesus tell me to receive His Word as truth by faith. By faith I read my Holy Bible and ask Jesus questions about His Holy Bible but I have never questioned the truth of His word. I ask Jesus for discernment, faith, compassion, and to help me understand enough of His word to help others come to a desire to know His love also.

I have met people that are questioning the truth of Paul's writings and trying to prove Paul's righting don't line up with the righting of Jesus. I simply will not spend my time trying to figure if God made a mistake putting Paul's writings in His Holy Bible.

In my Hoy Bible I have found I am loved by Jesus and taught by Jesus and knowing I am loved and taught by God is enough knowledge for me. Actually if you know you are His loved one you will know by faith you have the Holy Spirit of Jesus and Father God living in you already. They are the Spirit of truth and they dwell in you and so you have all knowledge already, for your loved one will never hold anything from you. If that seems to hard to understand or to accept as truth I wonder if you are reading your Holy Bible for knowledge and not accepting it as the truth from a loved one.

You see, I will not search for truth because I have found truth in the person of Jesus Christ and Abba Father God. By faith I accept their word as truth and by faith I believe Jesus teaches me on a need to know basis. This simple belief allows me to do the work of the kingdom every day knowing the Holy Spirit will give me everything needed to do and say to live a heart transforming lifestyle of being loved by Jesus and being the love of Jesus toward others.

If you or I studied for years and ended up with more questions than answers about Jesus, I pray Jesus would put someone in our path to give us revelation as to how we need to be studying. Again, we need faith to know Jesus is still our teacher and our teacher tells us He will never lie. We should have total faith in someone who has told us He will never lie and I believe we should have total faith in His Holy Bible also.

Trusting in God who said He will never lie is simple for me. Personally, I have a lot of questions about the Holy Bible as I read it. Truthfully, I don't understand a lot of the scriptures in the Holy

Bible but I don't question who wrote it and I will never question the truth of it. I simply take my questions to Jesus and if I hear from God then great, but if I don't hear from God I know by faith God will tell me when and if I need to know. Remember the manna from heaven in the desert was just enough for each day. I believe this is faith in God and with faith in God I know I am receiving the manna from heaven I need today. I love knowing I am already loved by God.

Did Jesus Give Us Two Types of Faith?

The scriptures prove faith is the right path to seek God. The apostles asked Jesus questions all the time and sometimes Jesus answered them directly and sometimes Jesus let them grow by faith into understanding. The number of apostles grew as long as Jesus taught things physically. I mean the apostles believed as long as they saw the miracles. Miracles built their faith but the moment Jesus ask the apostles to believe only in His words and with no physical proof most of His apostles left Him.

When the apostles questioned the truth of Jesus words, most of them left Jesus:

John 6:47-60 Verily, verily, I say unto you, He that believeth on me hath everlasting life. I am that bread of life. Your fathers did eat manna in the wilderness, and are dead. This is the bread which cometh down from heaven, that a man may eat thereof, and not die. I am the living bread which came down from heaven: if any man eat of this bread, he shall live for ever: and the bread that I will give is my flesh, which I will give for the life of the world. The Jews therefore strove among themselves, saying, How can this man give us his flesh to eat? Then Jesus said unto them, Verily, verily, I say unto you, Except ye eat the flesh of the Son of man, and drink his blood, ye have no life in you. Whoso eateth my flesh, and drinketh my blood, hath eternal life; and I will raise him up at the last day. For my flesh is meat indeed, and my blood is drink indeed. He that eateth my flesh, and drinketh my blood, dwelleth in me, and I in him. As the living Father hath sent me, and I live by the Father: so he that eateth me, even he shall live by me. This is that bread which came down from heaven: not as your fathers did eat manna, and are dead: he that eateth of this bread shall live for ever. These things said he in the synagogue, as he taught in Capernaum. Many therefore of his disciples, when they had heard this, said, **This is an hard saying; who can hear it?**

Right here we read how the apostles for the first time were questioning the truth of Jesus. I have heard preachers in churches today call the bread and wine a symbol. I think to myself, what a tragedy of unbelief. I have the bread of life living in me. I have the blood of Jesus Christ in me and I will not partake or believe in a stupid symbol. Where did the idea Jesus gave us a symbol of God come from? The symbol is from the devil who deceives those who will not believe the words of Jesus.

Some of the apostles said *'This is a hard saying; who can hear it?'* Jesus never said He came to give us a symbol. If you believe the body and blood of Jesus Christ is a symbol then maybe you will receive a symbol of heaven or a symbol of forgiveness or a symbol of love. I am sure the devil has a lot of other symbols for you nonbelievers. To you nonbelievers *'This is a hard saying; who can hear it?'*

Remember these apostles had been with Jesus for a period of time and may have been some of the seventy Jesus had sent out to do miracles and yet this saying of Jesus was so hard for them to expect. I believe the apostles struggled with this teaching because it is the first teaching Jesus taught them by faith alone. Yes, they had to accept this saying by faith alone for there was no physical evidence. Physical miracles are so much easier to believe than spiritual miracles. Believing what we see physically really does not require the depth of faith to believe compared to believing in a spiritual miracle.

We are all given a choice to simply believe by faith or to question the truth. Jesus changing bread and wine into the body and blood of Jesus Christ should not be that hard for us to believe. We have advantages the apostles didn't have at that time. We have the whole picture of the life of Jesus, we have been set free of the fear of dying, and we have the baptism of the Holy Spirit. For me, to believe this hard saying is just a choice of trust and faith I must make. I believe the twelve apostles made the right choice, for they trusted Jesus to speak truth and truth brings a reward of faith, I pray to be counted with the apostles for I believe the bread and wine is more than a symbol it is the actual body and blood of Jesus Christ for Jesus said it is.

Read on and see the rewards for believing.

John 6:61-71   When Jesus knew in himself that his disciples murmured at it, he said unto them, Doth this offend you? What and if ye shall see the Son of man ascend up where he was before? It is the spirit that quickeneth; the flesh profiteth nothing: the words that I speak unto you, they are spirit, and they are life. But there are some of you that believe not. For Jesus knew from the beginning who they were that believed not, and who should betray him. And he said, Therefore said I unto you, that no man can come unto me, except it were given unto him of my Father. From that time many of his disciples went back, and walked no more with him. Then said Jesus unto the twelve, Will ye also go away? Then Simon Peter answered him, **Lord, to whom shall we go? thou hast the words of eternal life. And we believe and are sure that thou art that Christ, the Son of the living God.** Jesus answered them, Have not I chosen you twelve, and one of you is a devil? He spake of Judas Iscariot the son of Simon: for he it was that should betray him, being one of the twelve.

I hope you heard the reward in this scripture? Our reward for believing is eternal life with our Abba Father and Jesus. I pray for the faith of the apostles that believed the words of Jesus, but even more I pray for the faith of Jesus to be my faith and with His faith in me to bring more people into the kingdom of God. Please pray to receive the faith of Jesus and Father God to come into your heart. They had to have great faith that one man could turn this world around. I pray and with the faith of Jesus in me I know my life will make a difference in the hearts of many for I have written the words of Peter on the tablet of my heart. **I believe and I'm sure that thou art that Christ, the Son of the living God.**

Again, Jesus showed us He had absolutely no fear of loss when He told us the truth, the bread and wine is transformed into His body and Blood. When the seventy-two left Him, notice Jesus didn't go after them and sugarcoat this teaching. Maybe Jesus could have kept them from leaving his flock by telling them the bread and wine is a symbol for believing the bread and wine to be a symbol requires no spiritual faith. Maybe Jesus could have kept the seventy-two from leaving if He just watered down His truth a little by compromising the truth to accommodate their feelings.

I believe Jesus transformed the bread and wine into His very own body and blood and I will believe the words of Jesus to be truth by faith. I have received the Body and Blood of Jesus Christ into my heart by faith for the bread and wine still taste like bread and wine to me but I know I have received the body and blood of my savior Jesus Christ. Remember the words of my Jesus to Thomas 'Blessed are those who believe and do not see.' Again, I say to believe the bread and wine is a symbol takes no faith and a symbol has no life changing power in it.

John 20:29 Jesus saith unto him, Thomas, because thou hast seen me, thou hast believed: blessed are they that have not seen, and yet have believed.

2 Corinthians 5:7 For we walk by faith, not by sight

I believe this teaching is the first teaching from Jesus the apostles had to accept on spiritual faith, not physical faith. I believe I have the Holy Spirit of Jesus and Abba Father in me and I believe with my spiritual faith to believe in the words of Jesus that the bread and wine are His Flesh and Blood. When the eleven apostles believed they started a life transformation into the image and likeness of Jesus. The seventy-two who did not believe are somewhere, but the believers in Jesus Christ are rejoicing in eternal life with the real Flesh and Blood of life, Jesus Christ and Father God.

John 6:54 Whoso eateth my flesh, and drinketh my blood, hath eternal life; and I will raise him up at the last day.

I seriously pray for the faith of Jesus and I know faith comes from knowing our Abba Father and Jesus love us. When we know we are loved we will have faith. Jesus dearly loved His apostles and His love shows all through His book of life, the Holy Bible. I pray the book in heaven being written about Ron Johnson's life here on earth is full of the love of Jesus flowing through me. I pray for the faith of Jesus Christ to be in me by faith in Him and I do not partake in symbols. Jesus never said this is a symbol, Jesus said

"THIS IS MY BODY AND THIS IS MY BLOOD" and I believe Jesus.

These scriptures should remove any doubt for they are the words of Jesus at His last supper.

> **Mar 14:22-24**   And as they did eat, Jesus took bread, and blessed, and brake *it*, and gave to them, and said, Take, eat: **this is my body.** And he took the cup, and when he had given thanks, he gave *it* to them: and they all drank of it. And he said unto them, **This is my blood** of the new testament, which is shed for many.

This is repeated in Luke.

> **Luke 22:19-20**   And he took bread, and gave thanks, and brake *it*, and gave unto them, saying, **This is my body** which is given for you: this do in remembrance of me. Likewise also the cup after supper, saying, **This cup is the new testament in my blood, which is shed for you.**

I just cannot find the word symbol here and I wonder why Jesus would come and do all that He did to give us a symbol. I know the coming of Jesus fulfilled the Old Testament prophesies which prove Jesus is real and not a symbol.

If you were really thirsty right now, I mean dying of thirst, would you want me to give you a big drink of water or just a symbol of a drink of water? Nonbelievers are dying of unbelief. You must choose belief for eternal life with God. I believe the symbol of eternal life without faith in the words of God is hell. I believe the apostles chose well and so do I.

> **John 6:68-69**   Then Simon Peter answered him, Lord, to whom shall we go? thou hast the **words** of eternal life. **And we believe and are sure that thou art that Christ, the Son of the living God.**

Jesus said our words have meaning - *This is my body and this is my blood* because our words reveal what is in our heart. We believers all know Jesus gave us his body and blood. Jesus said He will never lie and we who believe will never die.

Matthew 12:35-37 A good man out of the good treasure of the heart bringeth forth good things: and an evil man out of the evil treasure bringeth forth evil things. But I say unto you, **That every idle word that men shall speak, they shall give account thereof in the day of judgment.** For by thy words thou shalt be justified, and by thy words thou shalt be condemned.

I believe Jesus held Himself accountable to the scriptures and I believe Jesus when He said "THIS IS MY BODY AND THIS IS MY BLOOD." I know in my heart I want to be His hope of glory here on the earth for I know Jesus was the hope of glory to His Father and He succeeded and so will I by simply believing God when He says all things are possible. Jesus came to reap sons of God for His Father and I live to reap sons for my Father.

I will not be just a symbol of His glory or a symbol of a son for by the grace of God I can be a real Son of God and I can be the real hope of glory for Abba Father and Jesus said so. I want to be counted in the beloved of God who really believe with a whole heart Jesus is real.

I hope and pray you seek God to come into intimate relationship with Him so you are able to believe by faith God Himself will give you the words to transform hearts towards the love of Jesus every day. The tools you need to do the work of the kingdom are also our rewards of the kingdom of God.

Galatians 5:22-23 But the fruit of the Spirit is love, joy, peace, longsuffering, gentleness, goodness, **faith,** Meekness, temperance: against such there is no law.

The reward God freely gives us for living in these gifts is freedom from the law and freedom from fear to die to yourself. If you believe by faith you received these fruits from God you will see them operate in your life. But if you think I am not ready or I am not worthy or I must study for years and years to become ready and worthy you will probably never be ready or worthy because you haven't accepted His gifts. Seeking God is to seek to be His love here on the earth and His love will be witnessed to others by the joy in you walking in these gifts and watching these gifts flowing through you.

If you are seeking knowledge alone or truth alone you will probably become puffed up in your knowledge and you might become desirous of vain glory.

Galatians 5:26 Let us not be desirous of vain glory, provoking one another, envying one another.

Please remember we are to seek ye first the kingdom of God and His righteousness for when you do you will receive a Spirit of knowledge and truth in you. You will not be puffed up or envying one another but you will live to give glory to God and to God give the pure glory for the voice of God is speaking His loving truth through you. Actually there in is a great discerning tool. Does your knowledge bring glory to God or to yourself?

Do Our Accomplishments Bring Glory to God?

I met a girl who has a lot of talent to play musical interments. She has studied for years to gain the knowledge of playing these instruments perfectly. She gave me one of her CD's. She told me she writes her own worship songs. I tried to listen for the words of her songs but the music on the CD was louder than her signing. I just could not hear the words of the girl signing.

I finally just throw the CD away because I became frustrated with it, then I wondered if the beautiful music of life (our accomplishments) speak louder than our actions and beliefs in Jesus Christ. I thank God for transforming me away from the accomplishments of this world that held me in bondage most of my life and I thank God for giving me eyes to see the freedom of being loved by Jesus Christ will supersede the accomplishments of this world. I by faith know Jesus and I together make beautiful music and Jesus and you together will make beautiful music also.

Here is another way to discern if your love of accomplishments is a problem.

Galatians 5:24 And they that are Christ's have crucified the flesh with the affections and lusts.

Those of us who seek to be the love of Jesus will find the things of this world are momentary and we will willingly crucify our selfish gain and momentary vain glory. With the Holy Spirit in our heart we will crucify our own momentary lusts because we will not envy one another the way nonbelievers do.

Please let me clarify myself. If you were my friend and you were a millionaire and you gave me a million dollar camper to travel in then I would accept it. My point is I don't think about it, I don't seek after it, actually I think of it as the momentary junk of this world. I choose to focus on Jesus and what He needs done today. My priority will always be Jesus first and everything else second. I believe we have crucified our flesh when we seek first the kingdom of God and His righteousness.

Galatians 5:25 If we live in the Spirit, let us also walk in the Spirit.

Living in the spirit is such a delight. My spirit needs nothing for my spirit is in constant commutation with my Jesus. I have allowed my spirit to be the love of Jesus Christ in me and that allows me to walk in the spirit of love. I remember when Jenny and I first met. Our spirits needed nothing except to spend time together. We cherished our time together. We lived to be with each other. Now my Jenny is with my Jesus and I love Him and praise Him for giving Jenny her final reward. Accepting the outcome of your prayer is another sign of faith. I pray to have faith likened to the faith of Job. And in my trial, I pray to have the words of Job in my heart '*Who am I to question God?*' Thank you Jesus for giving Job words of faith for his words help my faith thousands of years later.

If we live our life knowing we are loved by Jesus we will live knowing Jesus will give us the words and the actions to help others become His love. This is so simple if you have faith God is with you in the form of the Holy Spirit. To me, walking in the Spirit of

God is to allow God through faith to give me the words He wants spoken at any given time. Jesus walked in the Spirit of His Father's love to show us by example.

Love never fails.

Are You Walking in the Spirit?

Here is a simple question that you can ask yourself. When you think about doing something for God or when you are prompted to do something for God and you put it off because you might lose what you already have like 'I have to go to work because I have big payments to make and I don't want people to think I can't afford all my stuff,' I wonder are you or could you be saying to God, 'What I already have is more important then what you are asking me to do Lord.'

You know when you fall in love with someone you will drop every earthly desire to be with that one person you love. We are saying to that person you are important and spending time together with you is my highest priority. Jesus tells us in His Word that He is the same way. Jesus tells us if we forsake the things of this world to spend time with Him we will reap an unexplainable joy that can only come from a loving intimate relationship with Him.

For example, In John 11 Jesus raised Lazarus from the dead. I haven't raised anyone from the dead yet but I have seen people healed and I have experienced the joy that comes only form God through believing in Him.

John 11 is a biblical example of belief and unbelief. Please look at the outcome of the loving actions of Jesus.

Then ask yourself, was the outcome of the actions of Jesus love or hate? Lazarus life was restored and his loved ones rejoiced (*love*). The Pharisees were afraid of losing their earthly position. Notice that they were willing to commit murder in order to keep their position (*hate*). Jesus listened to and revealed His Father's love and His Father's heart (*love*). The Pharisees wanted to kill Jesus. They listened to and revealed the evil of the devil (*hate*); they also revealed they had no discernment as to who they were listening too. Jesus and His followers had great joy and the Pharisees had total discontent. There in is another discernment tool. Walk with Jesus and walk in joy and contentment or walk with the devil and live in evil discontentment.

When the Pharisees heard Jesus had raised Lazarus form the dead they were complexed with what to do with Jesus, asking one another *"What do we?"*

> **John 11:46-48** But some of them went their ways to the Pharisees, and told them what things Jesus had done. Then gathered the chief priests and the Pharisees a council, and said, **What do we?** for this man doeth many miracles. If we let him thus alone, all men will believe on him: and the Romans shall come and take away both our place and nation.

The motive of the Pharisees was not to build the kingdom of God by being the love of God. It was not to bring more people to believe in Jesus being the son of God. They didn't care about the people being helped by the miracles. Their motive was fear of losing their positions and their fear led them to premeditate murdering Jesus in their heart. Please read John 11:48 again.

> **John 11:48** If we let him thus alone, all men will believe on him: and **the Romans shall come and take away both our place and nation.**

Is there any difference between the fear of loss the Pharisees had and the fear of loss some Christians walk in today? Are we Christians the Pharisees of today? We can prove our belief by how we walk, what we meditate on and by our hidden personal thoughts that no one else can see. The Pharisees hid their thoughts and in secret they plotted many times to kill Jesus. The Pharisees feared the loss of there place of royalty and they feared their loss of power over the nation. The fear of loss is another discernment tool.

Fear of loss is one of the greatest tools the devil still has. Fear of loss is so powerful. We read in the scriptures how the Pharisees (*men of God*) actually plotted and premeditated the killing of Jesus Christ because of their fear of loss.

Today, the devil is still using the same play book. People are always talking about what they read or hear in the news and how the fear of loss has caused someone to kill. People seem to walk in fear today and this is such a shame on our Christian belief especially when Jesus clearly tells us not to fear.

Matthew 10:28 And fear not them which kill the body, but are not able to kill the soul: but rather fear him which is able to destroy both soul and body in hell.

Jesus did not fear the Pharisees. Jesus talked plainly to them. Jesus did not sugarcoat His message to please them. Jesus did the miracles in front of them to help them come into belief. In Matthew 10:28, Jesus plainly tells us to fear not those who can kill our body (*men*) but to fear him which is able to destroy both the soul and body. The Pharisees walked around with authority, in white robes, commanding respect to themselves, they were in constant judgment of others and their hearts were far from the truth of Jesus.

The fear of loss turned the judgment of the Pharisees into a killing, murdering, deceitful, army of the devil. We read Jesus had no fear of those who could kill His body and the fearlessness of Jesus made an open show of the devil in the Pharisees and the evil in their ways. We have the same Holy Spirit of Jesus in us and with faith Jesus is in us; we can walk like Jesus walked, we will talk like Jesus talked, and be a fearless vessel of the transforming power of God every day.

Please know Jesus gave us purpose and value.

Continuing on in Matthew we read how we are protected by God and our value is explained.

Matthew 10:29-31 Are not two sparrows sold for a farthing? and one of them shall not fall on the ground without your Father. But the very hairs of your head are all numbered. Fear ye not therefore, ye are of more value than many sparrows.

I believe Jesus is using our value system to show us our worth. To us, a sparrow doesn't worth that much. I haven't ever heard of anyone having sorrow or being upset when a sparrow flies in front of our moving car and dies. I love my wife Jenny but I never took the time to count the hairs on her head. Yet Jesus tells us not one sparrow falls to the ground without the Father knowing and our Father knows everything about us and God loves so much and God is in our details so much that God has counted and numbered the hairs on our head. I believe Jesus is telling us we have value and we are valued to our heavenly Father.

Now we know we are valued just like Jesus knew his value to our Father. Jesus wants us to be fearless in our mission and Jesus explains our mission as we read on.

Matthew 10:32-33   Whosoever therefore shall confess me before men, him will I confess also before my Father which is in heaven. But whosoever shall deny me before men, him will I also deny before my Father which is in heaven.

Think about faith. Is your faith in God or in your conceal carry permit? How are we confessing our belief in Jesus if we put our faith in our guns? Are we actually confessing our unbelief by carrying a gun? Are we actually denying our God before men by caring our own protection or are we saying I believe in God but if you get in my face I will turn my love into hate and kill you if you threaten me or my family. Look at the words of Matthew 10:33:

Matthew 10:33   But whosoever shall deny me before men, him will I also deny before my Father which is in heaven.

Are we actually denying our faith in God by carrying a gun? Jesus only did what He saw His Father do and we are to only do what we read Jesus did. The way that seems right to a man has crept into our faith to such a degree there are some preachers who carry a concealed gun and some of them actually preach form a church pulpit. The fear of losing their life has gripped them to a point they will take the life of another to save their own life. I wonder if they have ever read the words of Jesus, '*And fear not them which kill the body, but are not able to kill the soul.*'

The truth is so simple to me. I know Jesus and Father God love me. I know Jesus and Father God don't carry guns. I know I am protected, and I know I will live forever in their love. There is no fear in love for perfect love cast out fear. Jesus said it and I believe Him and thanks to the love of my Jesus towards me I don't need a conceal carry permit or a gun. Can you imagine Jesus getting a conceal permit?

This past Sunday while I was at church, I was told of a married couple who both have a conceal carry permit and if the husband forgets his weapon his body will began to shake. In my opinion, everything about the conversation was gripped with fear and bondage. This is so sad. The scriptures are so clear. Jesus has made our life so simple if we believe. If you hope to be the hope of glory then you must believe Jesus is real and dwells in and with you.

Here is a short story about being the hope of glory for Jesus Christ. Today I received a phone call from my good friend Deb. Deb and James and their six children are in Texas right now. They are camping next to a church where they are helping in any way possible. The churchyard has chicken coop. Deb's children enjoy feeding the chickens and eating the eggs.

Johnny one of their young sons went down by an old fifth wheel camper to pull some tall grass, to feed the chickens. In his hurry to run back toward the chicken coop he cut under the front of the fifth wheel camper. He was running fast when he hit his forehead on the steel tow connection of the camper. The impact split his forehead open and blood was almost everywhere in seconds. He ran right to his mother and said "Momma, pray for me." Deb only prayed a short time when Johnny proclaimed Jesus did it. He then ran out to feed the chickens.

Deb said later that night she told her son she needed to shower him and wash all the blood off of him. Deb warned him the water might sting a little. She said as the blood dissolved she kept looking for the wound and could not find it. Jesus did a complete job of healing Johnny's forehead. Deb said she looked at Johnny surprised and in total amazement and Johnny looked at her and said "You prayed, momma!" Praise you Jesus and praise you some more! I want the faith of Johnny. I pray for the faith of a child.

Look at the faith Johnny has. He could have run in and said momma call 911 or he could have just screamed. Instead, he had total faith in God so Johnny asks for prayer and received a total healing. Come as a child, with the faith of a child and receive your complete healing. To me Johnny is a fine example of Christ in you the hope of glory. I pray to have the faith of Johnny. I believe Jesus Christ lives and is very comfortable in Johnny and the two of them are walking in the glory of God.

You might be wondering how a seven-year old has such faith. I know this family and they spend their time talking to their children about God and they are reaping the goodness of God. I had the privilege to camp next to them and I have been invited to set in on their every morning Bible study. I listened to their four-year old sound out big words in the Holy Bible that I struggle with. I listened to James, the father and Deb, the mother instruct their children in such a loving way I had to go back to my camper and I cried tears of joy as I thanked God I was next door to His children.

I love seeing the love of Jesus flowing through anyone but to see His love and faith in a seven year old, well, I simply had to thank Jesus for bringing this family into my life. I thank Jesus for allowing us to be His ambassadors and to be His apostles but it is more than awesome to witness His words of loving faith coming from His children so young.

Please read one more give the glory to God story. The other day, I met a man who complained about everything. I mentioned to him how I see Jesus in every detail of my life. He told me he finds himself cussing God in almost every detail of his life. Here is one example he gave me. He said that morning he wanted to put a new role of toilet paper on the holder. The little tabs that need to line up with holes in the holder looked like they lined up but when he went to pull some toilet paper off the role it fell on the floor. He said it happened three times that morning and he got so mad and he cussed god.

I asked him if he ever gave God the glory when the holes and post lined up. He said, "Hell no! God doesn't care if my toilet paper holder works or not." I asked him, "If God doesn't care, then why do you curse Him when it doesn't work?" He said, "I don't understand." I said, "You curse Him when the toilet paper falls on the floor but you don't give Him the credit when it works?" The simple truth is God desires to be in every detail of our life. I begged this man to please ask God to help him with everything that brings on such a reaction in his life.

I was thinking about this story when I thought about cars and how in some ways we all do the same thing this man did. Today, almost everyone will get ready to go somewhere and they expect their car to start. When the car starts they just go wherever they needed to go but if the car will not start, some of us Christians will automatically get mad at God and ask Him, "God, why didn't my car start?" Or even worse they might cuss God.

I believe this proves we know God is in our details for we acknowledge Him the second things go wrong but we almost never take time to praise Him when things go right for us. Acknowledging Jesus with a scream 'God why did not the car start' is really saying we expected you to start our car for us Lord. If this has ever happened to you please pause for a moment and thank God for forgiveness. Purposely turn away from these outburst by acknowledging God in your details of life.

To summarize, please come to know God through reading your Holy Bible but remember the Holy Bible will never replace your relationship with God. The Holy Bible will only tell us what is possible with faith in God. The Holy Bible will teach you who God is and that Abba Father sent His son to show us the love of Himself. Yes, Abba Father desires to have a relationship with you personally. They have given us their Holy Spirit and in John we read the words of Jesus:

John 14:26-27 But the Comforter, which is the Holy Ghost, whom the Father will send in my name, he shall teach you all things, and bring all things to your remembrance, whatsoever I have said unto you. Peace I leave with you, my peace I give unto you: not as the world giveth, give I unto you. Let not your heart be troubled, neither let it be afraid.

Contrast the lives of the people in the two stories above and you choose which walk you want to be on. Deb and James and family are walking in total peace, enjoying the Joy of the Lord, giving glory to God in word and actions or you can choose to be the man who is angry and up set with God. The choice is clear, the results are on display either way and people are watching all the time. We are either helping God build the kingdom of God or we are helping the devil add to the number of people going to hell! I know there is not any middle ground.

With the Holy Spirit in us, we walk in the love of God as Jesus did and Johnny does, we have peace knowing Jesus is our teacher, our comforter and Jesus will give us the words to help others come to know His love is true.

Here is an easy discernment. The Holy Bible will not tell you to cuss God if your car doesn't start or if your toilet paper falls on the floor but we Christians know who will tell us to cuss God. If your relationship with God is simply to read and study His Holy Bible you will probably burn out and backslide and you will not think to thank God every time the car does start. The relationship I am talking about is in your heart to heart relationship where you set time aside to hear and receive the heart of your best friend.

Father God and Jesus are in heaven but their Holy Spirit is here with us. My Holy Bible tells me so and they wake me up every morning to talk to me personally. Sometimes, I cannot sleep at night because I am so excited to see what we are going to do tomorrow. I ask Jesus how you will top today. My heart is full of joy and I simply cannot backslide because their joy has over taken me. Their love is flowing through me and I love it. John spoke the words to show how we overcome the world.

1 John 5:4-5 For whatsoever is born of God overcometh the world: and this is the victory that overcometh the world, even our faith. Who is he that overcometh the world, but he that believeth that Jesus is the Son of God?

We prove our belief by our walk and our words. Jesus took fear, and tells us to testify our testimony to show people what God is doing today and every day of our life. Part of the snare of the devil is the lust of Man's knowledge. Jesus tells us over and over in the Holy Bible.

1 John 2:15-17 Love not the world, neither the things that are in the world. If any man loves the world, the love of the Father is not in him. For all that is in the world, the lust of the flesh, and the lust of the eyes, and the pride of life, is not of the Father, but is of the world. And the world passeth away, and the lust thereof: but he that doeth the will of God abideth forever.

I have come to know the will of God through studying my Holy Bible and I have come to know the heart of God by my personal relationship with God. I prove everything I hear by asking my Holy Spirit to show me what I am hearing in the word of God. I can back up every detail of this book in His word except the vision I talked about. The apostles lived this way. When Jesus taught them in parables they often went to Jesus privately and ask Jesus to explain the parable to them and Jesus always did. We can do the same thing today but you must be listening. If we are to busy then we will miss the joy of the Lord that comes from walking and living in His presents.

I am seeing in my mind right now a picture of a switch. The switch is in the form of a pointer. On the left is lust of the world and on the right is Jesus Christ and joy. Then Jesus pointed out to me that the devil never makes you choose between the devil and Jesus. The devil always makes the choice between lust of the world and believing in the goodness of God. The devil came into our life through the fall of Adam but we keep him in our life by our personal choice. I choose to seek God with my whole heart, mind and soul and Jesus responds with His love for me. Yes, I know I am loved by God and I know His choice is to love me.

Again, we need to ask God into every detail of our life by seeking to be every detail of His life. Simply pray knowing God has an answer. God is the answer and by faith God will deliver His answer. You know with faith in God we can sometimes be His answer. Allow God to talk through you and God will flow His answer through you. This is God in our details.

Please people if there are seemingly little things going on around you that cause you to curse God, please I beg you to take these matters to God and then you will see God does care. You will see God is in your personal details of life and these seemingly small details will become a praise God moment and not a curse God moment. You will see yourself being transformed in to the love of Jesus and Abba Father God.

Please if you find yourself cursing God for anything at all, please ask God to put a check in your spirit to help you see the moment for what it is. For when you ask God for a check in your spirit, your spirit will hear a gentle reminder from God and you will thank God you have peace and joy instead of frustration and cursing. You will thank God for being with you and your whole day will grow better.

The toilet paper man told me that might work for you but it doesn't work that way for him. My heart hurts as I realized what he just said. I asked him, to take out the words *'that'* and *'it'* in his statement and put God in his statement where *'that'* and *'it'* was. Now your statement reads *'God might work for you but God doesn't work for me.'* Nothing could be further from the truth of God but in man's knowledge *'that'* and *'it'* sounds like truth.

Our words have meaning. Our thoughts have power and asking God into the details of our life will remove frustration. With the Holy Spirit of God in our life we will not be ready to curse God for every little problem. Instead, we will thank God for the blessings. Cursing God is a sign we don't know God at all.

While we have life in us, we have time to choose God. Without God in you there is no hope of glory for God or you until God comes back. Think for a moment. Man's wisdom could have you standing in front of people at a banquet celebrating a victory and holding a gold medal and in a few days no one remembers your name. I want to celebrate in front of God as I hear the word *'Well done my good and faithful servant.'* Where are your goals? Where are your treasures?

Matthew 25:23 His lord said unto him, Well done, good and faithful servant; thou hast been faithful over a few things, I will make thee ruler over many things: enter thou into the joy of thy lord.

I believe the joy of the Lord is a gift we enter into and we live through by turning off the distractions of this world and turning into His love for us. We do this by faith in His love for us and allowing His love to flow toward others. The glory of the Lord in us is useless unless we allow His glory to flow through us and into the hearts of others. I hope you see God is glorified when we become His hope of Glory by being so intimate with Holy Spirit. His words become our words and His thoughts become our thoughts and we will see as Jesus sees.

We will recognize our heart transformation when our loved ones start asking us where our joy comes from. We will notice our eyes have been opened to see Jesus in the details of our life. Love will not be something we seek after but something we freely give. Our earthly wants will simply be replaced with an intimate love so satisfying our hearts desires will overflow into everyone we meet. The love of Jesus will be so real to us; we will willingly lay down our life and ask Jesus to let us go to the cross for the sins of others.

Our goal will not just be saving souls but our goal will be blessing others with His love today and His love will transform others. Yes we will bring heaven to earth and the gates of hell will be afraid to come against His love in us. We believers will understand there is no force on earth to stop us, no walls to contain us for this is the freedom Jesus came to give us. The love of Jesus will shine in us and we will bind the evil in this world and all we need to do is believe the love of God toward us is real.

Here is a question I hear a lot: "Ron, how did you get this walk with the Lord?" Today in my quiet time, I ask the Lord to explain my walk to me. I heard in my heart this story. If your dad had his own business and you were ten years old and one evening you ask your dad, "Can I go to work with you tomorrow and work for you dad?" I bet your dad could find something simple for you to do at work. Even without skills your dad can find something for you to do. I believe your walk with Jesus is the same way. If you make yourself available to God, He will use you.

The little boy only knew he loved his dad and wanted to please his dad. That is all that is required of us, for with a desire to show our love we will make ourselves available. The little boy laid down his life to go to work with his dad. The cross is whatever his dad asks him to do. The pay is the sheer joy of being with his dad. Please note the little boy did not try to please his dad in his own strength but he ask his dad can I be of help to you dad.

The Samaritan woman at the well is like the little boy. She was like a baby in Christ. She only knew Jesus a few minutes but she found the loving forgiveness of God came into her heart and she had to run and share this love with everyone in her town.

As the little boy grows up and his wisdom increases his jobs will become more complex but Father God will never give him more then he can handle. Come as a child needing nothing but having a desire to spend time with God and let God grow you up. The proof of belief is in your love life.

Jesus, Jenny and I love you forever and I pray this book gives you a desire to have an intimate love relationship with my Jesus.

Made in the USA
Charleston, SC
20 January 2017